The Play of Goodness

Series Board

James Bernauer

Drucilla Cornell

Thomas R. Flynn

Kevin Hart

Richard Kearney

Jean-Luc Marion

Adriaan Peperzak

Thomas Sheehan

Hent de Vries

Merold Westphal

Michael Zimmerman

John D. Caputo, *series editor*

Perspectives in
Continental
Philosophy

JACOB BENJAMINS

The Play of Goodness
Creation, Phenomenology, and Culture

FORDHAM UNIVERSITY PRESS
New York ▪ 2025

Copyright © 2025 Fordham University Press

All rights reserved. No part of this publication may be reproduced, stored in a retrieval system, or transmitted in any form or by any means—electronic, mechanical, photocopy, recording, or any other—except for brief quotations in printed reviews, without the prior permission of the publisher.

Fordham University Press has no responsibility for the persistence or accuracy of URLs for external or third-party Internet websites referred to in this publication and does not guarantee that any content on such websites is, or will remain, accurate or appropriate.

Fordham University Press also publishes its books in a variety of electronic formats. Some content that appears in print may not be available in electronic books.

Visit us online at www.fordhampress.com.

Library of Congress Cataloging-in-Publication Data available online at https://catalog.loc.gov.

Printed in the United States of America

27 26 25   5 4 3 2 1

First edition

To Kristin

Contents

	Introduction: It Is Good	*1*
1	Entangled Topologies	*21*
2	The Givenness of Creation's Goodness	*47*
3	Transfigured Goodness	*72*
4	Obscured Goodness	*94*
5	Not Good Enough	*117*
	Conclusion: The Credibility of Creation's Goodness	*140*
	Acknowledgments	*147*
	Notes	*149*
	Bibliography	*199*
	Index	*215*

The Play of Goodness

Introduction
It Is Good

If there is something good about creation that is ongoing and definitive, then it will appear in experience and be describable to some degree. My conviction is that describing this goodness does not require one to overlook pain and suffering or oppose the rise of secular modernity. It is possible to trace the play of goodness within the flux of experience and shifting cultural dynamics. This book sketches various ways in which creation's goodness appears and commends it as a helpful theological concept for understanding one's place. Affirming creation's goodness has the potential to animate an abiding affection for one's place, accentuate our reasons to care for it, and confirms that what happens in our lives is of genuine significance.

The primary method I use to describe creation's goodness is phenomenology. This approach does not establish phenomenology as the normative discourse in which to understand the meaning of a good creation, but it offers a means to examine critically the ambiguities, limits, and richness of experience in relation to theology. From this point of view, I turn to phenomenology for expressly theological interests and purposes but explore topics broadly relevant to philosophical discourse: the interplay of hermeneutics and phenomenology, reality and relativism, as well as commonalities and diversities in experience. My hope is that one does not need to hold a particular set of theological convictions (or a confession of faith) to find the following of interest.

One of the basic premises of this book is the idea that there is something like a quality of "goodness" at play in experience that is quite general. We encounter qualities in temperature, comfort, voice, and taste, and the idea that one might more or less recognize and describe these should be uncontroversial.[1] These are qualities that one does not project onto experience but may be "'affective signs' of real sensible *qualities* out there in the world."[2] As Paul Ricoeur explains in his early work, there is a basic level of need wherein "values *emerge* without my having posited them in my act-generating role: bread is good, wine is good. Before I will it, a value already appeals to me solely because I exist in flesh; it is already a reality in the world, a reality which reveals itself to me through the lack."[3] Of course, not all qualities are reducible to a category of "goodness," but it is enough to acknowledge these potential realities within material, embodied life that broadly appear as good.

Critically, however, not only does this book describe the appearing of a general play of goodness, but it also relates it to a broader horizon of place. This latter task introduces some of the more complicated aspects of a phenomenology of creation's goodness, since it involves several multifaceted hermeneutical issues. If I am walking through the park on a winter day in Ontario, it is easy enough to see how snow settles on the branches of a birch tree and note that it appears with a certain quality of goodness. It is quite another thing to know what this small-scale encounter indicates about the world more generally. There is a significant degree of complexity involved in relating a particular experience (noticing snow on the branches) to a wider sense about the kind of place in which I find myself (whether or not it is a "good creation"). And so, exploring this exchange (or the inextricable relationship) between small-scale encounters and one's broader understanding of place is one of the defining problem-contexts of this book.

Although I foreground a theological concept (creation's goodness), it is not my intention to prove the existence of a Creator (phenomenology does not prove the existence of anything).[4] A Creator and an originary moment of creation (for example, a first cause) may be implicit to many theologies of creation; however, the presence of these "realities" does not impinge on appearances like an ordinary object of perception.[5] At the same time, over the course of this study, I argue that a phenomenology of creation's goodness does not require one to *impose* theological concepts (like a Creator) onto experience. In fact, there is substantial coherence between the ambiguities of experience and a nuanced theology of creation that leaves room for diverse horizons of place. A phenomenology of creation's goodness opens space to wrestle with the appearing of goodness rather than forecloses differing perspectives. As I will explain, this accommodating and open account of creation's goodness does not end with an overly simplistic relativism but actually lends credibility to what it means to encounter one's place as a good creation.[6]

The central authors I engage in order to develop a phenomenology of creation's goodness are Jean-Yves Lacoste, Claude Romano, Emmanuel Falque, Jean-Luc Marion, and Jean-Louis Chrétien. One reason for working with these authors is explained by what Christina Gschwandtner describes as the "striking" similarities in the method employed by these French phenomenologists (Romano notwithstanding).[7] She notes that they offer "primarily phenomenological depictions of religious experience in a variety of registers." And while these descriptions often differ from one another, Gschwandtner proposes that there are "significant areas of overlap, such as an emphasis on abundance and excess."[8] I would add to her analysis that even the differences in their descriptions are often a matter of emphasis rather than contradiction. Marion engages with *apophatic theology*, whereas Falque focuses on the concept of *kenosis*. Lacoste accentuates the *partiality* of experience, whereas Chrétien emphasizes the *excess* of experience (or the excess of the call over the response). Romano examines the significance of transformative *large-scale* events, whereas Marion tends to consider the *small-scale* structure of events.

Because there is substantial coherence within this relatively small group of authors working in French phenomenology, it is possible to build on the complementary nature of their work while noting differences and developing potential criticisms along the way. My primary focus, however, is neither to compare and contrast their work nor to provide a comprehensive summary of developments in contemporary French philosophy. I examine these authors because their work offers insight into the experiential dynamics of creation's goodness. For the most part, this implies that I develop an argument consistent with their broader philosophical and theological projects, but there are also times when I push back on specific positions these authors develop. As I will explain shortly, this critical dimension of the book is partially attributable to a lack of engagement with phenomena that can be associated with creation's goodness in French phenomenology. While French phenomenology has done substantial work on religious themes like liturgy, eucharist, and revelation, there has been a tendency to overlook the ordinary sense in which one's life may be defined by a creation that is good.

Defining Creation's Goodness

Before explaining in more detail how I plan to develop a phenomenology of *creation's goodness*, it is helpful to have a working theological definition of the concept so that there is some clarity about the kind of phenomena I seek to describe. My aim is to identify features of creation's goodness that are malleable enough to appear in a variety of theological contexts yet specific enough to establish a starting point for thinking about how creation's goodness might appear in experience. This means that I build on the idea that there is a "surplus of meaning" in the concept: It "may mean more than one thing at any given time" and speaks to "different audiences in varying ways through the centuries."[9] I do not intend to adjudicate differing theologies of creation's goodness in any detail, since my central interest is in whether phenomenology can provide some insight into the experiential dynamics of the doctrine as it is broadly understood.

The primary meaning of creation's goodness in this study is derived from the first chapter of Genesis. Despite the long, variegated, and at times reticent reception of the text in Christian history, there is enough commonality between different understandings to propose that creation's goodness can be outlined as follows:

(1) Creation's goodness is *capacious*.
(2) Creation's goodness is primarily a *quality* rather than an *ethic*.
(3) Creation's goodness includes the affirmation of *materiality*.
(4) God is the *source* and *sustainer* of this goodness.

In order to understand how creation's goodness is first of all "capacious," it is helpful to note that there is substantial ambiguity in the Hebrew term for "good" (*tôb*). The word has a range of meanings that are "as broad as that of 'good' in English."[10] This range of meaning can, in part, be illustrated in the connection between creation's goodness and the concept of *blessing* implied in the first chapter of Genesis. As Othmar Keel and Silvia Schroer explain, "The people of ancient Israel, and probably other peoples of the ancient Near East, quite reasonably began with the fact that blessing (*berakah*)—or, to put it even more simply, 'good' (Heb. *tôb*)—is present in and can be experienced in much that is created."[11] They offer a wide range of biblical references in order to illustrate this connection between blessing and creation's goodness:

> In the Old Testament understanding, blessing is present wherever life prospers to the fullest extent; it is through blessing that life and prosperity advance. Rain that falls in its season and causes the seed to sprout is an embodiment of blessing (Gen 27:27; Ps 84:7, 85:13; Isa 45:8; Ezek 34:26; Joel 2:14); and so are the verdant tree, the good harvest (Ps 65:10–14, 67:7f.; Jer 31:12), the lavish table and warm clothing (Ps 132:15, Hag 1:6), the land that may be inhabited in peace, spared by war (Lev 26:6), the pregnant (Luke 1:42), the multiplication of offspring (Ps 37:26), the woman's full breasts (Gen

49:25; cf. also Luke 11:27), health (Deut 7:15), long life (Job 21:7), sound sleep (cf. Ps 127:2), increasing flocks (Deut 7:13 etc.), the nursing animal with her young, a neighbor's friendly greeting, and the day of rest from hard work (Gen 2:3, Ex 20:11).[12]

Creation's goodness is capacious, therefore, in the sense that it is involved in "God's original blessing" and in God's "assignment of fertility to all living things (Gen 1:22, 28, 2:3)."[13] This "goodness" is not an ephemeral spiritual reality but rather a "concrete gift" that seems to touch on "much of what is created."[14] Wherever life is flourishing or enjoyed one might relate it to the affirmation of goodness in the first chapter of Genesis. The capaciousness of creation's goodness does not imply that it *appears* with more commonality than negative or mundane phenomena but rather that it is integral to living things.

While there are ethical considerations involved with promoting the various dynamics of creation's goodness, the biblical concept maintains a primarily qualitative meaning. Walter Brueggemann emphasizes this sense by relating it to aesthetics. He suggests, "Blessing theology defines reality in an artistic and aesthetic way," so that when God judges that creation is good, it "does not refer primarily to a moral quality, but to an aesthetic quality. It might better be translated 'lovely, pleasing, beautiful' (cf. Eccles. 3:11)."[15] Ellen Davis offers a similar interpretation of what is "good" about creation by proposing that the writer of Genesis 1 "is inducting us into the practice of what the theologians of the early Greek church called 'natural contemplation': looking at the world with a view to discerning 'the inner principles in accordance with which things were created and are organized.'"[16] She suggests that the aesthetic purpose of the text (referring to it as a poem) is to teach readers to "stand 'in mute awe before the wonder of being.'"[17] And Claus Westermann, likewise, submits that the Hebrew word for "good" can also mean "beautiful" and that the joy that God expresses in the text "contains within itself all joy in what is beautiful."[18]

The idea that there is an aesthetic quality to creation's goodness is illustrated in diverse theological contexts. For instance, Hildegard of Bingen expresses sensitivity to the quality of creation through the image of *greenness* in her theology. The image symbolizes "the energy of life evident in grasses, trees, flowers and vineyards. It is the fruitfulness of the earth itself. Greenness is associated with moisture, with dew on the grass and with rainfall."[19] It stems from the "life-giving life" of the Holy Spirit, which "is the root of the whole creation and cleanses all things from impurity, scrubbing out sins and anointing wounds."[20] Working in a very different theological context, John Calvin encourages "his readers to use the good things of this world 'with a clear conscience, whether for necessity or for delight.'"[21] He develops a theological aesthetic that is focused on "God's works and his word" by using the metaphor of a *theater* in order to understand the created world as "a grand aesthetic spectacle" where "God's glory shines on every side, and whatever is seen above or below invites us to the true God."[22] And, in a comparably different context, the aesthetic dimension to creation's goodness can be found in the early writings of Charles Darwin, who "found the natural world created by God beautiful and full of wonder; close observation of it brought him intense joy."[23]

The sense in which creation's goodness is a dynamic quality also has been understood in relation to God bringing *order* out of chaos in the first chapter of Genesis.[24] R. W. L. Moberly proposes that the text offers the image "of God as a craftsman fashioning initially shapeless material into something pleasing that evokes his delight in his handiwork—hence the repeated pronouncement that what has been made is 'good,' and indeed, when taken as a whole, 'very good' (Gen 1:31)."[25] Some scholars argue that the preoccupation with *ordering* undermines the constructive role of *chaos* in the text. Catherine Keller, for instance, argues that chaos offers a "creative edge" to creation and undermines imperialistic temptations to try to control everything.[26] She observes how the creatures of the sea are part of YHWH's creation in Psalm 104: "To love the sea monsters and their chaos-matrix is consonant with affirming their 'goodness' within the context of the whole. It doesn't make them safe or cute."[27] The tension between order and chaos, therefore, suggests that the meaning of creation's goodness is not easily reducible to a pristine or sublime concept of beauty and introduces the sense in which creation's "goodness" is not always self-evident—an issue I return to throughout this book.

The idea that creation's goodness is not always self-evident indicates a fundamental complexity within the concept that is related to the affirmation of *materiality*. As David Fergusson explains, "The creation narratives do not allow a denigration of the material world or a dualism that depicts the world as a battleground between rival cosmic powers. Even while it is the arena of decay, suffering, conflict, and sin, this world remains God's good creation. Its goodness is not limited to some past golden age in Eden."[28] While the physical world is clearly included in what is affirmed as good in the first chapter of Genesis, suffering and death also seem to be inherent to materiality. This problem contributes to the rise of a tradition in Christianity that seeks to explain suffering and death as the result of a primordial Fall (a position I consider more closely in the fourth chapter). However, scholars like Moberly argue that Genesis 1 "is not a picture of a world that ceased in the next couple of chapters, when humans sinned, but a picture of the world familiar to the writer and his intended audience. As such, it incorporates the writer's understanding of the way the world is—as is most obvious in the depiction of the waters and the barrier that holds much of them back."[29] While I adopt an interpretation of the text in line with Fergusson and Moberly's analysis, questions clearly remain about the extent to which one might legitimately call creation good, because of the extensive suffering and death in the world.

Irenaeus represents one of the earliest Christian theologians working through the challenge of affirming the materiality of creation.[30] Writing in opposition to the Gnostic teachings of Valentinus and Marcion, he emphasizes "the earthiness and physicality of the creation, with the human molded from mud."[31] Denis Edwards explains that Irenaeus is well known for "his idea of the immediacy of the Creator to each creature; his insistence on the goodness of creation, of matter, of flesh; his concept that it is our bodies that are made in the divine image; his defense of the bodily reality of the incarnation and of the human death of Jesus; his position that not just humanity but all things are recapitulated in Christ."[32] But perhaps no figure exemplifies the difficulties involved with affirming the goodness of the material world in the face of suffering, sin, and death more than Augustine.[33] In the *Confessions* Augustine identifies matter as something "close to nothing" rather than "very good."[34] Yet, in the *City of God* he contemplates "the manifold and various loveliness of sky, and earth, and sea; of the plentiful supply and wonderful qualities of the light; of sun, moon, and stars; of the shade of trees."[35] Commentators like Peter Brown and Rowan Williams maintain that Augustine became "ever more deeply convinced that human beings had been created to embrace the material world."[36] No matter how one interprets the wider Augustinian corpus, however, his struggle to affirm the material world represents an enduring Christian issue—one that continues today as authors like Elizabeth Johnson reflect on how to affirm "the intrinsically worthy quality of what has been created" while at the same time acknowledging the "terrible cost" implicit to the evolution of life.[37] Creation's goodness is a capacious quality that includes materiality itself, but there are times when this goodness is not self-evident and is difficult for Christians to explain.

God as the Source and Sustainer of Creation

An additional layer of complexity with respect to creation's goodness stems from the fourth feature indicated earlier—namely, that God is the *source* and *sustainer* of this goodness. The status of God's ongoing relation to creation is particularly noteworthy in a study that actively engages with phenomenology. While it may be obvious to Christians that creation implies a Creator, this connection raises questions related to onto-theology in the context of post-Heideggerian philosophy. The threat of onto-theology is not *the* defining issue in the following; however, because of its relevance to philosophies of religion from the first half of the twentieth century onward, it is important to offer some preliminary remarks on how I situate my account of creation's goodness in relation to onto-theology. As I will explain, my aim is to avoid the worst theological caricatures associated with an onto-theo-logical God, while maintaining that creation's goodness (in some way) finds its source in a Creator.

Heidegger borrows the language of onto-theology from Immanuel Kant's *Critique of Pure Reason* and offers his most decisive treatment of the issue in *Identity and Difference*. Heidegger identifies metaphysics with a conceptual framework based on the following premises:

> When metaphysics thinks of beings with respect to the ground that is common to all beings as such, then it is logic as onto-logic. When metaphysics thinks of beings as such as a whole, that is, with respect to the highest being which accounts for everything, then it is logic as theo-logic.[38]

According to Heidegger's account, then, the onto-theo-logical constitution of metaphysics occurs when "God" is understood as a logical concept that functions as the *first cause, highest being,* and *ultimate ground* of all being. Merold Westphal argues that at this level of description, Heidegger's understanding of onto-theology has the potential to imply that "any theistic discourse, whether scholarly or not, that affirms God as Creator of the world would be an instance of onto-theology."[39] According to Westphal, however, such a claim is abstract, and "only the narrowest sect in the Heideggerian church needs to take it seriously."[40] The more interesting issue arises from a related question posed by Heidegger in the same text: "How does the deity enter into philosophy, not just modern philosophy, but philosophy as such?"[41] With this question, Heidegger situates the concept of onto-theology in a wider discussion about the interaction between philosophy and theology by questioning the legitimacy of any "deity" understood primarily according to the norms of philosophical discourse.[42] He proposes that "the deity can come into philosophy only insofar as philosophy, of its own accord and by its own nature, requires and determines that and how the deity enters into it."[43] This kind of philosophy has the danger of inscribing God into "abstract, impersonal categories" (such as *causa sui*) and eliminating mystery by explaining everything in "the light of a cause-effect coherence."[44] Alluding to Nietzsche, Heidegger writes: "Man can neither pray nor sacrifice to this god. Before the *causa sui*, man can neither fall to his knees in awe nor can he play music and dance before this god."[45]

The desire to avoid a mere "concept" of God has inspired philosophers like Richard Kearney and John Caputo to reflect on how "God" may not be reducible to the conceptual framework of onto-theology. This includes questioning aspects of creation theology that they view to be problematic (creation *ex nihilo* and God's omnipotence). Kearney, for instance, argues that "the concept of God as absolute Monarch of the Universe stems from a literalist reading of the Bible along with unfortunate misapplications of a metaphysics of causal omnipotence and self-sufficiency."[46] He argues that this approach "has led to the ruinously influential notion of theodicy, namely, the belief that God as Sovereign *causa sui*, as immutable Emperor of the world, exercises arbitrary and unlimited powers over his creatures. Every-thing—even the worst horrors—could thus be justified as part of some divine Will (the ultimate Will to Power)."[47] Similarly, Caputo proposes that the "delicate balance between God's lordship and the chanciness of creation . . . is upset by an excess of metaphysical zeal, by an overzealous extension of the concept of God's power to an 'omnipotence' that had a tin ear for life's contingencies and would thereafter have the effect of laying the horrors of this life squarely at the feet of God."[48] Authors like Kearney and Caputo exemplify a concern that onto-theology leads to the image of an all-powerful God who sits on the throne of the universe, arbitrarily controlling every moment of "his" creation. This is a God who functions at the top of a causal chain and fits into predetermined categories of reason and logic.

Some scholars question the significance of onto-theology for understanding the history of Christian thought and practice. Anthony Godzieba, for instance, argues that surveys of Christian history inspired by Heidegger may "miss the bodily intentionality of Christian practices and beliefs, how essential that intentionality is to the lived tradition, and how it creates rifts and disruptions in the second-order ontotheological framework."[49] Emmanuel Falque submits, "Onto-theo-logy is like the quest for a soul mate: the more one searches for it, the harder it is to find."[50] He proposes that there is an "'insoluble tension' between the metaphysical and the theological that God's 'entrance' into the horizon of human reflection demands."[51] Meanwhile, Jean-Luc Marion offers a historical account of onto-theology in which the onto-theo-logical constitution of metaphysics is a specifically *modern* philosophical project associated with the reception of Scholastic thought. He argues the concept of metaphysics "appears only relatively late, but with a clear definition . . . the system of philosophy from Suarez to Kant as a single science bearing at one and the same time on the universal of common being and on the being (or the beings) par excellence."⁵² Marion challenges Heidegger's reading of philosophical and theological history but at the same time gives him credit for identifying how the meaning of being may be obscured when God is understood as both a first cause and the being par excellence.⁵³

I have no intention of settling different historical assessments of ontotheology, although I do aim to avoid the worst caricatures associated with the conceptual God depicted here. This position does not imply that I evade anything resembling metaphysics in relation to a theology of creation's goodness. For instance, I do not question classical theological distinctions (which one may or may not call "metaphysical," depending on your definition)—such as the idea that it is possible to affirm "*that* God is good" but not the "*manner* of God's goodness."⁵⁴ I do not explicitly avoid the language of ontology when speaking about creation's goodness, since, for instance, I describe the phenomenological dynamics of this goodness in relation to a primordial "ontological duplicity" in the first chapter.⁵⁵ Furthermore, I am partial to the idea that a doctrine like creation *ex nihilo* has the potential to protect the *apophatic* dimensions of theology by placing God "totally outside any genus or hierarchy of being (q. 3.5) in a realm beyond our ability to conceptualize" even if it has not always been used in this way.⁵⁶ My aim, therefore, is to explore the relationship between God and creation's goodness in a way that is sensitive to the complexity of traditional creation language and to the dangers of depicting God as a "Monarch" who has a "tin ear for life's contingencies." As Westphal proposes, Christian faith is always metaphysical in the sense that there is a "'world behind the scenes' and thus a God who remains hidden in the midst of self-revelation to whom in awe and wonder one might well pray or sacrifice or sing or even dance."⁵⁷ As I describe the phenomenological contours of creation's goodness, my intention is to respect the hiddenness of God, while seeking to remain upfront about how a nuanced creation theology affirms God as the source and sustainer of this goodness.

The Genesis definition of creation's goodness noted earlier is not derived primarily from Christian Neo-Platonist or Aristotelian metaphysical traditions. As such, I do not defend Augustine's classic definition of evil as the privation of the good or Aquinas's transcendental conceptualization of the "good" as the proper "end" of being. At the same time, there may be areas of coherence between my phenomenological descriptions and traditions that emphasize the idea that creation's goodness somehow "flows" from God.⁵⁸ In the latter half of this study, the idea that God is the source and sustainer of creation becomes a much more prominent theme, since I focus on how God's relation to creation affects what it means to encounter "goodness." The kind of theology I engage with to explore this possibility is represented by Pope Francis's proposal that Christians "are called to recognize that other living beings have a value of their own in God's eyes: 'by their mere existence they bless him and give him glory,' and indeed, 'the Lord rejoices in all his works' (Ps 104:31)."[59] This idea implies that the *intrinsic value* of creation (its goodness) is defined in relation to God before its appearing in my experience. Not only does this theology lead to an expansive concept of "goodness," but it opens up broader questions about how the relation between God and creation might appear (or not) within the contours of experience. These issues remain my focus rather than an analysis of how the language I use to describe God's relation to creation interacts within the diverse Platonist or Aristotelian Christian traditions.

In summary, then, creation's goodness is a dense theological concept that relates to a variety of complex theological issues (Christology, original sin, metaphysics, creation *ex nihilo*). While these issues are engaged further in the following chapters, I primarily identify creation's goodness with a capacious, qualitative affirmation of materiality that finds its source in God. This definition is malleable enough to be found in a variety of theological contexts, and, moreover, it leaves open the possibility that one might identify how creation's goodness is at play within experience. This possibility is considered by means of phenomenological description, seeking to explain how the features outlined earlier appear (or not) and may be described to some degree.

Phenomenological Hermeneutics and Creation's Goodness

The primary benefit of turning to phenomenology is that it offers a critical approach to examining how creation's goodness might appear in experience. Using phenomenology to describe the appearance of creation's goodness does not establish a philosophical method as arbiter of the doctrine's truth but rather provides resources for understanding the category of experience and its relationship to theological concepts. In order to clarify how phenomenology can help with this task, some introductory remarks on the methodology's relation to hermeneutics and its function in this project are necessary.

In the first place, there is not one agreed-upon definition of phenomenology. Already in 1945, Merleau-Ponty pointed out that there are many different ways of practicing phenomenology—these differences have only increased since the middle of the twentieth century.[60] Merleau-Ponty offers a broad and open-ended definition of the method, proposing that "*phenomenology allows itself to be practiced and recognized as a manner or as a style, or . . . exists as a movement, prior to having reached a full philosophical consciousness.*"[61] He also suggests that its first rule is "to be a descriptive psychology" that does not involve "explaining or analyzing" phenomena.[62] More recently, Claude Romano broadly affirms Merleau-Ponty's definition of phenomenology(ies), stating: "The idea of a descriptive philosophy seems to be their lowest common denominator." However, he also warns that "description can be understood in so many ways that it alone can hardly provide us with the requisite guideline" for determining what constitutes phenomenology.[63] Romano recalls that phenomenological description is not the kind of description one might associate with scientific, literary, or sociological description. It aims to describe a world upon which these discourses depend. Unique to phenomenology is an interest in *pre*-predicative, *pre*-scientific, *pre*-thetic, or a *pre*-hermeneutic level of understanding—with the prefix "pre-" variously implying a world that exists prior to our knowledge of it.

One of the central questions about phenomenology is whether or not one's understanding of a prelinguistic (or pre-predicative) world can be simply *described* or is necessarily *interpreted*. The tension between description and interpretation is already evident in the early history of phenomenology through the differences between Husserl and Heidegger. As Romano explains, Husserl seeks to establish phenomenology "as a science 'grounded on an absolute foundation'" that achieves a "genuine freedom from prejudice [*die echte Vorurteilslosigkeit*]."[64] Conversely, Heidegger argues that the desire to be free from prejudice is impossible, since one's "description is always an account" that is never fully faithful to what is "given."[65] Heidegger argues "not only that we could not have most of our thoughts, beliefs, or opinions if we did not have language, but that we could not have certain feelings, goals, intentions, desires, and so on, either."[66] The differences between Husserl and Heidegger illustrate a problem that becomes even more pronounced with the "hermeneutic turn" in continental philosophy in the 1960s.[67] On one end of the spectrum, Ricoeur argues for a "gulf" between phenomenology and hermeneutics and insists that a linguistic, cultural, and historical detour is necessary in order to describe religious phenomena; on the other end, Michel Henry develops an "anti-hermeneutical" approach to phenomenology through his reflections on the words of Christ.[68]

More recently, several authors have sought to bring phenomenology and hermeneutics into closer relation. For instance, Kearney argues for the development of a "carnal hermeneutics," which emphasizes the interpretive function of the body through the integration of flesh (*Leib*) and body (*Körper*). This includes exploring embodied encounters with a qualitative dimension of material existence that involves some level of interpretation. Romano directly opposes Ricoeur's rendering of phenomenology and hermeneutics by arguing that "*genuine hermeneutics is phenomenology and phenomenology is only achieved as hermeneutics.*"[69] And Falque integrates several of Romano's positions—suggesting that phenomenology and hermeneutics "are each dependent on the same 'sap,' as it were, although in different modalities."[70] Critically, the method used throughout this book is derivative of these more recent approaches to phenomenology and hermeneutics. I locate aspects of creation's goodness in certain prelinguistic experiences of goodness, while at the same time I acknowledge that my "descriptions" are also "interpretations."

In order to clarify the phenomenological hermeneutic employed in this study, it is helpful to consider further Romano's assertion that genuine phenomenology "is only achieved as hermeneutics." He argues that both a recognition of prelinguistic experience and an acknowledgment that language forms understanding is necessary for phenomenology today. He explains, "Phenomenological hermeneutics can only formulate itself coherently if it accepts the pre-hermeneutic level of a spontaneous understanding at work in experience itself, a *perceptual* experience not mediated by signs."[71] "Otherwise," Romano adds, "what would be exactly the meaning of this constantly maintained reference to 'the things themselves' to which phenomenology's task is to lead us back?"[72] At the same time, naming this "spontaneous understanding" *follows* the prehermeneutic moment (in a sense it comes too late) and as a result, description must be held in balance with several hermeneutical principles:

> A description always involves (1) interests, that is, implicit questions; (2) given that it is formulated in a specific language, conceptual schemes, which may also be called a (linguistically articulable) pre-comprehension of the phenomena; (3) in the majority of cases (especially in instances of a complex description with underlying philosophical stakes), beliefs or presuppositions, sometimes even an entire tacit theory.[73]

Romano's principles help clarify the approach I take in the following, since it should be clear that I am *interested* in phenomena related to creation's goodness. I seek a reduction to "goodness" precisely because I am exploring the capacious quality of goodness indicated in the first chapter of Genesis. And by acknowledging this broader interest, I therefore also acknowledge that there is an "entire tacit theory" (which is really a theology) at work in the language of goodness (I will return to this point shortly).

It is important to note that Romano does not identify prelinguistic experience by freezing or pinpointing a moment within the flux of perception. He explains, "The relevant sense of priority here is not chronological but logical."[74] A phenomenological reduction to goodness therefore follows from reflecting on the contours of experience, which in turn shows "a meaningful order of our experience that does not coincide with that of our 'grammar.'"[75] Returning to Ricoeur's example of "good" bread illustrates the point. As one eats a slice of bread, it may become noticeable that the bread is soft, savory, tangy, chewy, and salty and satisfies hunger. These characteristics appear within a *perceptual* experience capable of *pushing back on one's expectations* and offering a unique taste that may be broadly described as "good." There is an embodied (perceptual and prelinguistic) encounter with a "reality in the world" (bread) that does not undermine the necessity of hermeneutics but helps give shape to experience. As I explain in the following chapters, examining this kind of prelinguistic experience provides an important source for identifying various features of creation's goodness.

Horizons of Place

At the risk of compartmentalizing what may be inextricably related, then, I aim to make a *descriptive* distinction between general qualities of goodness in *prelinguistic experience* and the way that it is understood in a *Christian horizon of place*. A substantial amount of philosophical and theological nuance is needed in order to make this distinction, and much of the following is dedicated to this task. But several points of clarification are worth noting from the beginning.

First, as acknowledged earlier, my decision to use the language of "goodness" in reference to prelinguistic experience is suggestive. I self-consciously use the word in relation to a historically, linguistically, and culturally situated theological concept (creation). However, "goodness" also has exceptionally broad connotations in English and does not necessarily point toward the first chapter of Genesis or its Jewish and Christian heritage. Throughout this book I make an ongoing effort to describe various prelinguistic experiences of goodness with ordinary examples that seem to transgress cultural and linguistic barriers. It would be hard to argue, for instance, that an enjoyable taste (like good bread) is the exclusive terrain of Western English-speaking cultures. At the same time, it is important to acknowledge that my reflections in the following are limited to atheistic, agnostic, Jewish, and Christian horizons of place. While it may be productive to explore the relevance of prelinguistic experience for interreligious dialogue (I think it would be), this book focuses on perspectives one typically finds in so-called secular Western contexts. I hope to show that a phenomenological reduction to goodness has the benefit of opening up conversation about commonalities in experience without essentializing it or undermining diverse horizons of place—but this "benefit" remains carefully delineated and limited.

Second, in the latter half of the book I provide more detail on what I mean by a specifically *Christian* horizon of place. There is a whole range of theological concepts that have the potential to shift (and even transform) the general meaning of "goodness" associated with prelinguistic experience. The concept of "creation" itself implies a degree of theological knowledge that unfolds what is good in relation to a Creator. But as the book progresses, I show how the descriptive distinction between prelinguistic experience and its integration in a Christian horizon of place can clarify how various contours of experience mutually inform one another. On the one hand, a theology of creation's goodness is informed by persistent and ordinary encounters with a prelinguistic qualitative dimension of life that is at play in experience regardless of one's confessional stance. On the other hand, a theology of creation's goodness can initiate one's attentiveness to this goodness, mediate, and potentially broaden its significance for understanding one's place.

Throughout the study I refer to this "mediated" Christian horizon of place as a *topology of creation*. In the context of phenomenology, "topology" provides relatively neutral language for describing some of the experiential contours of encountering one's place. The way I use the term may be associated with Heidegger's "world," Christianity's "creation," or any other concept that indicates how people understand the place in which they find themselves. The language of "topology" has the advantage of guarding against any tendency toward locating the appearing of creation's goodness exclusively with "interiority" or the "relation of the 'I' to itself."[76] As Abraham Olivier explains, a common misconception about phenomenology is that it is "merely a first-person description of consciousness, only accessible via the mind's inward reflection on its own contents, in short introspection."[77] However, phenomenological description "is always directed to or about the meaning of an extramental, publicly accessible reality."[78] I associate creation's goodness with topology because it is part of this publicly accessible reality in a highly qualified sense.[79] No one is forced into adopting a horizon of place that is defined by its relation to a Creator—at the same time, I will argue that phenomena that Christians associate with creation's goodness may be recognizable regardless of one's confession of faith.

Third, the idea that creation's goodness is part of a Christian horizon of place (or a topology of creation) is related to a distinction made by Lacoste in *Experience and the Absolute*. Therein, he argues that the most important aspects of being human are not always reducible to what is most "initial" in experience (for example, prelinguistic experience).[80] He introduces a reference to the "Absolute" in order to argue for the significance of "secondary evidence" that mediates one's relation to the world.[81] This is not an argument that is predicated on the existence of God but rather an investigation into how placing oneself before the Absolute (Lacoste's definition of liturgy) discloses something essential about being human. Introducing the Absolute implies a kind of theological knowledge that may help guide the interpretation of one's experience (or "nonexperience," in the case of Lacoste's account of liturgy). As I will explain in more detail, this distinction between what is "initial" and "secondary evidence" has similarities with Romano's account of the difference between *understanding* and *interpretation* and Marion's account of the gap between what *shows itself* and *gives itself*. These distinctions create substantial complexity for understanding the relationship between phenomenology and hermeneutics. But for now, it is enough to note that creation's goodness involves "secondary evidence" related to theological knowledge, and so it is not synonymous with a prelinguistic experience.

Finally, working with an experiential distinction like "initial" and "secondary evidence" does not separate what is undeniably linked in theology (nature and grace or the natural and supernatural). I submit that it is possible to outline an encounter with certain aspects of creation (its goodness) without immediately pointing out that confessional Christians understand this goodness to be sustained by God. This descriptive distinction is a practical outcome of the idea that God's relation to creation may not appear in the same way as the "concrete blessings" outlined in the first chapter of Genesis. As I explain in Chapter 3, creation's goodness should not be associated with "pure nature," but a whole series of theological tensions are introduced if one seeks to explain how God's relation to goodness appears (if it appears) within the contours of experience.

The Structure of the Argument

I develop a phenomenology of creation's goodness over the course of five chapters. In the first half of the book, I explore the possibility of a prelinguistic quality of goodness that appears regardless of one's confession of faith. In the second half, I examine how this "goodness" may be integrated within an explicitly Christian topology of creation—although I continually evaluate this integration throughout the study.

The first chapter introduces the appearing of a prelinguistic goodness by considering the experiences of joy and enjoyment (a distinction based on Lacoste's work that is explained in the opening pages of the chapter). Both experiences disclose a prelinguistic goodness to varying degrees—however, I do not suggest it is self-evident that one is living in a good creation simply because of a joyful experience. The chapter examines hermeneutical challenges that follow from offering a particularly Christian interpretation of goodness in a pluralistic context. It affirms a wide spectrum of interpretations of "goodness" without falling into a simplistic relativism. To this end, I put forward the idea that a Christian concept of creation remains *entangled* with a variety of atheist or agnostic horizons of place at a prelinguistic level of experience. Not only does this entanglement challenge various aspects of Lacoste's account of "creation," but more importantly, it facilitates the identification of commonalities in experience between people who think differently, which in turn creates space for argumentation about the "real" to proceed.

Chapter 2 continues to outline the experiential contours of a prelinguistic goodness. I engage with Marion's work in order to show how givenness and the gift define part of what it means for "goodness" to be at play in prelinguistic experience. The chapter also outlines why the phenomenological contours of a prelinguistic goodness can be a helpful source for theological interpretations of culture. This position is drawn in contrast to Marion's reoccurring assertion that the current era is defined solely by nihilism and that only Christians have the solution to this problem (since they have knowledge of the gift). While nihilism is a relevant concept for understanding certain sociopolitical issues today (such as the climate crisis), a more complex account of contemporary life is needed. To this end, the chapter demonstrates how the dynamics of creation's goodness consistently push back on the threat of nihilism.

The third chapter marks a point of transition in the book, since it begins to describe how a prelinguistic experience of goodness is integrated and transfigured within a topology of creation. Describing this integration is challenging because it is relatively common to experience the world without reference to a Creator. However, throughout the chapter I argue that a topology of creation does not impose the idea of God onto experience but leaves room for the ambiguities and limits of experience. Irresolvable theological tensions such as nature and grace, activity and passivity, knowing and unknowing mediate and cohere with experiential ambiguities. This coherence does not prove God's presence in the world but offers some depth and credibility to what it means to inhabit one's place in relation to God. The concluding sections of the chapter then return to the central theme of the study by introducing how goodness may be *transfigured* within a topology of creation—which, as noted earlier, implies that all of creation has *an intrinsic value*. The potential appearing of this transfigured goodness is the focus of the remaining chapters.

Chapter 4 examines how a transfigured sense of creation's goodness relates to the immense amount of pain and suffering in the world. Rather than address the problem of evil as it is classically formulated, however, my method remains phenomenological. The chapter examines how the appearing of creation's goodness becomes obfuscated in the midst of bodily suffering and death by engaging the work of Falque and Romano. In response to this obfuscation, I propose that affirming the intrinsic value of all creation (a transfigured goodness) does not require one to diminish the significance of suffering and death but affirms that all suffering life is worthy of compassion and care. This position is reinforced with a Christological reading of the relationship between God and creation. The chapter concludes by explaining that creation's goodness validates a wide spectrum of experiences and is not dependent on evaluating the weight of self-evidently good versus bad phenomena in one's life.

The final chapter acknowledges that affirming creation's goodness often remains strangely disappointing. Not only does it expose one to the burden of care and compassion for creation, but it also offers few reasons as to why there is so much pain and suffering. Within the Christian tradition this disappointment (which may include forms of anger, sadness, grief, and lament) implies an eschatological structure to God's relation to creation. While Christian forms of eschatology have been challenged within phenomenology (especially by Heidegger), I propose that Lacoste's account of being-at-peace demonstrates that there can be a variety of authentic forms of eschatological anticipation. In order to develop this possibility, I explore the interaction between the "goodness" of the first six days of creation and the "holiness" of the seventh. Drawing on the work of Søren Kierkegaard and Abraham Joshua Heschel, the chapter concludes that the Sabbath both *qualifies* the gifts of creation and *transfigures* them by exposing one to a temporal duration not defined by my existential temporality. Within the liturgical context of the Jewish Sabbath, in particular, the value of creation participates in an eternity that encircles all of life and dissipates in relation to the holiness of God.

Throughout these chapters, three scholarly contributions to a thinking of creation in the context of philosophy of religion (or philosophical theology) are developed. First, a phenomenology of creation's goodness has the potential to counterbalance what Brian Treanor identifies as a melancholic tendency in continental philosophy. He argues, "It seems that melancholic disposition, or some variation thereof, has come to serve as a watermark of sorts for serious continental philosophy, which is concerned with otherness, alienation, inauthenticity, angst, anxiety, dread, melancholy, finitude, mourning, and death."[82] While this focus is understandable given that "suffering, tragedy, and death are unavoidable," Treanor warns that "a certain *hyper*-sensitivity, which, in its fixation on these unhappy phenomena, misses or deemphasizes other phenomena and occludes other, equally significant truths."[83] By focusing on phenomena associated with creation's goodness (particularly at a prelinguistic level), this study aims to elucidate the significance of phenomena otherwise overlooked or undervalued in continental philosophy. Identifying the pervasive appearing of goodness at a prelinguistic level of experience suggests that it is an integral aspect of understanding one's place. While my focus is on phenomenology, the capacious appearing of goodness indicates it is a noteworthy theme for continental philosophy in general.

Second, some of the conclusions presented by central figures in French phenomenology are challenged. A substantial part of the book's argument is indebted to the work of authors like Lacoste, Falque, and Marion, but there are times when the phenomenal content of creation's goodness pushes back on various positions they develop. I aim to nuance different aspects of their work by focusing on the appearing of creation's goodness—an approach that, perhaps, only underscores the previous point regarding melancholic tendencies in contemporary continental philosophy. For instance, I will argue that Lacoste and Marion create untenable binaries along confessional lines that fail to account adequately for the way goodness defines one's place regardless of one's confession of faith. I also question Falque's contention (following Heidegger) that finitude is an accurate summary of what is first given and most ordinary to experience. In each case, accounting for the phenomenology of creation's goodness complicates key positions outlined by French phenomenologists of religion.

Third, focusing on the appearing of creation's goodness has the potential to contribute to a nuanced theological reading of culture. In some ways, this aspect of the book is developed in relation to the aforementioned critiques (for example, critiquing Marion's assertion that the contemporary era is defined by nihilism is part of my questioning the confessional binaries he describes). But thinking about the importance of creation's goodness for understanding culture also leads to the broader aim of this study—namely, to commend creation's goodness as a helpful category for understanding one's place. To this end, I do not seek to identify specific aspects of a given culture that are "good," but as I will explain, it is necessary for those who confess a Christian faith to account for the persistent appearing of creation's goodness regardless of the shifting cultural moment. Making this case with credibility will depend on closely examining the interactions between the contours of experience and a nuanced theology of creation.

1

Entangled Topologies

The first chapter of Genesis portrays creation's goodness as a capacious quality that affirms materiality and finds its source in God. This provides a definition that is malleable enough to be represented in various theological contexts in Christian history but specific enough to provide a framework in which to consider how (or whether) creation's goodness appears in experience. In what follows, I argue that *aspects* of a Christian understanding of creation's goodness appear within prelinguistic experiences that are not reducible to one's confessional stance—yet remain open to a specifically Christian understanding mediated by a degree of theological knowledge. Making this case requires examining some of the hermeneutical complexity between a prelinguistic experience of goodness and a self-consciously Christian interpretation of it. My aim is to both affirm the inextricable diversity of people's experiences but also leave room for exploring various forms of commonality in prelinguistic experience.

In order to introduce the idea of a prelinguistic goodness, I engage with the work of Jean-Yves Lacoste. While he is best known for his reflections on liturgy in *Experience and the Absolute* (1991), Lacoste's more recent work remains relatively overlooked in the context of English philosophy of religion (likely because of the slow rate of translation). His reflections on affectivity offer a rich resource for evaluating the category of experience in relation to theological concepts. Always a judicious philosopher, Lacoste's phenomenology often explores mundane and uncontroversial examples that tend to emphasize the limits of experience while also maintaining its importance for theological knowledge. I am particularly interested in his account of experiences like *joy* and *enjoyment* (I will explain the distinction shortly), since these affectivities exemplify different aspects of a prelinguistic experience of goodness. Building on Lacoste's account of affectivity allows for a phenomenological reduction to goodness that can be associated with an expansive range of phenomena reflective of the Hebrew term "good" (*tôb*).

After describing the experiential contours of a prelinguistic goodness in relation to joy and enjoyment, I will develop the concept of *entangled topologies* to address several hermeneutical challenges that follow from affirming an explicitly Christian horizon of place. If there are prelinguistic experiences of goodness (as I argue in the first half of the chapter), then such a goodness necessarily remains open to a wide range of interpretative categories. I explore several examples of how differing horizons of place commonly encounter a prelinguistic goodness at play in experience—Heidegger's world and earth, agnostic and atheistic concepts of the sacred, as well as explicitly Christian concepts of creation. My central point is that a broadly articulated prelinguistic goodness opens up ways in which to explore commonality between people even amid inextricable differences.

Arguing for the entanglement of topologies based on a prelinguistic experience of goodness underscores one of the crucial positions in this book, namely, that one does not need to affirm a Christian horizon of place in order to identify phenomena theologically understood to be part of creation's goodness. Critically, the legitimacy of diverse interpretations does not lead to a simplistic relativism, since, to the extent that my descriptions of joy and enjoyment accurately sketch the contours of a prelinguistic goodness, they constitute a step toward the "real" and open up further avenues of argumentation—one might further explore various modes of theological rationality from within the inextricable limits, ambiguities, and diversities of experience. In the context of this chapter, however, the theological insights derived from outlining a prelinguistic goodness are substantially qualified. As I will explain, the phenomenological contours of a prelinguistic goodness do not adequately represent or demonstrate creation's goodness but help clarify the relationship between experience and theological concepts.

Joy and a Prelinguistic Goodness

Lacoste's account of joy and enjoyment are not the only instances in which one might identify a prelinguistic goodness at play in experience, but they offer some of the clearest examples. He distinguishes the two affectivities by defining *joy* as an existentially significant experience capable of shifting the entire way in which we relate to our surroundings (similar to

Heidegger's *Erfahrung*).[1] Conversely, Lacoste relates *enjoyment* to simple pleasures that are tied to particular things or objects like a good book or a cup of tea. The experience of enjoyment is closer to Husserl's understanding of experience as "mental states relating to objects of consciousness or intentionality: what the self is 'living through' in any given instance (*Erlebnis*)."[2] As I will explain, both affectivities help one recognize a prelinguistic goodness at play in experience that is related to the biblical affirmation of creation's goodness—albeit in different ways, which are nonetheless linked.

Lacoste develops his phenomenology of joy as part of a broader critique of Heidegger's prioritization of anxiety as *the* fundamental disclosing mood (*Grundstimmungen*). Joy stands as one of several "counter-existentials" that demonstrate how various moods are capable of disclosing the meaning(s) of being.[3] By exploring a diverse range of moods, Lacoste aims to develop a modest phenomenology that actually says "very little of being as such apart from its appearing fragmentarily in various modes of being."[4] He seeks to nuance and limit the role specific moods (or affectivities) might play in disclosing the meaning of being, while leaving open the possibility that they still indicate something about what is originary (or perhaps prelinguistic) about existence.

Lacoste's account of joy is clarified by its relation to Heidegger's concept of *Befindlichkeit*. As Thomas Sheehan explains, *Befindlichkeit* refers to "the condition of affective familiarity with a given context of meaning and its contents. Such affective attunement is the primordial way that a world of meaning is opened up to us."[5] In other words, *Befindlichkeit* relates to the way different moods influence one's perception of the world. Boredom, for instance, can affect not only what I think about the television show I am watching, but it might impact my impression of the entire world of watching television.[6] Heidegger, however, is less interested in ordinary moods like boredom than he is in ones that help people understand their situation more fundamentally (*Grundstimmungen*). In other words, Heidegger is interested in moods that not only disclose the world but disclose *Dasein* to itself and offer "a way of understanding oneself."[7] In Chapter 5, I will explain why Heidegger prioritizes anxiety as *the* fundamental mood in more detail, but for now it is enough to note that Lacoste argues that there are a variety of disclosing moods that *counter* anxiety—none of which have the final or decisive insight into the meaning of being.

While Lacoste's account of joy is contextualized within his argument for a modest phenomenology, he emphasizes that joy can have an expansive influence on how one relates to the world. He submits:

> When I find my joy to be, or to exist, then the phenomenon has nothing fragmentary about it. Not only is joy present, but also its present, if it is invested in a future or a past, can confer on them its proper tonality: the one who lives in the pure and simple phenomenon of joy lives there as an "I am," an "I was" and an "I will be."[8]

In Lacoste's account, the experience of joy is not permanent, since it can be interrupted or "deconstituted" like any other experience.[9] But when one finds oneself in joy there is less concern over duration or what may have been experienced in the past or will be in the future. Being-in-the-world simply becomes "'well-being' in the world."[10] Joy accommodates the entirety of existence by "reflecting on everything inhabiting the world and on all dealings with the world."[11] In other words, Lacoste's account of joy has an *expansive* (or capacious) quality that discloses a general sense that "it is good."

Although the kind of experiences Lacoste associates with joy may be relatively rare, he presents it as an almost universal phenomenon. He acknowledges that joy is subjective in the sense that it is always "mine" (I am, I was, and I will be), but this does not change that "when I find myself in joy, the 'I' in question engages, beyond my experience, a universal aptitude for experience."[12] Joy in being is not simply the result of one's circumstances or prior beliefs but "is to itself its own reason."[13] The agnostic person with little money on a crowded subway may find herself in joy, while the first-class airline passenger who believes in the Christian God may be irritated. And while there are things a person can do to try to cultivate something like joy, ultimately, it is not a feeling that can be attained on demand or traced to a particular cause (such as privilege or wealth).

Now, Lacoste's account of joy relates to what I have described as a prelinguistic goodness in the sense that it is associated with an *originary possibility*. He argues that there is no reason to foreclose the "origin" to Heidegger's "pure fact of existing," but instead, one must also consider the significance of counterexistentials like joy.[14] There is a "primordial rhythm of affection" that intimates the diverse meaning of being over the course of affective experience, and a joyful sense of "well-being" is included in this rhythm.[15] Critically, relating joy to an originary possibility does not deny the significance of language for disclosing phenomena or its obvious role in describing it but (as indicated in the Introduction) simply indicates "a meaningful order of our experience that does not coincide with that of our 'grammar.'"[16] Claude Romano explains:

> If there is one claim that seems to be shared by almost all phenomenologists—perhaps the only one—it is that according to which

phenomena are presented to us with an autochthonous meaning that is not projected onto them by our language patterns. Whether it be the face, which, in Levinas, speaks to us before any word, the flesh and expressive gestures, which are, according to Merleau-Ponty, at the root of language itself, affectivity, the event, and even Heidegger's *Sinn des Seins*—in all these cases, it is indeed with a prelinguistic meaning that we are dealing.[17]

Joy helps disclose an important dynamic within this meaningful order of prelinguistic experience. Even if it is not the most frequent experience, joy intimates the originary possibility that there is goodness (very broadly defined) at play in experience.

Lacoste connects joy to a specifically Christian concept of creation's goodness in *Être en danger*; however, he does so almost in passing. The text is one of his most philosophically focused, so while he makes theological observations, the transitions from philosophy to theology are often clearly demarcated and uncontroversial.[18] And this remains the case with respect to the connection between joy and the affirmation of creation's goodness when he writes: "*Joy recaptures for itself the divine words saluting the completed creation: it is good. (And it pronounces in this way on the 'meaning of being')*."[19] The connection here is illustrative rather than dogmatic. Lacoste does not take the opportunity to develop further theological explanation but simply indicates that joy offers a point of contact between the biblical account of creation's goodness and one's potential experiences. More recently, he further clarifies the connection between joy and creation's goodness when he warns that the Genesis text describes a moment *before* history and that one should not consider personal experiences like joy to be equivalent to the anthropomorphized feelings of God expressed in the text.[20] Lacoste proposes that when "what is, appears to us as well and good and these only," then this is only an intimation of a moment that is before human history.[21] There is no equivalence between individual joy and God's apparent pleasure in the goodness of creation, but affective experience at least introduces the context in which one might consider what it would mean when God affirms "it is good" throughout the opening Genesis poem.

Enjoyment and a Prelinguistic Goodness

If joy suggests an originary possibility that can be related to the expansive affirmation of creation's goodness in the biblical text, enjoyment is a more ordinary experience, one with fewer existential implications and offering minimal insight into creation's goodness.[22] Nonetheless, as I will explain, there are times when it is difficult to distinguish the two affectivities, and more importantly, enjoyment uniquely offers additional insight into a pre-linguistic goodness at play in experience.

In *The Appearing of God*, Lacoste uses the term "enjoyment" (*jouissance*) in order to describe the "joy of" something. Unlike joy, enjoyment does not accommodate the entirety of being; rather, it operates as a "mixture" of pleasure and joy.[23] It is not a "fundamental" disclosing mood, since it is closer to a feeling "like interest, sympathy, fear, or disgust."[24] And while lasting joy is at least conceivable, enjoyment is "fleeting," since it requires the *presence* of something that "takes possession of our consciousness, making us, as it were, one body with it."[25] When we enjoy this presence, everything else is put on hold because nothing is missed in the "immediacy" of the experience—there is a temporary immersion with the object of enjoyment.[26] Lacoste explains, "We do not enjoy everything at once, only this at one moment and that at another, but while we enjoy it, our satiated consciousness and body seem to expend all their capacity upon it."[27] For example, when I enjoy a beer at the end of a day, the stress of completing my assignments becomes marginalized. Or, when I enjoy reading a book to my nieces and nephews, we put aside the fact that it is their bedtime soon and that I have to go back to Belgium in the coming weeks. These enjoyable moments provide rest and comfort after a period of activity and might even be understood as a form of distraction.

While enjoyment is a phenomenon of the here and now, Lacoste notes that it is not strictly defined by the present—but rather, a *living present*. One's relationship to a thing that is enjoyed often initiates remembering and even hope for its reappearance. Lacoste calls maintaining a relationship to enjoyment *fidelity* (although he suggests that the "language of love is not quite right for enjoyment"). His point is that there is "a bridge from enjoyment to an experience of time not centred exclusively on the present."[28] As such, fidelity to enjoyment encompasses the capacity to *feel the absence* of things. Absence is defined affectively in this context because we are not capable of feeling the absence of everything that is not present, but we do tend to feel the absence of something that was enjoyed. Lacoste writes:

> I can remember what I did an hour ago—leaving my home, having a cup of coffee, etc.—without any sense of absence. (Or of presence, either, since memory gives presence only to what creates a *feeling*.) Absence, as now defined, is given to be felt, as a kind of suffering, to be more precise.[29]

As such, when I am living in Belgium I often feel the absence of my nieces and nephews who remain in Canada; however, I have never *felt* the absence of Toronto's traffic even though it is also unavailable. The contours of enjoyment are not defined simply by the pleasure of a present moment but also by the affective absence of this pleasure.

As I have indicated, there are times when Lacoste's analysis of enjoyment incorporates characteristics of joy, and it becomes hard to distinguish between the two. The integration of the two affectivities is most evident in Lacoste's reflections on drinking tea in his office during a moment of rest in *Le monde et l'absence d'œuvre et autre études*. Therein, he describes a moment where he is not worried about the past or future but is simply experiencing the "peaceful joy" of the present.[30] He introduces the language of comfort or ease (*l'aise*) in order to describe the experience and goes on to propose that the moment "can be received with gratitude, as part of what, in the beginning, was declared 'good,' and 'very good,'" while also adding that one does not need "biblical legitimation" in order to accept this kind of experience.[31] Critically, joy and enjoyment seem to be mutually informing each other in this example. Lacoste *takes a break* from work and *enjoys a cup tea*, which in turn influences a much *wider sense of joy* wherein Lacoste *finds himself* in a more existentially significant mood. There is no guarantee that tomorrow's cup of afternoon tea will lead to a similar experience that recalls the biblical affirmation of creation's goodness.

The ambiguity between enjoyment and joy in Lacoste's example underscores an important complexity related to the role of *intentionality* in affectivity.[32] In some circumstances the role of intentionality seems clear—I plan to have a beer after work because it is typically enjoyable. However, as Robyn Horner explains, if one considers carefully Lacoste's example of rediscovering an old friend, the role of intentionality becomes less clear. Following Levinas, she notes the difficulty one might have in "constituting another person in intentionality" and "wonders whether the intentional feeling of joy [enjoyment] that has another person as its object is ethically possible, since it would involve the indulgence of possession and egoistic pleasure at the expense of the other" (the qualification can be extended to my example of enjoying a moment reading with my nieces and nephews).[33] Moreover, she asks whether Lacoste's rediscovery of a friend may in fact be closer to existential joy on occasions if it is "the rediscovery of a friend once thought lost or dead or in grave danger." According to Horner, there is "a continuum implied in the very distinction between ordinary and deep joy, which in itself is problematic, unless it is explained in terms of a very flexible use of language."[34] As such, joy and enjoyment are often "mixed" (as Lacoste acknowledges) to the point where it is difficult to distinguish between the two affectivities or the role our own intentionality plays in creating the feeling.

It is critical to acknowledge the way enjoyment and joy are mixed, in part, because it opens further implications for the experience of enjoyment. A helpful example can be found in Jean-Louis Chrétien's *Spacious Joy*, wherein he does not distinguish joy and enjoyment but rather defines his analysis by the movement between *interiority* and *exteriority*.[35] On the one hand, joy is an interior state that is capable of transforming how we relate to our surroundings: "As soon as joy wells up in us, everything expands. Our breathing becomes more ample, and our body suddenly stretches out of its self-confined corner and quivers with mobility. Feeling more alive in a vaster space, we want to leap, skip, run or dance."[36] On the other hand, Chrétien also notices how the presence of particular things in the exterior world are capable of transforming one's interior space. For instance, he proposes, "A new relationship with the world starts with a pleasing smell. Nothing stops a smell from spreading since it penetrates everywhere."[37] He notes that its "ambient, atmospheric dimension" can travel "long-distances" and bring us into "unison with the atmosphere" that surrounds us.[38] Something as simple as a pleasing smell is capable of shifting one's mood (or interior space), which in turn suggests that the enjoyment of a particular presence can contribute to a more substantial or expansive sense of joy. This mixture of joy and enjoyment remains less a question of cause and effect and more an exploration of the ongoing interaction between bodily life and the world.

Critically, then, the interaction between bodily life and the world reinforces the contours of a prelinguistic goodness at play in experience. Enjoyable experiences (which are often mixed with joy) demonstrate a general quality of goodness that permeates experience in a variety of ways—a pleasant smell, reading with my nieces and nephews, the touch of a partner, a cup of tea—all of which (again) become part of what Romano describes as the prelinguistic "meaningful order of experience." These are *perceptual* (embodied) experiences that one encounters in various phenomena in the world. Even if one has concerns with the language of "goodness," the enjoyment of particular things should at least signify ordinary ways in which there are agreeable qualities at play in experience that are rarely questioned.[39] This perceptual (prelinguistic) experience does not undermine the importance of hermeneutics but points toward real, sensible qualities out there in the world.

For those who confess a Christian faith, these "qualities" relate to the concrete blessings associated with a theology of creation's goodness. However, as I explain in the following section, there remains a significant degree of complexity within the interaction between affectivities like enjoyment and theological concepts. The experience of a prelinguistic goodness does not necessarily imply that one is living in a good creation since that experience remains open to diverse horizons of place.

Affective Experience and Theological Knowledge of a Good Creation

Up to this point, I have argued that Lacoste's phenomenology of joy and enjoyment discloses a prelinguistic goodness at play in experience that is recognizable regardless of one's confessional stance. While Lacoste relates joy/enjoyment to the biblical affirmation of creation's goodness, he does not expand on the connection in detail. In order to elucidate some of the issues that arise in making the connection, it is helpful to examine his account of affective experience in relation to theological knowledge. Lacoste's approach is helpful because he emphasizes the limits and ambiguities of affective experiences (like joy/enjoyment) while also maintaining their significance for understanding theological propositions (like creation's goodness). The emphasis on ambiguity underscores why there are a variety of interpretative possibilities that arise in relation to a prelinguistic goodness. Moreover, his description of theological knowledge helps clarify why the claims of theology are not reducible to how a person might feel at a particular moment in time. Each of these points will inform my argument for "entangled topologies" in the latter half of this chapter.

It is worth noting that Lacoste often relays skepticism regarding philosophies of religion that rely on a concept of "experience as religious sentiment"—an approach that he associates with Friedrich Schleiermacher and William James.[40] While focusing on feeling or sentiment "has the advantage of providing an easy entry into the subject," he argues it has "the drawback of assigning narrow limits to the relationship of man to God."[41] Moreover, Lacoste warns that relying on how a person feels in order to talk about God can risk "threatening the confessional and propositional contents of the Christian faith."[42] In order to offer a more credible account of religious experience and the role of affect in Christian life, therefore, Lacoste draws a distinction between intuitive knowledge (*connaissance*) and propositional knowledge (*savoir*). This distinction runs throughout Lacoste's work, and as Horner points out, it can be difficult to keep track of how the two ways of knowing are performed in his various texts.[43] But near the conclusion of *The Appearing of God*, Lacoste offers one of his clearest accounts of the role of *connaissance* and *savoir* with respect to theological knowledge. As I will explain, his analysis in this context helps clarify the way affective experiences like joy/enjoyment interact with the biblical affirmation of creation's goodness.

Lacoste describes *propositional* theological knowledge as a formal, conceptual discourse about God, based on God revealing God's self through scripture, tradition, history—all of which is necessary in order for theology to speak about God.[44] The definition of creation's goodness I provided in the Introduction of this study can be identified with this kind of propositional theological knowledge. I identified a set of propositions (or "features") that define creation's goodness based on the first chapter of Genesis and its subsequent reception in Christian history and tradition. I emphasized the variety of theological contexts in which the following propositions are maintained: (1) creation's goodness is capacious; (2) creation's goodness is primarily a quality rather than an ethic; (3) creation's goodness includes the affirmation of materiality; (4) God is the source and sustainer of this goodness. It is not necessary to *feel* like we are living in a good creation in order to understand how I developed these propositions. As Lacoste explains, theology is perfectly capable of organizing itself as a propositional discipline even if this emphasis tends to marginalize the "element of praise" (a form of theological expression that is closer to intuitive knowledge).[45]

Conversely, Lacoste suggests that intuitive knowledge is attained through "affection, familiarity, and 'knowledge by acquaintance.'"[46] It develops *prior* to the language that describes it and often "paves the way for propositional knowledge without a break."[47] In certain instances of religious experience intuitive knowledge can be "a strictly unrepeatable experience, a wholly interior event, stubbornly indescribable and resistant to all categorization."[48] Elsewhere, Lacoste associates "knowledge by acquaintance" with *la parole*— which can be identified with "the quality of being affected" or a point of "'contact between consciousness and what enters into its field' as present."[49] With respect to understanding creation's goodness, intuitive knowledge is related to the phenomenology of joy and enjoyment I noted earlier. An experience of profound joy discloses the *capacious* sense of goodness that is also affirmed in the first chapter of Genesis. Or, more ordinarily, the enjoyment of particular things like a cup of tea or a glass of beer suggests a quality of goodness that one might associate with specific manifestations of creation's goodness. The important point is that both experiences help form an intuitive knowledge (*connaissance*) that offers affective insight into the propositional content of creation's goodness.

Lacoste insists both forms of knowledge are necessary and eventually come together for theological knowledge. While it is possible to separate them for the sake of explanation and clarity, one's knowledge is incomplete without access to both forms of knowledge:

Propositional knowledge can survive without intuitive knowledge, as intuitive knowledge can survive without knowledge of the facts. Yet in the end there are two non-negotiable points of reference: (i) conscious life cannot be described without both kinds of knowledge, (ii) there is a rhythm in the life of the self that links the two kinds without creating an opposition between them.[50]

Creation's goodness, therefore, should include a set of understandable concepts and propositions, but those concepts are enriched by encountering something like a prelinguistic goodness in the rhythm of affective life. Theological knowledge requires both a sense of being affected and our efforts to make sense of this affection through language, concepts, propositions, and so on.

While acknowledging the necessity of both propositional and intuitive knowledge is important, Lacoste quickly points out that the two forms of knowledge do not always work together seamlessly. He explains that a common instance of confusion regarding intuitive and propositional theological knowledge relates to speaking about God—who is unlike any other "object" of propositional statements. In response, Lacoste proposes that certain conceptual norms for theology have arisen in order to define the relationship between intuitive and propositional theology. He explains:

> Whenever the question of intuitive versus propositional knowledge of God arises, it is wise to make one thing clear at the start: God is known to us (*connu*) as unknown (*inconnu*). We may attribute any emotion we call "religious" to the presence of God, but when we try to analyze it, we shall quickly learn that we hardly know what it is that has moved us. . . . The tradition that has used the words "God known as unknown" acknowledges, before all else, God's unknowability. He is more than could lie within the compass of our feeling. But that leads on to speaking of his knowability, too. To say "unknowing exceeds knowledge" paradoxically focuses on the knowledge of God. In this context "I feel an absence of feeling" says something quite precise: the unknown cannot pass unnoticed. I know what it is I do not feel, though I would like to. Feeling, on the other hand, is not denied.[51]

For a person interested in knowing God, it would be hard to bracket feeling or desire from that interest—nor should one necessarily want to bracket those things, since intuitive knowledge informs propositional statements about God.[52] But because it is common enough for one's feelings to have a complicated relationship to theological propositions, Lacoste suggests that as a "safe rule" one should "let propositional knowledge be the judge of intuitive knowledge to the extent that it is capable of it."[53] While both forms of knowledge are necessary, propositional knowledge can help one examine or discern one's feelings or desires and integrate them (ideally) into more understandable theological content.

The principles of theological knowledge Lacoste outlines are particularly important for thinking about the fourth feature of creation's goodness—God as the *source* of goodness. For instance, one might consider the statement in Psalm 34: "O taste and see that the Lord is good" (Ps. 34:8).[54] The psalmist makes use of intuitive knowledge that seems to be a mixture of joy and enjoyment. The statement draws on the experience of something particular from creation (an enjoyable taste) in order to describe an expansive sense of gratitude and joy in God.[55] A point of connection with propositional theology then arises when the psalmist relates creation's goodness to the Lord's goodness. While this connection is perfectly legitimate within the context of praising God, if one moves toward a more critical analysis of the analogy that is offered, then further propositional knowledge becomes important. Within the broad history of Christian thought God's goodness is not synonymous with creation's goodness but is rather contextualized by statements like God is "always greater (*deus semper maior*)" or by the idea of an "infinite qualitative difference" between God and creation.[56] The "infinite qualitative difference" offers a "safe rule" in which to integrate the knowledge (*connaissance*) that arises in a moment of joyful praise into propositional knowledge (*savoir*) about God.

Of course, what constitutes an acceptable "proposition" about God is controversial. There are enduring debates about the degree of equivocity involved in using analogies or metaphors for God—some of which are related to the dangers of onto-theology noted in the Introduction. But the point of connection I am seeking to clarify in the context of Lacoste's thought is less metaphysical than phenomenological. In his account, the movement from joy/enjoyment (intuitive knowledge) to creation's goodness (propositional knowledge) would not be the result of a logical deduction but rather a particular understanding of that which appears. He explains:

> It may be perfectly clear that there is an ashtray on my desk, perfectly clear that $2+2=4$ (if we know what we are talking about and understand the meaning of the terms, etc.). It is not perfectly clear, on the other hand, that what is seen owes its being to an invisible First Cause, and even when we have done our utmost to prove it, our proof, unlike a logical or a mathematical proof, will not constrain us. But it

will allow us, perhaps, to see the world differently, and it will allow that by offering such a possibility to us. It is up to us to take the step of saying that, as a result of the proof, the Absolute *can* be known, and *is* known.[57]

Similarly, when it is suggested that a quality of goodness finds its source in a Creator, then it appears as a "possibility to us" that we might adopt. The suggestion here might arise in a variety of circumstances—reading Genesis 1, Psalm 34, or contemplating Aquinas's five ways. The important point with respect to God's appearing as the source of creation's goodness is that it is not a presence that forces itself on people like an ashtray or an equation. Yet, if one "takes the step" of saying that creation's goodness ultimately comes from God, it has the potential to change how one perceives the world. One might more readily relate the goodness of creation to the goodness of God, but this will require substantial qualification within the context of propositional theology.

Secondary Evidence

Seeing the world differently relates to Lacoste's account of *secondary evidence*—a concept I alluded in the Introduction. Therein I suggested that Lacoste develops the concept of secondary evidence in order to argue that the most important aspects of being human are not always reducible to what is "initial" or first given to experience. This is an issue that is specific to the phenomenological tradition, since phenomenology is broadly concerned with experiences of a *pre*-predicative or *pre*-linguistic world that exists *prior* to our knowledge of it. I have sought to engage with this concern by exploring a prelinguistic goodness at play in experiences of joy and enjoyment. However, like several of his contemporaries in French phenomenology, Lacoste seeks to expand the range of phenomena that might be available to phenomenological description beyond what is initial in experience.[58] This includes "secondary evidence" that is explicitly related to theology and capable of shifting the way in which people relate to their surroundings.

Lacoste describes secondary evidence within the context of his reflections on liturgy in *Experience and the Absolute*. I return to his account of liturgy in the fifth chapter of this book, since it raises important issues for thinking about topology (one's horizon of place). But for now, it is helpful to focus on the concept of secondary evidence and, more specifically, on how this implies a degree of theological knowledge that *mediates* one's surroundings. Lacoste explains:

> In stark contrast to the initial manifestation of the "life-world," the field of liturgy is governed by knowledge. Only a fundamental presupposition—that the Absolute is a subject, with which a relation has been promised—enables it to open itself up and organize itself. The logic that precedes here is not that of primitive acts of consciousness and the raw appearances of phenomena: on the contrary, it unfolds within the order of mediation, and this mediation is a critique of the antepredicative evidence of life.[59]

The significance of secondary evidence to liturgy offers a tentative analogue for understanding how creation's goodness might mediate one's encounter with a prelinguistic goodness. By introducing God as the source of the blessings associated with creation's goodness, a new horizon emerges that shifts and potentially even functions as a "critique" of what "initially" appeared. Even if it is ordinary to live in the "sphere of antepredicative evidence," the introduction of God (or the Absolute) suggests the possibility that one's experience might not be solely defined by what is first given.

Lacoste's concept of secondary evidence reinforces (even radicalizes) what Romano describes as a gap between *understanding* and *interpretation*. Romano associates "understanding" with prelinguistic meaning and "interpretation" as that which arises in response to it.[60] He argues that if interpretation does not follow from an originary understanding then "all interpretation must refer back to yet another interpretation, and an infinite regression is inevitable."[61] While Romano acknowledges that interpretation can "*shed light on* our experience of phenomena," he emphasizes that phenomena can also be "ricocheted back onto their interpretation, reorienting and enriching it."[62] A prelinguistic meaning, then, is necessary in order to avoid "perspectivism," wherein everything is reducible to interpretation (I will return to this issue near the conclusion of this chapter).[63] An initial encounter with meaningful phenomena (like goodness) opens the door for a more complex hermeneutic associated with creation's goodness—which has the potential to reorient and enrich the notion of goodness.

Lacoste's account of secondary evidence, therefore, is necessarily *hermeneutic*, and he acknowledges as much when he states that it produces mediating concepts:

> This secondary evidence will perhaps install a second immediacy that will enable us to perceive in the world, such as it is presented to us, the clear and distinct reflection of the divine glory. But we must never forget that this perception is the offspring of the work of interpretation, and projects onto phenomena a light and a univocal meaning

not actually given in conjunction with the phenomena . . . God must be named beforehand for the heavens to sing their glory.⁶⁴

It is important to emphasize the considerable shift taking place in the transition from a prelinguistic experience to a more specifically Christian interpretation wherein one perceives the world as "a reflection of divine glory." Reading a book to my nieces and nephews may display a general play of "goodness" in the contours of experience, but with increasing degrees of theological knowledge, that experience might be integrated into a Christological horizon wherein our entire lives are defined by God's relation to creation. I intimated the wide-ranging theological implications (or possibilities) of this relation already in the Introduction when I noted examples like Hildegard of Bingen's image of greenness as the "life-giving life" of the Holy Spirit or Calvin's understanding of creation as God's "theater of glory." One might encounter goodness through the "primordial rhythm of affection," but the specifically Christian experience of that goodness appears in the context of secondary evidence that includes a degree of theological knowledge.

Critically, although Lacoste describes secondary evidence as an "interpretation" that projects a certain "light" onto phenomena, this emphasis on interpretation is not a complete theological summary of what is happening when one begins to understand the world to be a good creation.⁶⁵ In Chapter 3 I consider what happens when we "see the world differently" by examining a Christian concept of transformation that introduces the centrality of *God's initiative*. This possibility noticeably complicates the category of experience by suggesting that it is not only *my decision* to interpret the world in a particular way that unfolds a Christian horizon of place. For now, however, I am principally concerned with introducing the hermeneutical complexities related to the movement from a prelinguistic goodness to a more explicitly Christian understanding of that goodness amid legitimately diverse horizons of place.

Entangled Topologies: World and Creation

In order to further address these hermeneutical complexities, it is helpful to examine the potential of a prelinguistic "goodness" to appear within differing topologies. In the following two sections, I explore this possibility by turning to Lacoste's evaluation of Heidegger's concepts of "world" and "earth" in relation to the Christian concept of "creation." While Lacoste emphasizes substantial differences between these topologies (which I do not question), one might also identify the persistent presence of a prelinguistic goodness within each of these horizons of place. In order to make this case, the central theme I develop is the *entanglement of topologies*, which allows me to acknowledge both the legitimacy of a wide spectrum of interpretations and avoid an overly simplistic relativism. The entanglement that I describe looks different depending on whether one is referring to "world" or "earth." In fact, as I will explain, the entanglement of *earth* and creation is particularly complex and requires additional explanation—in part, because I question aspects of Lacoste's account by considering different ways in which to understand the concept of "sacrality." As such, it is productive to begin with Lacoste's account of world and creation, which establishes clear differences while also leaving room to articulate their entanglement around the appearing of a prelinguistic goodness.

While there are manifold differences one might point out between Heidegger's world and a Christian concept of creation, Lacoste identifies two distinctions that are particularly important. First, and most obvious, Lacoste notes that Heidegger's world entails "no relation to God, no presence before God."[66] He proposes that the silence concerning God is a nonnegotiable outcome of a "philosophical hermeneutics of facticity," which assumes that "there is nothing beyond; it measures all presence in the last instance."[67] Such a horizon of place clearly differs from Christian concepts of creation, according to Lacoste, since creation implies a God who is never reducible to the *immanence* of experience. Theologically speaking, he explains that creation and Christology form a "horizon for one another" wherein the Word is the "internal foundation" for the covenant (*l'alliance*) between creation and God.[68] The Word is not synonymous with creation yet remains "internal" to it and therefore marks an obvious point of difference with Heidegger's world.

A second distinction that Lacoste draws between world and creation relates to the status of sin. In *Note sur le temps* (one of his more explicitly theological texts), he suggests that the world represents "the refusal of the covenant, that is to say sin, and its consequences introduce a new order of being."[69] Lacoste has been challenged on this characterization of the world by several commentators. Emmanuel Falque, for instance, argues that identifying sin with the "world" condemns the logic of facticity too quickly.[70] He worries that associating the world with sin leads to a theology of "redemption" that overlooks Christ's "solidarity" with finitude.[71] Pushing the issue even further, Joeri Schrijvers argues that Lacoste offers "a somewhat one-sided valuation of creation," wherein creation speaks of a certain "relationality" or "rapport" with things (such as art, resting, liturgical experience), while the absence of such a relationality is "de-creation."[72] He contends that in Lacoste's account "everything that is good and meaningful must be conceived of as creation," and "all that there is to the world can only be the negativity of death and sin."[73] I will return to the concerns registered by Falque and Schrijvers shortly, since I think that Lacoste has a complicated rendering of the relationship between world and creation. But it is important to acknowledge that Lacoste clearly associates the world with sin in his first book (*Note sur le temps*), and this marks another obvious point of difference between the two topologies.

Despite these substantial differences, Lacoste does not exclusively draw a binary distinction between the world and creation. A close reading of his work also shows how world and creation remain fundamentally entangled. For example, in the same paragraph in which he associates sin with the world, Lacoste also writes, "Real difference cannot and must not mean the total annulment of creation by the world."[74] He foreshadows the development of his modest phenomenology by asserting that there is a fundamental "ambiguity" in experience that withholds the possibility of a decisive philosophical meaning to being.[75] Both an "atheistic enclosure of the self" and "a theological sense of experience" are transcendental possibilities that cannot be excluded.[76] They are both implicit possibilities that do not cancel each other but instead underscore the diverse meanings of being human.

Pushing the point even further, Lacoste does not always give the atheistic enclosure of the self a negative evaluation. He identifies the "ontological duplicity" that stems from the "profane or demythologized" world as a helpful account for theologians.[77] As Jeffrey Bloechl emphasizes, Lacoste is interested in Heidegger's works in part because he thinks they "offer us the best possible understanding of dimensions of our being that do not (yet) know God."[78] These dimensions have an "integrity all their own," which in turn can be related to what contemporary discourse often calls "secularity."[79] While Lacoste does not hesitate to criticize Heidegger, he also recognizes that the implied atheism of the world can be authentic and rational, rather than a topology that should only be criticized so that one might be brought into relation with God.

The legitimacy of a "profane or demythologized" world is further endorsed by Lacoste because it helps establish the possibility of human freedom. He argues that the world reinforces a "primordial structure that would be dangerous to decompose" and remains the "*a priori* condition of a freely desired relation."[80] Lacoste summarizes the position stating:

> The world is our unique introduction to creation. This introduction is problematic and ambiguous, because creation is not another name of the world, because it is what people have always lost or forgotten.

But behind the erasures of history, we do not exist in the world without also revealing the government of creation. Neither being-in-the-world nor holiness defines us completely. The dialectical interplay of creation and the world is the place of our existence. Creation and the world are interwoven for us.[81]

Together, the concepts of world and creation are capable of working in a way that is complementary and noncontradictory (at least to a certain degree). The ambiguity of experience holds within it the reality and accessibility of creation; however, that is not the only legitimate interpretation (there is freedom). The world and creation are necessarily entangled (they are *interwoven* in us), even if they are differentiated in experience and understanding.

Critically, then, because the world and creation are entangled in Lacoste's account, it is not surprising that he recognizes phenomena in the "world" that might be associated with what I have described as a prelinguistic goodness. Even in *Note sur le temps* Lacoste recognizes room for *joy* and *benevolence* in the "world," while still emphasizing that death has the "last word."[82] This recognition of joy and benevolence foreshadows Lacoste's subsequent argument in *Être en danger* that affective experiences (like joy) disclose something important about the meaning of being regardless of one's confession of faith. This is important in part because it pushes back on the assertion that "everything that is good and meaningful must be conceived of as creation" in Lacoste's account. But more importantly, it indicates the possibility that there is *entanglement* between world and creation around the prelinguistic play of goodness in moments of joy and enjoyment. Of course, this goodness is understood very differently depending on whether one's horizon of place is defined in relation to God. The appearing of a prelinguistic goodness simply initiates entangled interpretations from within diverse topologies.

Entangled Topologies: Earth and Creation

The entanglement between Heidegger's earth and creation's goodness is more complicated, in part, because Heidegger uses religiously inflected language in order to describe the earth's topology.[83] Perhaps in response to this more spiritually accommodating terminology, however, Lacoste warns against collapsing the concepts of "earth" and "creation." Similar to my analysis of world and creation, it is not my intention to question the broader distinctions he identifies; however, "earth" and "creation" also remain linked in ways Lacoste does not acknowledge. As I will explain, the *sacrality* of Heidegger's earth is not fully separable from what Christians describe as creation's goodness, and this connection helps illustrate a much broader uncertainty related to what constitutes a distinctively "Christian" or "secular" experience.

Lacoste explains that Heidegger describes a topology of the earth in his later work as a way to contradict fruitfully the anxiety and homelessness associated with being-in-the-world.[84] If being-in-the-world implies a feeling of "house arrest," then the language of "mother earth" alludes to a sense of dwelling and being-at-home.[85] The earth is "the paradoxical intervention of the numinous in the world," offering shelter, protection, and the "all-sustaining [*omniportante*] ground" on which human beings might encounter the "sacred."[86] While Lacoste acknowledges that Heidegger's emphasis on sacrality "substantially enlarges the sphere of immanence," he argues that it emerges from the same ground as the world.[87] According to Lacoste, Heidegger's account of the sacred guarantees "proximity" to the divine, whereas there is an "infinite distance" that defines one's relation to the Absolute in Christianity.[88] As a result, the sacredness of the earth cannot be correlated with a Christian understanding of creation, since it remains coordinated exclusively by immanence.

Lacoste further distances the sacrality of the earth from Christianity with reference to the holy. He builds on the classic French distinction (*sacré* and *saint*)—which is also represented by its historical usage in English, wherein the sacred rarely refers to God, but "the holy is of God, and as such reflects the purity of the transcendent."[89] Lacoste reinforces the point by turning to the image of a "holy fool" who refuses to be at home in the world or take comfort in the "numinous" treasures of the earth.[90] And he proposes that the holy fool's "spectacular marginality" expresses in "concrete form" the peculiarity that affects "anyone subordinating this being-in-the-world to his being-before-God."[91] The holy fool understands that God is not found anywhere in the sacred but instead waits for God within an eschatological horizon.[92] It is important not to overlook the significance of this distinction, and I will return to its centrality for thinking about creation's goodness in the final chapter. For now, it is enough to identify (and affirm in principle) the difference between the holy and the sacred, based on the immanence of Heidegger's topology of the earth and the transcendence of God from creation in Christianity.

Despite the validity of these distinctions, one might also identify ways in which "earth" and "creation" remain entangled by reassessing the role of the "sacred" in relation to creation's goodness. To this end, it is helpful to consider Jeffrey Kosky's *Arts of Wonder*, which borrows from Heidegger in order to reflect on a contemporary dissatisfaction with "the immanent self-assertion of reason through the mastery and alteration of reality" often associated with secular life.[93] He considers works of art in order "to linger in the majesty of things that do not appear in the light of reasons rendered" and to inhabit "places where we might adopt 'a pensive nature' and discover a 'daily majesty of meditation, / that comes and goes in silences of its own.'"[94] Kosky avoids Christianizing "secular" art or attempting to show how it might be embraced and reinterpreted within Nicene Christianity.[95] Instead, he addresses his reflections to "people who are sensitive to human longings and experiences that might traditionally have been located in religious traditions," while at the same time suggesting that "these longings exceed such a location and might also be encountered, and cultivated in, and by, contemporary works of art."[96] Kosky does not aim to affirm a traditional Christian concept of divine transcendence, but at the same time, he is dissatisfied with "immanent self-assertion" and finds Heidegger's framework a helpful way to push its boundaries.[97] At the very least, Kosky's reflections on contemporary art put into question where one might locate the beginning of transcendence and the end of immanence both in Heidegger's work and in so-called secular contexts more broadly.

Kosky's appropriation of Heidegger foregrounds a much broader issue, one in which the lines between the sacred and secular, religious and profane, immanence and transcendence, are often difficult to draw for scholars.[98] His dissatisfaction with immanent self-assertion points to what Charles Taylor describes as *cross pressures*:

> The salient feature of Western societies is not so much a decline of religious faith and practice, though there has been lots of that, more in some societies than in others, but rather a mutual fragilization of different religious positions, as well as of the outlooks both of belief and unbelief. The whole culture experiences cross pressures, between the draw of the narratives of closed immanence on one side, and the sense of their inadequacy on the other, strengthened by encounter with existing milieu of religious practice, or just by some intimations of the transcendent.[99]

What Taylor describes as "intimations of the transcendent" includes a wide range of possible experiences that might tentatively be associated with "sacrality." By using terms like "immanence" and "transcendence" Taylor is not suggesting that these concepts adequately distinguish what is religious from the secular or Christian from non-Christian, but rather, he proposes that the distinction is "tailor-made for our culture."[100] It conceptually represents what Kosky describes as a sense of *longing* or the desire to participate in something outside the strict immanence of self-assertion—again, putting into question where immanence ends and transcendence begins.

One of the reasons it is important to note the ambiguity around terms like immanence and transcendence is that it leaves space in which to understand how creation's goodness remains entangled with secularized concepts of sacrality. Critically, however, this entanglement is not only based on uncertain intimations of transcendence; it also stems from the sense in which creation's goodness remains on the level of immanence—at least to a degree. As I explained in the Introduction, the Genesis affirmation of creation's goodness is not an ephemeral or abstract quality but rather a "concrete gift" that relates to a wide variety of phenomena: "rain that falls," "a verdant tree," "lavish table," "health," or simply a "neighbor's friendly greeting."[101] Of course, as I noted earlier, the source and sustainer of this goodness remains defined by an "infinite qualitative difference" within a Christian horizon of place. But whether one refers to the sacrality of the earth or the goodness of creation, there is enough phenomenal overlap (or entanglement) to outline the immanence of a prelinguistic goodness in both topologies. The enjoyment of particular things, such as those I just described, is especially relevant here, since Christians clearly are not the only ones to enjoy the rain that falls or the verdant tree.

Central to the entanglement of topologies, then, is an affirmation of the idea that there is only *one world* (the language of "world" here is a general term for *place* rather than a reference to Heidegger's world). As Lacoste argues, there is not "a world of reason and a world of faith, with a boundary between them" but only different aspects of the same world.[102] In other words, there is not *my* world, *your* world, or *our* world but simply different "aspects of the same phenomenon, *the* world."[103] Despite the inevitable differences in interpretation, there remains a common encounter with the world, which I propose includes phenomena defined by a quality of "goodness" at a prelinguistic level of experience. Because this goodness appears quite generally, it naturally engenders a variety of interpretative possibilities that nonetheless remain entangled.

There is a sense in which I am advocating for something like a theological rejoinder to the agnostic philosophical position laid out by Bradley Onishi in *The Sacrality of the Secular*. Similar to Kosky, Onishi searches for "non-secularist visions of secularity" and identifies this possibility in continental philosophy of religion that historically precedes the secularization theses and their recent demise.[104] He notices a "disenchantment with disenchantment," which "does not mean refusing secularity; it means complicating our understanding of it in order to make such an understanding more expansive and vibrant, which is, or can be, carried out by way of encounter with religious phenomena."[105] His approach does not "return" to religion in the sense that philosophy submits to the authority of religion but rather seeks to think *with* religion.[106] To this end, Onishi aims to let religious phenomena enlarge and enrich secular space.[107] By emphasizing the entanglement of topologies, I similarly aim to identify a more generous theological encounter with categories like the "sacred." As a rejoinder to Onishi, my position assumes that experiences that are not self-consciously religious still enlarge and enrich a Christian understanding of creation.[108] Agnostic or atheistic topologies can also identify a prelinguistic quality of goodness that is integral to a theology of creation. This more open account of secularity does not imply that each person's way of explaining the world is equally true, but it begins with the assumption that those who do not confess a Christian faith still encounter what the biblical text affirms as a good creation. It is a matter of thinking with those who do not affirm creation's relation to a transcendent God while at the same time refusing to submit theology to the authority of an agnostic philosophical starting point.

Relativism and the Real

Acknowledging the legitimacy of diverse interpretations based on a prelinguistic goodness is not the same thing as adhering to a simplistic relativism. This point is already implied by my insistence that a prelinguistic goodness is integral to the place in which we find ourselves. But more can be said about the kind of claim I am making and, in particular, how it builds on a certain *phenomenological realism*. While phenomenology is concerned with the category of experience, it does not need to leave aside the category of "reality." Phenomenology might still associate the real with what is given or with that which appears.[109] This commitment to appearances does not imply that religious phenomena like creation's goodness achieve a de facto status as reality in-itself simply because that is what appears to some people. Instead, phenomenology "opens a field of research on the relationships between our discursive intelligence and our sensible, embodied intelligence."[110] Associating the real with appearances, therefore, is a means for philosophical argumentation to proceed rather than a solution to all its problems.

In order to further clarify what I mean by argumentation, it is helpful to consider Romano's analysis of Husserl's classic phenomenological example of a vase sitting on a table. As I walk around the room and do my best to describe the most essential features of the vase, my perceptions of the vase will change based on where I stand in the room. As my perceptions change, this engenders questions like whether or not they are "objective, subjective, or neither—relational, that is, belonging to the relation that, in perception, is established between this vase and me."[111] These questions eventually lead to further questions about the accuracy of my perceptions; however, as Romano argues, the naïve acceptance of *what appears* (my adumbrations) is not misplaced. He explains:

> I may be wrong about this vase, about its determinations and even about its existence, but I cannot be wrong about the adumbrations themselves. I may believe that this vase is porcelain, while in fact it is earthenware or glass; there may not even be a vase before me; but I cannot be wrong about the fact that I perceive at this moment this opalescent, bluish form, continually changing its aspect, its look, its perspective, as I move toward it or away from it . . . the adumbrations are subjective, while the vase being adumbrated in them is objective. The former belong to consciousness, the latter to reality. The adumbrations are given "adequately," in an infallible evidence; reality is given inadequately, so that it is always possible to raise a doubt about it: a doubt about the existence of the vase, the objects surrounding it, and even the world as such.[112]

Phenomenology, therefore, does not escape classic philosophical questions about what is real. It begins by accepting appearances, which then opens up "argumentation" about the various descriptions of that appearing.[113] Romano suggests, "Naturally, considerations concerning the subject of perception immediately impinge on the way we will describe the object perceived and its adumbrations. The more distant these considerations are from the point at which the description is anchored in essential truths, the more urgent the question of whether we have correctly described things becomes."[114] It is important to note that the principles outlined by Romano do not identify what is initially given (a naïve commerce with things) as the *arbiter* of what is real. Instead, he simply acknowledges that the more complex and layered the description, the greater the "urgency" of questions regarding the adequacy of the description.

Romano's analysis helpfully contextualizes my account of a prelinguistic goodness and more explicitly Christian interpretations of it. The general play of goodness intimated in moments of joy or enjoyment are closer to "essential truths," in a Husserlian sense, than a Christian interpretation of that goodness, which implies mediation by means of secondary evidence based on a degree of theological knowledge. The difference between these different kinds of descriptions may raise questions about the relationship between creation's goodness and "reality," but it is not capable of determining whether the Word forms a covenant with creation even prior to history. I turn to phenomenology primarily in order to evaluate critically the category of experience rather than establish it as an arbiter of theological claims.

One of the reasons phenomenology cannot adjudicate the reality of a theological claim like creation's goodness returns to God's unique mode of appearing (this is an issue I will return to throughout the study, especially in Chapter 3). The *source* of creation's goodness will not appear anything like the vase sitting on a table (or any other object in the world). Lacoste emphasizes throughout *The Appearing of God* that one does not become "familiar with God in the same way the natural attitude makes us familiar with the world."[115] This is why theology "is never built exclusively on the narrow base of the experience of God. . . . When religious experience takes possession of us, it will be a good strategy, existentially and theoretically, not to leap to the conclusion that what has happened originates beyond our consciousness and bears the stamp of divinity."[116] Theological knowledge, therefore, is not solely dependent on a particular experience of creation's goodness: "There are limits to religious knowledge-by-acquaintance, and the phenomenology of experience cannot segue seamlessly into theology."[117] As I note in the first half of the chapter, religious experience can certainly inform theological knowledge, but it is far from exclusively defining it.

If creation's goodness is to be more fully evaluated in relation to the "real," criteria internal to theology also need to be evaluated. Romano notes: "We must not reject, in the field of hermeneutics, the existence of rules and criteria; but neither must we assume that there are more exact criteria than those actually accepted in a given interpretive community."[118] In other words, phenomenological hermeneutics does not do away with rules or criteria but instead puts into question "the existence of *exact* norms and criteria that it would suffice to apply mechanically without appealing to discernment, judgment, and experience on the part of the interpreter."[119] This leaves room for a specifically Christian concept of creation's goodness to be offered that builds on theological knowledge and rationality (the criteria of a given interpretive community). If one is to evaluate the relationship between creation's goodness's and the "real" when it is one interpretative option among many, then it is necessary to consider its place within a much broader context of reason and argumentation. So, for example, Jean-Luc Marion writes:

> Christianity rests on the Revelation of God, through himself and in person, as triune and as one. On the basis of the Father and as the absolute gift, the Trinity unfolds the Word as *Logos*, that is to say, as

first and ultimate reason of all things that were created in Him, according to the communion of the Holy Spirit, namely by the charity he allows, according to a unity that reinforces the singularity of individuals sanctified in God. Consequently, the Word, in whom everything receives being, life, and movement, displays reason.[120]

The important point here is that the validity of *creation's* goodness (its relationship to the real) is not determined solely by the content of religious experience but according to its participation in a wider "rationality."[121] One would need to evaluate the rationality of the Word (which Marion argues is defined by charity).

As I explain in the latter half of this book, the broader rationality of the Word plays an important role in transfiguring the meaning of "goodness." Something as "small" as being given a refreshing glass of water can be transformed into something more within a horizon of creation.[122] While the appearing of this "something more" takes place within a particular interpretative community, this only opens further discussion about what appears and how it appears.

Conclusion: Diversity and Commonality

The prelinguistic goodness outlined in this chapter is contextualized by the categories of "reality" and "relativism" in two ways. First, to the extent that my description of joy and enjoyment accurately sketches the experiential contours of a prelinguistic goodness, it constitutes a step toward the "real." One of the reasons for affirming the legitimacy of such a step stems from the idea that a prelinguistic goodness appears regardless of one's confessional stance or socioeconomic situation. The widespread (almost universal) experiences of joy and enjoyment disclose a persistent play of goodness in the place in which we find ourselves. While sociopolitical factors evidently impact the appearing of goodness in significant ways, joy and enjoyment are not the exclusive terrain of the privileged. Small pleasures associated with enjoyment (a nourishing rainfall, holding a small child, a pleasant smell, or the way light falls in the evening) may appear in diverse situations. Even more important and surprising (as I explain in Chapter 4) is that joy has the potential to arise in some of the most difficult and painful circumstances. Goodness *appears* to be a *reality* at play in the place in which we find ourselves.

At the same time, because the prelinguistic appearing of goodness is quite general, it remains open to diverse interpretations, and there is a degree of *relativism* with respect to how one will understand and integrate this "goodness" in a broader horizon of place. The concept of entangled topologies models a helpful way in which to maintain a "quest for the real" from within this diversity of interpretations. By starting with a commonly encountered quality of goodness, it becomes easier to have a more precise discussion about differences in interpretation. In other words, a description of prelinguistic phenomena has the potential to help organize commonalities and differences in experience in a way that is productive for thinking about what is "real." While respectful dialogue can seem futile in certain hyperpolarized contexts, the entanglement of topologies based on a prelinguistic experience of goodness suggests there may be a degree of shared experience that operates *beneath* various discourses. Hiking through the Canadian Rockies with a person who holds sharply opposing political or religious views may do more to affirm a shared sense of being human than any extended discourse. Identifying this commonality in the context of a philosophical argument is not a practical solution to pressing divisions, nor does it adjudicate our most complex differences (for instance, whether or not there is a Creator who remains in relation to creation). But as I noted earlier, a phenomenological realism linked with appearances is a means for argumentation and thinking to proceed, and this is precisely the purpose behind outlining the appearing of a prelinguistic goodness in this chapter. I have foregrounded the importance of a prelinguistic goodness for understanding how one might think about the manifestation of creation's goodness amid the diversity of interpretations.

There is more to be said with respect to *how* this prelinguistic level of experience appears and its importance for understanding creation's goodness. The following chapter expands on the experiential dimensions of a prelinguistic goodness by engaging with Marion's phenomenology of givenness and also explains why a phenomenology of creation's goodness may be helpful for theological interpretations of culture.

2

The Givenness of Creation's Goodness

If there is a degree of phenomenal overlap between a Christian understanding of creation's goodness and prelinguistic experiences of goodness, one might identify how it ordinarily appears and is recognizable in a wide variety of contexts. Even in the midst of so-called secular contexts, the expansive presence of phenomena associated with creation's goodness would have the potential to be a defining feature of life. Broadly applying a theological concept like creation's goodness to culture should not require one to impose a Christian self-understanding onto the experiences of those who think differently; however, it is possible to articulate how creation's goodness is a category that can help confessional Christians (and potentially others) make sense of the place in which they find themselves. To this end, the phenomenological dynamics of a prelinguistic goodness can be a resource for theological interpretations of culture that do not threaten the legitimacy of diverse horizons of place.

In order to explain how a phenomenology of creation's goodness (in particular, its prelinguistic dimensions) might inform a theological interpretation of culture, I will engage with the work of Jean-Luc Marion. A leading figure in French philosophy and theology, Marion has generated substantial debate on issues including the history and status of metaphysics, the relationship between philosophy and theology, and the role of hermeneutics in phenomenology—to consider just one vector of his extensive corpus. My interest in his work, however, is focused on its relevance to a phenomenology of creation's goodness and theological readings of culture.

For readers familiar with Marion, this emphasis may be surprising, since creation and culture are not prominent points of reference throughout much of his writings. In fact, it is not until his extended reflections on Augustine's *Confessions* (*In the Self's Place*, 2008) that he provides a detailed account of how creation fits within his broader phenomenological and theological projects. And it is not until his even more recent comments in *A Brief Apology for a Catholic Moment* (2017) that Marion's cultural concerns have become clear. Nevertheless, as I explain over the course of this chapter, both themes play an important role in the overall development of his work and are worthy of critical evaluation.

More broadly, there are two central reasons for considering Marion's approach to creation and culture in this book. First, his work raises the significance of a confessional hermeneutics for understanding one's place as "creation." Marion exclusively associates creation with a confession of faith, which in turn establishes a strict binary between those who self-consciously describe themselves as Christian and those who do not. He then reinforces this binary when he (problematically) asserts that contemporary culture is defined solely by *nihilism* and that only Christians have the resources to address the problem. The second reason I examine Marion's work is that his phenomenology of givenness and the gift offers an internal corrective to his misreading of culture. His phenomenological work undermines aspects of his confessional hermeneutics and further clarifies the *entanglement of topologies* around prelinguistic experiences of goodness. The phenomenology of givenness suggests that there are aspects of creation's goodness that may be at play regardless of the cultural moment.

Focusing on theological interpretations of culture presents an important angle from which to consider the significance of creation's goodness as a topological category. Of course, "culture" is not synonymous with "topology." Contemporary theories of *culture* understand the term to "refer to a multitextured network of relations or total way of life encompassing the myriad relations, institutions, and practices that define a historical period or specific geographical location or formative community or subgroups within larger fields."[1] And as Kathryn Tanner explains, "It seems less and less plausible to presume that cultures are self-contained and clearly bounded units, internally consistent and unified wholes of beliefs and values simply transmitted to every member of their respective groups as principles of social order."[2] *Topology* is a phenomenological concept that is related to the *contours of experience* roughly defining one's broader horizon of place. My intention is to explore how creation's goodness (an integral part of a Christian topology) is crucial for any theological interpretation of a culture. I do not define any given culture as "good," nor do I locate where and when creation's goodness appears within the various dimensions of culture. Instead, I argue that phenomena Christians understand in relation to creation's goodness are at play regardless of the cultural moment based on its phenomenological dynamics (in particular, its prelinguistic appearing). Not only does this approach push back on Marion's emphasis on nihilism, but more broadly, it underscores the centrality of creation's goodness for a nuanced theological interpretation of culture.

The Hermeneutics of Confession

In the Self's Place appears relatively late in Marion's career and assumes knowledge of important concepts and strategies developed in his earlier texts. As I noted in the Introduction, Marion's work is part of a movement in continental philosophy of religion that is focused on the onto-theological constitution of metaphysics. His reading of Augustine clearly reflects this interest, since Marion proposes that Augustine functions as "the privileged interlocutor and, in a sense, inevitable judge, of the project of accessing phenomena irreducible to the objects and beings of metaphysics."[3] He attempts to "read and interpret the *Confessions* of Saint Augustine in a resolutely nonmetaphysical mode, by using to this end the major concepts that I had just elaborated in a logic of radically phenomenological intent."[4] As I will explain, this nonmetaphysical reading not only defines Marion's reading of Augustine but also his understanding of creation theology that is developed within the same text.

Marion holds a nuanced interpretation of the history of metaphysics and its relation to onto-theology. He credits Heidegger with recognizing the onto-theological constitution of metaphysics but ultimately questions Heidegger's account of when metaphysics is represented in the history of thought. According to Marion, metaphysics is located within a specifically *modern* philosophical tradition (particularly that of Descartes).[5] He argues that modern metaphysics creates a *conceptual idol* by understanding God primarily in the terms of efficiency and foundation (*first cause* and *supreme being*).[6] This "God" does not "refer back, like the icon, to the invisible," nor is it capable of a "creation," since it is rather the philosopher who engenders the concept.[7] One can recognize Marion's understanding of the "mirror" function of the idol in this interpretation of metaphysics. He locates the problem of idolatry not in the object to be worshiped but in the *disposition* of the one who views it. While one may intend toward the divine that pursuit stops at the point of intention, since, in Marion's account, the idol becomes "a mirror that reflects 'the image of its aim and . . . the scope of that aim.'"[8] This is precisely the kind of idolatrous metaphysics that Marion proposes Augustine avoids in the *Confessions*.

The primary strategy that Marion uses to distinguish Augustine from metaphysics (and subsequently idolatry) is based on his account of "*confessio*." He proposes that the *Confessions* are neither autobiography nor a theological treatise that speaks *about* God; instead, they are defined by the *hermeneutics of confession*. And *confessio* introduces a "precise and complex language game" of praise, which guards against an idolatrous conception of God.[9] He writes:

> In an extraordinary rupture with the metaphysical mode of speech as the predication of something *about* something, praise no longer pretends to say anything *about* God, but signifies precisely that I am saying nothing *about* God, or rather it signifies *to* God that I acknowledge him alone as God, by saying it to him and by acknowledging myself a non-god.[10]

Because the *Confessions* operates within the context of *confessio*, it leaves behind the "metaphysical mode of speech" and resists making God "another myself more or less dominating, more or less comparable, therefore commensurate to myself—in any case, not God."[11] In other words, according to Marion, Augustine's *Confessions* guards against idolatry because it is not merely engendered from Augustine's personal aims or intentionality (a mirror reflection).

Marion's reading here repeats aspects of his 1997 debate over Jacques Derrida's essay "How to Avoid Speaking" at Villanova University.[12] At the heart of the debate was a disagreement over apophatic theology—or, more specifically, whether one can "find a way of thinking what is greater than thought."[13] Marion argues for a *surplus* at the heart of the apophatic theological tradition and accuses Derrida of using the terminology of absence and presence in a way that fails to include the crucial third sense that Denys the Areopagite incorporates into his thought.[14] He insists that the third way can "nominate" and "undo" at the same time, which is the way of "*de-nomination*" and operates pragmatically as a *language of praise*.[15] He goes on to suggest that even if "praise attributes a name to a possible God, one should conclude that it does not name God properly or essentially, nor in presence, but that it marks God's absence, anonymity, and withdrawal— exactly as every name dissimulates every individual, which it merely indicates without ever manifesting."[16] Praise, in Marion's account, never constitutes a univocal conceptualization of God but remains traced with a negativity that protects the name of God from the mirror function of the idol.

Within his reading of Augustine's *Confessions* Marion identifies a similar function within the language of praise through an emphasis on its *call-and-response structure*. He explains, "The one who praises—me, you, or us—is only responding to the prior call of God, which we read in the scriptures and to which we respond possibly as the last, in response, after the fact, by citing it."[17] According to Marion, the *Confessions* exemplifies this call-and-response structure because Augustine continually cites the Psalms in order to respond to God.[18] Augustine does not *decide* to adopt the language of praise after careful reflection on the meaning of being; instead, the language of praise is engendered *only after* he has been called by God through the scriptures. The call from God is never statically present but is intimated "after the fact" through Augustine's response.

Marion then proposes that the implications stemming from *confessio* go beyond issues related to the proper language for God. He argues that *confessio*'s call-and-response structure defines Augustine's *situation before God* quite broadly. He explains, "The issue is no longer what I say to him, but what I am before him—how I carry myself (*Haltung*) and find myself (*Befindlichkeit*) before him."[19] This wider situation before God is exemplified in Augustine's conversion story. Therein Augustine finds himself "before God" yet feels that he cannot speak "*to* God" because of his guilt.[20] Then, despite hesitancy over the inadequacy of his speech, Marion notes that Augustine finds a word of response in the Psalms: "'And you, Lord, how long? How long, Lord, will you last in your anger to the end? Keep not alive the memory of our former iniquities' (VIII, 12, 14, 65)."[21] Again, Augustine's response to finding himself before God is not engendered from the resources of his own creative capacity or careful reflection on the proper name for God but is a response born from a prior call on his life through the Scriptures.

The call-and-response structure that defines *confessio* underscores an important (and controversial) aspect of Marion's thought—*l'adonné*. This is a term that is generally translated as "the gifted"; it signifies the one who stands at one "pole of the givenness" and "whose privilege is confined to the fact that he himself is received from what he receives."[22] The concept implies that phenomena are capable of inverting one's ordinary way of relating to objects in the world, so that the "I" is constituted by the phenomenon, becoming a me, a witness of the excess of givenness.[23] Marion tends to reverse the logic typically applied in modern philosophical accounts of the subject by emphasizing what is *given* and how that modifies the one to whom it is given, rather than the capacity of the subject to make appear or anticipate the meaning of phenomena. This is also the logic Marion identifies in Augustine, who does not find answers to his questions in the depths of his own inner life but rather in that which is precisely *not* him:

> For the inner man does not constitute the dwelling place of truth, since, in contrast, he inhabits himself in He who opens truth to him: "*ipse interior homo cum suo inhabitatore . . . conveniat*" (the inner man himself is found with he who inhabits him). Truth dwells in the inner man but not in the sense that the inner man would have truth in him, since in fact it dwells rather in he who is invited and invited the truth into him.[24]

The idea that Augustine does not go out and search for God but rather finds himself already in God (or in God's truth) is a critically important conclusion for Marion's theology—one to which I return later in this chapter. For now, my point is simply to introduce the centrality of *confessio* in Marion's argument for a nonmetaphysical reading of Augustine.

Confessio and Creation

When Marion finally examines the concept of creation in the fifth chapter of *In the Self's Place*, his analysis is defined by these same concepts and strategies. For instance, his commitment to a nonmetaphysical reading of Augustine leads him to argue that creation theology has very little to do with ontology. While he has been questioned on this interpretation of Augustine by Emmanuel Falque and Jean Greisch, Marion maintains that the biblical account of creation does not answer the question "why is there something rather than nothing."[25] He contends that it may be tempting to interpret the Genesis text with this question in mind, since we are "inevitably caught in a metaphysical and Greek position" that associates creation with the "imprecise and cursory" category of the "totality of beings"; however, creation theology will always be an "inept" answer to an ontological question because it was never meant to answer that kind of question.[26] He asserts that Heidegger was wrong to draw that connection and any association between a theology of creation and onto-theology "does not stand even for one minute."[27] While Marion does not make a totalizing distinction between ontology and the concept of creation, he clearly downplays the relationship and differentiates philosophical modes of approaching being/beings from the biblical text.[28] If there is a relationship between ontology and creation, then it is secondary to the explicit concerns of Genesis 1 according to Marion.

Although his account of creation is openly theological in *In the Self's Place*, Marion rehearses aspects of the logic developed in his phenomenology of givenness (*Gegebenheit*)—a theme I explore in more detail near the conclusion of this chapter.[29] Integral to Marion's argument for a phenomenology of givenness is his insistence that *there is no underlying reason why anything is given* (it does not answer the "why question"). Givenness has a "factual character, imposed de facto and always already achieved: the given, whatever it may be, indeed admits of no exception; the de facto is always already there, or rather always already *here*, as close as possible, we are straightaway caught in it, our feet in it, enmeshed unto nausea in the horror of the ground that glues us to it."[30] According to Marion, creation theology does not contradict this nausea by imposing a "theological giver" as the explanation for why things exist (despite the persistent suspicions registered by a number of critics).[31] Instead, any concept of a theological giver or, more precisely, a Creator only follows from within a context of *confessio*. In fact, he goes so far as to argue that one can only recognize creation, as such, starting from within the context of *confessio*:

> Creation, therefore, responds to the question of the possibility of *confessio*, and creation gives place to *confessio* by defining *where* those who must do so—in other words, all that is not confused with God—can do so. Creation does not define only what happens to be created but, first of all, that in view of which the created is created—accomplishing a *confessio* by praise of the creator. Creation gives place (*ubi*) to *confessio* by opening the dimensions where the created can direct itself toward the creator of a *here* (*ibi*) turning toward an *over-there* (*illic*).[32]

Within the context of *confessio*, creation is the place in which one can unequivocally relate to the Creator as the created.[33] It is synonymous with an expansive theological horizon that "embraces indifferently the angelic choirs (celestial hierarchy), the terrestrial church (ecclesiastical hierarchy), the eschatological mass of the elect, and the intelligible heavens, indeed the world of idealities, provided that with the *confessio* of God the intelligible is put into operation everywhere by intellectual creatures."[34] Recognizing one's place in and as creation, therefore, follows from *confessio*, wherein one finds oneself before God, responding in the modality of praise even prior to recognizing creation, as such.

Marion is not concerned with arguing for creation as an event in primordial history. Instead, the issue is whether or not one *sees* or *recognizes* the place in which one finds oneself as created, in creation. And critically, he suggests that the question of "seeing" creation extends from a personal experience implied in the language of praise toward participation in the broader *community of believers*:

The community of believers, of those who confess God in faith, is therefore the sole thing that permits seeing and saying things as created, therefore as not subsisting (non-*vorhanden*) because it alone hears and sees in them the goodness of God. . . . The exegesis of Genesis in fact ends at a hermeneutic, by the community of believers, of heaven and earth as gifts given by God—in other words, the interpretation of the creation story leads to interpreting the world as created. This is possible only by a universalized *confessio* of God, by all believers, with regard to all things, as so many gifts.[35]

The *sole* way to recognize oneself as living in creation is by entering into praise for the gifts of God within the community of believers. Once the "believer" (Augustine) finds himself before God (*confessio*), then his response of praise is "confirmed in the response of the community of believers (and of readers), which is in turn ratified by the response of the world, interpreted as created, to God, himself acknowledged as creator."[36] One of the results of Marion's account of *confessio*, therefore, is "a *liturgical condition* for the possibility of recognizing creation."[37] By entering into the community of believers and participating in the language of praise, the world finally appears as creation (I will also return to this point).

It is important to note that the hermeneutic centrality of *confessio* extends to the recognition of creation's *goodness* in Marion's account. He proposes that for Augustine, "the pure and simple acknowledgement of the goodness (therefore also the beauty) of created things is equivalent in actuality to a praise, which no longer need be qualified explicitly as such."[38] Marion writes, "The entire '*ordo pulcherrimus rerum valde bonarum*' (perfectly beautiful order of very good things) (XIII, 35, 50, 14, 520) that concludes all the *Confessiones* completes the initial praise of God *laudabilis valde* (I, 1, 1, 13, 272)."[39] The world does not appear to be good and beautiful based on philosophical reflection on the meaning of being but rather unfolds within a context of praise that participates in the community of believers—all of which constitutes a confession of faith and the necessary condition from which to recognize creation's goodness.

While I will identify several difficulties that stem from Marion's emphasis on *confessio*, my intention is not to question every aspect of the position I have outlined here. After all, it would be unlikely that people would embrace angelic choirs or the celestial church "indifferently" without also affirming God's prior self-revelation, a confession of faith, or a community of believers. Moreover, it is helpful to note that the basic outline of Marion's account of *confessio* has similarities with what I have already indicated is constructive for defining the experiential contours of creation's goodness in Lacoste. Specifically, Marion's reference to a "liturgical condition" mirrors the logic of *being before God* that Lacoste describes in *Experience and the Absolute*. For both philosophers, creation unfolds as a horizon of place only after you find yourself in a broadly defined liturgical situation ("God must be named beforehand for the heavens to sing their glory").[40] My intention is not to question this condition for the appearance of a more fully developed topology of creation.

Before moving on to consider Marion's interpretation of culture, however, I want to emphasize the clear "either/or" that is implied in his hermeneutics of confession, since I will come back to it as I develop various arguments in this chapter. According to Marion, *either* you find yourself before God confessing faith in the language of praise and subsequently recognize yourself to be living in creation *or* you do not hear the call and subsequently fail to recognize the place in which you find yourself as creation. Marion allows for some ambiguity with respect to how clearly one might "see" within the context of *confessio*.[41] But he does not acknowledge the possibility that aspects of creation's goodness might define the place in which we find ourselves regardless of confessional stance. There is no space for what I described in the previous chapter as the entanglement of creation (in particular, its goodness) with other topologies that do not employ the strict language game of praise or involve participation in the community of believers. Critically, as I explain in the following section, Marion repeats this binary when he asserts that nihilism is the *sole* category in which to understand our contemporary setting and that Christians *alone* have the resources to respond to this situation.

The Logic of Nihilism

Marion's understanding of nihilism (and more broadly his interpretation of culture) begins to develop in the context of being Roman Catholic in Paris in the 1960s and 1970s. This period is marked by a relatively combative relationship between the church and French society, especially following the student riots of 1968. Some of the openness and dialogue with culture that was endorsed by Vatican II was left aside for a more defensive stance and entrenched Catholic identity by the church.[42] Church leaders like Cardinal Lustiger (with whom Marion aligns himself) adopted the point of view that Catholicism was a "minority institution working to make inroads in a secular society that had lost itself morally and intellectually on the turbulent seas of modernity."[43] Much of the Vatican leadership during this period represented similar views, seeking to challenge a declining church authority in the West and reassert a moral consensus around Christianity.[44] And while Marion's position cannot be characterized as a simplistic endorsement of conservative church leadership, he does adopt the tendency to understand the cultural developments of the period negatively—specifically through the lens of nihilism.

Marion's concern with a culture of nihilism is made explicit in his analysis of the student riots in 1968. As a young student at l'École normale supérieure in Paris in the late 1960s, he was immersed in the riots yet remained abstracted from the fervor of the revolts and skeptical of the social changes associated with the movement.[45] While Marion's experience of the riots should not be assessed as purely critical, he explicitly states that the underlying *logic* of the moment was nihilistic and constituted a spiritual and cultural crisis. In the "English Preface" to *God without Being* he states:

> Written at the border between philosophy and theology, this essay remains deeply marked by the spiritual and cultural crisis in which it was thought and written. That crisis, shared by an entire generation (at least), had a time and a stake. A time: the test of nihilism which, in France, marked the years dominated by 1968. A stake: the obscuring of God in the indistinct haze of the "human sciences," which at the time were elevated by "structuralism" to the rank of dominant doctrine.[46]

This passage is offered almost in passing (it is not included in the French edition), and Marion does not explore the riots explicitly in the main body of the text. However, as I will explain, the connection between a culture of nihilism and his philosophical and theological analysis in *God without Being* becomes more explicit if one considers his comments on the student revolts in *The Rigor of Things* in light of the earlier text's account of nihilism.

In *God without Being*, the topic of nihilism arises soon after his phenomenological description of the mirror function of the idol. Within this context, he aims at once to affirm Nietzsche's statement that "God is dead" and move beyond it, since the only God that has died is a conceptual God (an idol) based on Kant's "moral God." According to Marion, this moral God is part of what leads to the rise of nihilism:

> Only the "moral God" can die or even be discovered as already dead; for he alone, as "moral God," is amenable to the logic of value: he himself operates and is comprehensible only in the system of values of morality as counternature; thus does he find himself directly hit the moment that, with nihilism, "the highest values are devalued."[47]

He then goes on to explain:

> This moral God remains trapped in a Kantian understanding of the subject because it implies an actual experience of God . . . but founded on a finite determination of "God" (from the sole practical point of view), starting not from the nature—if there is one—of God, but indeed from human *Dasein*'s experience of it.[48]

Any concept of a God that is determined according to the experience of "human *Dasein*" is idolatrous. As such, according to Marion, the moral God cannot really be God and should indeed be killed. But what is particularly important in the context of this study is that the "moral God" also leads to *nihilism*, since it is "amenable to the logic of value," which is based on the limits (impassably immanent) of human experiences. The "moral God" is a value like any other human value and is therefore reducible to the will of the one doing the valuing.

The language and concepts that Marion uses to describe nihilism in *God without Being* correspond to the comments he makes years later looking back on the student revolts in *The Rigor of Things*. Marion states that the period was primarily a matter of *values*, and "values, whether one is for or against them, never hold in and of themselves, because they depend on whoever gives them worth. What is particular to values lies in the fact that they have nothing of their own but depend entirely on evaluation, hence on the evaluator."[49] The language regarding the riots overlaps with his description of the moral God that is amenable to the logic of value. What is at stake in both instances is the capacity of the subject. Kant's moral God dies because it relies on *Dasein* and requires individuals to be capable of grounding the moral God. Similarly, but in a more general cultural sense, Marion finds the values of '68 tenuously grounded in the evaluators, and as such they fall into the same "logic of values."

The relevance of nihilism for Marion can also be identified in texts from the 1990s—although to a lesser extent. In his essay "In Defense of Argument" (1992), for instance, Marion relates his philosophical analysis of nihilism to the broader culture while locating his argument within the context of an "event." He asserts at the beginning of the essay that "in fact, for at least a century, whether we like it or not, we have been living in the situation that Nietzsche diagnosed as nihilism. Nihilism is defined by an event; the highest values are devalued."[50] The central problematic of the essay then proceeds to describe a philosophical crisis of *grounding*:

> Before and beyond the "death of God," which only results from it, Nietzsche deconstructs the foundations of rationality—and first the

possibility in general of any primordial grounding.... Admittedly, Nietzsche announces in grand style another, a "greater" reason. But he did not manage to capture it, even in his utmost progress, as was also the case for the "new gods." To the contrary, what became established was the crisis of grounding. And we are still there.[51]

Marion then argues for a Christian approach to reason that remains "strictly rationalist" but is also pragmatic and aware of the limits of argumentation. Christians, Marion indicates, follow another kind of reason based on what "Revelation has given us—and given us to comprehend."[52] At this point Marion is working toward developing the logic of givenness and the gift that does not depend on an individual subject to create or "ground" values.

While Marion's texts on the phenomenology of givenness are implicitly related to his warnings about nihilism, he rarely deals with the concept of nihilism in these texts. In fact, the concept does not play a significant role (or at least it remains in the background) in *Being Given* (1997) and *In Excess* (2001). In *Being Given*, for instance, nihilism is briefly considered within a technical discussion of phenomenology, wherein he critiques Heidegger and suggests that "Givenness alone uncovers beings in (and without) their Being, therefore the ontological difference as well as nihilism."[53] Then in *In Excess*, he relates the concept to the particular philosophical problematic of "first philosophy" as it arose in late-nineteenth- and early-twentieth-century philosophy.[54] Marion's references to nihilism, however, begin to increase in his more recent texts, which also display the significance he attributes to it for interpreting culture more explicitly. For instance, in "Faith and Reason" (2005) he suggests that nihilism is the defining feature of contemporary Western culture (the text was originally offered as a lecture for a series organized by Cardinal Lustiger). Therein, Marion remarks that "nihilism expands its dark sun by insinuating into each of us this disarming question: 'What's the use?' What is the point of the humanity of humans, the naturalness of nature, the justice of the polis, and the truth of knowledge?"[55] He then relates the "sole program of the ideologies that have dominated history since the beginning of the last century" to nihilism.[56]

By the time of *Negative Certainties* (2010), Marion employs the term with even greater frequency and ties nihilism explicitly to particular sociopolitical situations.[57] While his analysis of the concept remains related to philosophical critiques of the modern subject (suggesting nihilism is an extension of a Cartesian interpretation of the "I"), he also connects nihilism to contemporary modern economic and political interpretations of the

"I." He identifies a strategy that attempts to define *what* is humanity or the *essence* of being human in order to give access to "an ob-*jected* me [un moi ob-*jecté*] or to an *object* of the other."[58] According to Marion, these definitions are established in order to exclude or deny a person's humanity—for example, an undocumented worker who does not have the proper digital definition necessary for inclusion.[59] Such "a reduced reason," Marion concludes, "is found in the state of nihilism."[60] Marion's references to nihilism in *Negative Certainties* usually remain related to his precise philosophical and theological project, but the frequency with which he uses the category to understand his broader political, cultural, and economic situation also displays his growing concern over a broadly conceived culture of nihilism.

In summary, then, over the course of Marion's career he often contextualizes his work with references to the concept of nihilism. Much of the time, these references remain specific to philosophical history, and he develops a rather precise conceptual response. At other times, Marion seeks to expand the relevance of the concept and reveals the conviction that nihilism defines the current era (for instance, in his comments on the student riots or "Faith and Reason"). As I will explain, this latter opinion and its implications for understanding culture have become increasingly evident in some of Marion's recent work.

A Moment of Crisis

Marion's concerns with a culture of nihilism are most clearly articulated in a short book, *A Brief Apology for a Catholic Moment*. While his reflections are specific to the French context, the important passages on nihilism seem to refer to the West more generally. For instance, when Marion refers to Nietzsche's statement that *we* are in an era of nihilism, he transitions from Nietzsche's nineteenth-century German context to a twenty-first-century French context without reservation.[61] He argues that for more than a century, nihilism "has invaded the entire house, to the point of moving in for good." Nihilism "inhabits us" and "gnaws at us."[62] It is a "prison" we have constructed for ourselves, but we have not yet measured the deadly "perpetual growth of universal evaluation deployed by nihilism."[63] Marion makes no caveats regarding possible exceptions to this prison, nor does he suggest it is restricted to the French context.

Marion's dramatic rhetoric is representative of his tendency throughout the text to depict a moment of "crisis" (echoing his understanding of 1968) that Christians alone have the resources to address. He writes, "Only Christians, and first of all Catholics . . . know what it is to give their soul in order to give a communion to a community that, without them, would no longer be one and indivisible."[64] Moreover, he states that Christians form the "best citizens" because of their "disinterestedness toward earthly power" and the fact that they make "honest" and "reliable" workers.[65] Although Marion acknowledges this latter claim may come across as conceited, he suggests that the "danger of the present moment" requires greater "effort, courage, and resources than we seem to see."[66] Christians, according to Marion, are the ones who can "identify the danger" (nihilism), and this understanding of the problem is what makes them the most "useful."[67]

Aspects of Marion's analysis of nihilism in *A Brief Apology for a Catholic Moment* are conceptually familiar given his preceding texts. He argues that the highest values are devalued today because "all value depends first of all on an evaluation" and that as a result, these values possess "no value *in itself*."[68] *Evaluation*, according to Marion, is the only thing holding the value of values today. He insists that the *evaluator* or even the *evaluation* itself has taken on the supreme role of "totalizing" reality.[69] And "growth" (*croissance*) has become the empty name of evaluation, reducing all things to one value. The military, technology, and especially the economy represent the culture's subjugation to the desire for perpetual growth that marks the *value of evaluation* itself.[70] Those who object by "proclaiming values" miss the point, since Marion states that "the value already and precisely is not, not in itself, not at all."[71] The possession of values remains subject to the will of the evaluator and as such makes evaluation itself the supreme value.

Marion draws a connection between nihilism and a *metaphysics of presence*—which he proposes is the implied philosophical orientation of nihilism. Metaphysics in this context is not just an aspect of philosophical history associated with his reading of Descartes. Marion now relates metaphysics to an orientation that remains stuck in the "natural attitude of ordinary consciousness," wherein "being or remaining in the present, then, means to persist in presence in order thus to preserve one's being the best one can, to be in the mode of conservative perseverance, to preserve oneself identically to oneself in the endurance of presence."[72] In other words, the conservation of the *will* in the present, as a presence of oneself to oneself, remains the final and only goal.

Marion's analysis of a metaphysical orientation repeats an argument that he makes near the conclusion of *God without Being* when he proposes: "We, who privilege the point of view of the *here and now* as the preeminent dimension of time and hence of (the) Being (of being) . . . we can hardly conceive that a reality should unfold outside of the available and permanent *here and now*."[73] Critically, in both texts, Marion turns to the resources of Christianity in order to offer a way out of this metaphysics of presence. In *God without Being* Marion offers a reading of "the eucharistic gift that is not at all temporalized starting from the *here and now* but as memorial (temporalization starting from the past), then as eschatological announcement (temporalization starting from the future) and finally, and only finally, as dailyness and viaticum (temporalization starting from the present)."[74] From this point of view, Marion argues the present does not order "temporality as a whole" in the eucharist "but results from it" and, perhaps, also explains why he thinks only Christians "know what it means to give, to give a communion to a community."[75] In *A Brief Apology for a Catholic Moment*, Marion addresses the issue with a similar logic. He proposes that in order to get beyond the "will to will" (the need to preserve one's presence in the present) it is necessary *to want another will*, which is not mine and comes from elsewhere.[76] To this end, the way out of nihilism is exemplified by Christ on the cross when he relinquishes his will to the Father. Christ wills another will and thereby moves beyond nihilism and accomplishes metaphysics.[77] In both cases, Christianity appears as the solution to the nihilistic tendencies of a culture that has lost its way. The major difference between the two texts is that in *A Brief Apology for a Catholic Moment*, Marion's widespread cultural concerns are made more explicit.

The centrality of nihilism in *A Brief Apology for a Catholic Moment* is further confirmed by Marion's remarks on nihilism offered near the end of *The Rigor of Things*. Again, he insists that Nietzsche was right when he "announced in 1888 that nihilism must cover two centuries."[78] He then goes so far as to claim (again) that the category of nihilism is the *sole* key to interpreting society:

> Our era is characterized by nihilism. From Nietzsche to Heidegger, from Valéry to Husserl, everyone saw it, at least among those who think about what they are saying. But surprisingly (unless that itself *is* nihilism) the category of nihilism does not seem to be used by current commentators and observers of society. This is a grave mistake, because if for example we want to establish a link between the economization of society and the technologization of industry or the production of knowing (because technology becomes the engine of knowing and knowledge one of the products of the technological enterprise), if we wanted to understand ideologies and their equivalence or understand the motives for the famous "return of the religions" (as if they had left—where to?), if we wanted to provide a serious account of the ecological crisis, the demographic question, of

the ethical situation of our societies, then we would have to consider all these phenomena as symptoms of the same situation, which finds its logic and its setting solely in nihilism.[79]

Marion places a vast swath of the West's most pressing problems into the category of nihilism—to the point where he finds the situation's "logic and its setting solely in nihilism." His position does not imply nostalgia about things getting worse, but he is making a claim regarding "what model of interpretation of society and history" should be used.[80] Marion leaves little room for additional factors that could explain the cultural moment. Simply put, nihilism is the all-pervading crisis of the modern era.

The Logic of God

Given this overview, it should be clear that Marion's philosophical analysis of nihilism transmutes into a much broader claim. In what follows, my aim is not to question his arguments based on philosophical history—such as critiquing Kant's "transcendental I" or Nietzsche's "will to power." Nor do I intend to question the idea that nihilism is a relevant category for thinking about specific sociopolitical issues today—particularly the climate crisis or the economization of politics. However, I do think it is important to challenge the *extent* to which Marion uses the category of nihilism in order to understand contemporary life, as well as the way in which he applies it to people who do not share his Christian confession.

One way to clarify my concerns is to analyze several of Marion's more explicit claims about the differences between "Christians" and "non-Christians." The idea that Christians are the "best citizens" who do not seek power, or the suggestion that they are the "only" ones to be able to address the present danger of nihilism—these statements are simply too broad to represent adequately the mixed history of Christian praxis. Christians are implicated in the economization of society, the ecological crisis, to say nothing about the ongoing sexual abuse scandals of the clergy or churches' involvement in colonial activity. At the very least, before criticizing contemporary culture, Marion might acknowledge reasons to be critical of his own religious affiliation or emphasize the various ways in which Christians have abused the gift and continue to contribute to a culture of nihilism. In other words, he might recognize that the binary he draws along confessional lines breaks down on the level of praxis.

Critically, however, the problems with Marion's interpretation of culture go beyond a few overreaching statements or an overly positive evaluation of Christian citizenship. A more fundamental issue is that his account seems to contradict several of his own philosophical and theological positions. In particular, there is an unresolved tension between his analysis of nihilism and the position he adopts in the following:

> The people who search for God delude themselves: We do not search for God, because we are already within God, at the heart of God. We are within God—either we know it or we don't, either unwillingly or willingly; in short, our consciousness of it is more or less open. But one shouldn't reverse the roles: It is God who searches for us and not we who search for God. Consequently, the world has only a single logic, that of God. But this logic appears to us or does not appear to us; that's a different issue, which one can really debate. It is normal that it does not appear to us very clearly, but nevertheless there are no other kinds of logic. In short, this turnaround was and remains decisive for me.[81]

The tension arises when the *logic of God*, which is the only real logic in the world according to Marion, runs against the *logic of values*. In other words, it is a matter of determining how the "logic of values," based on the will of the one who evaluates and therefore falls within the unstable limits of *Dasein*, interacts with the "logic of God," which reverses the priority of things so that one receives oneself precisely by relinquishing oneself. Marion attempts to explain this tension with reference to a particular form of knowledge: "We are within God—either we know it or we don't, either unwillingly or willingly." But this emphasis (like his emphasis on *confessio*) seems to underestimate the possibility that the logic of God might continually undermine nihilism—*at least to a certain extent*—regardless of confessional stance.

A good way to explain how the logic of God might complicate the threat of nihilism is by reconsidering Marion's framing of the student riots in 1968. Instead of exclusively associating the events with nihilism and a crisis of the human sciences, one might also acknowledge how the human sciences that emerge from the period uncover forms of marginalization and injustice—insights that Christians seeking to follow what "Revelation has given us" can find good reason to support.[82] This is precisely the kind of theological reading of culture offered by other Christian writers in France during this period. Michel de Certeau, for instance, recognized the student revolts as a "symbolic revolution" that brought workers and students together and created a new space to expose the lies and exploitation of a republican democracy.[83] He understood the shifting cultural moment as an opportunity to return to a more *originary Christian* experience that relinquishes its authority within the social body.[84] Whether or not de

Certeau's account is more accurate than Marion's, at the very least, his analysis leaves space to acknowledge that God remains at work in ways that are outside the bounds of confessional Christianity—a possibility that seems to be overlooked and underappreciated in Marion's comments on contemporary culture.

There are some instances when Marion does recognize something like the "logic of God" at work in contemporary life. He alludes to this possibility when he suggests that further attentiveness to the *gift* is an answer to nihilism.[85] In an interview with Richard Kearney, he suggests that in response to Nietzsche's point regarding the "vicious circle of nihilism," it is important "to show how, in our everyday lives, we are already experiencing real things which cannot be experienced or represented as values but only as the 'impossible': birth, death, Eros, God. These are events, impossibilities from the point of view of metaphysical or humanist 'evaluation.'"[86] He then goes on to suggest that something like a "new hermeneutic" is needed in order to "pick out what is irreducible to the question of value," which is a hermeneutic he associates with the "gift."[87] Precisely employing a hermeneutic that picks out "what is irreducible to the question of value," however, is also a way of identifying aspects of the culture that have not been defined solely by nihilism. The "impossible" events that Marion identifies complicate the "natural attitude of ordinary consciousness." The birth of a child has the potential to bless a parent and initiate hope for future "gifts" (that is, further intimacy, love, grandchildren, and so on). In these ordinary yet "impossible" events the question of values does not solely dictate what is happening, regardless of one's orientation to the logic of values. These events might become the starting point for mundane participation in culture—taking children to sports practice or saving money for their university fees. While the logic of values may define these practices in certain instances, the point is that they also remain entangled with the gift to some degree. Based on Marion's own philosophical and theological position, his interpretation of the current "era" should not be defined solely by nihilism but also by an attentiveness to the ways in which the gift structures ordinary life (and in turn corresponds with the logic of God).

In *Negative Certainties* Marion aims to carry out the strategy of being attentive to the gift as a response to nihilism. However, he does so in a way that tends to set up a conceptualization of the gift on the one hand and nihilism on the other—which at least implicitly reinforces the binary that follows from his hermeneutics of confession. Christina Gschwandtner notes precisely this issue as she criticizes the excessive character of Marion's treatment of the gift. She states that for Marion, "a gift is a gift only if it is completely and utterly gratuitous," whereas "*any* definition or determination of the human or the divine or the gift (or indeed any rich phenomenon) is entirely reductive and nihilistic and must be radically excluded."[88] While she suggests there is a sense in which these absolute distinctions can be the case, it is not true of all gifts or instances.[89] Gschwandtner offers the example of shopping during the Christmas season amid a culture of consumption and economic exchange that defines a considerable amount of the gift giving during that time of year. While it is true that aspects of economic exchange (a desire for gratitude and recognition of the gift) likely define much of the giving in these contexts, she proposes that there is still a "'purer' or more abundant giving, one that is unconditioned and beneficent with no expectation of return," which "still underlies this culture of giving."[90] On some level (or perhaps to a certain "degree") then, the absolute gift that Marion emphasizes structures giving even amid the economy of exchange.

Although Gschwandtner confirms Marion's tendency toward a binary between nihilism and the gift, it is important not to overstate the case against him. In *Negative Certainties*, Marion seems to anticipate the event that Gschwandtner has in mind when he writes, "The gift succeeds . . . when, from the innumerable crowd of beings and objects that are available but undistinguished or ruled by possession, there is one that detaches itself and imposes itself by appearing as the one that I must accept."[91] Even in the frenzied experience of the modern consumer, the gift is capable of complicating or interrupting the logic of nihilism. As I will explain in more detail, Marion's phenomenology holds within it the *potential* for recognizing greater diversity with respect to how the gift structures ordinary experience—which, again, is why it is all the more surprising when he overextends the applicability of a concept like nihilism.

Part of the issue I am attempting to clarify here returns to the problems Robyn Horner highlights in *Rethinking God as Gift*. Alongside Marion (at least in "orientation if not entirely in method"), she suggests, "If God gives Godself without condition, then we will not be able to identify that gift *as such*: it will never be present. The relationship must rest on a freedom that risks the possibility of misunderstanding or rejection, or else it will not be a relationship of love but one opening onto coercion."[92] In other words, the gift, if it is in fact freely given, *still needs to be received in some way*—which is also the crux of the issue with respect to the "logic of values" and the "logic of God." I propose that the gift is operative in a noncoercive way, even amid those who find themselves participating in a logic of values. Within Marion's own framework it should be expected that people move in and out of a disposition of economic exchange to a certain extent and that the purity of the gift would manifest itself ambiguously (it will never be present) in everyday experience. But this giving would be the case whether people recognize it clearly or not and whether they confess a Christian faith or not. The structure of givenness and the gift would continually pull people back from the logic of values at least in various times and places—never letting any given culture enter an era solely defined by nihilism or the gift.

Creation's Goodness in the Field of the Given

The possibility of a noncoercive reception of the gift regardless of one's confessional stance is clarified by returning to the phenomenology of creation's goodness. If, as proposed in the previous chapter, creation's goodness is operative within prelinguistic experience, then it has the potential to define broadly the place in which we find ourselves. And as I already intimated, Marion's own fundamental philosophical and theological positions are capable of accommodating this *prelinguistic* goodness and, in fact, contribute particular insights into how it appears. Moreover, identifying aspects of creation's goodness within prelinguistic experience will not only help correct some of the overextended differences Marion draws along confessional lines but also lead toward a more nuanced theological interpretation of culture.

It is helpful to recall that the previous chapter linked the appearing of a prelinguistic goodness with moments of *joy* and *enjoyment*. Building on Lacoste's work in *Être en danger*, I explained that *joy* functions as a counterexistential to Heidegger's anxiety and intimates a goodness within the primordial rhythms of life. The *enjoyment of* particular things, I suggested, indicates a more mundane goodness that we generally accept without reservation in the course of an ordinary day. In both examples, my aim was to affirm a prelinguistic goodness at play in experience that remains open to a wide variety of interpretations. One does not need to confess a Christian faith to "recognize" this goodness—although Christians might credibly integrate it into part of a broader horizon of creation.

Marion's analysis of a lecture hall in *In Excess* is a good place to consider how his phenomenology of givenness might accommodate (and refine) the aforementioned prelinguistic experience of goodness. Therein, Marion describes the phenomenon of the hall as being marked by a past, present, and future that starts "from within itself" and has a phenomenality that "rose up from the self of its givenness."[93] He argues for this givenness by explaining that what a phenomenon *gives* is prior to what it *shows* and that therefore its *self-givenness* can never actually be seen, as such.[94] In order to recognize what "gives itself," he proposes that one "try to circle, in the space of manifestation, regions where phenomena *show themselves*, instead of letting them be shown simply as objects."⁹⁵ The example of the lecture hall clarifies what he means by what a phenomenon "shows." He points out that the hall takes on the character of an *event* because it "pre-exists us"; it is "already there, rising from a past of which we are ignorant, restored many a time by forgotten initiatives, charged with a history exceeding memory (is it a converted ancient cloister?), it imposes itself on me in appearing to me."⁹⁶ The hall also appears in a particular way in the present, since it no longer looks the same way it would in between lectures, when the hall is empty.⁹⁷ And finally, the evening of his lecture is a unique event that is "unrepeatable and for a large part unforeseeable." No witness could reconstruct it in the future "stone by stone, epoch by epoch, onlooker by onlooker."⁹⁸ Marion concludes that the lecture hall has its own self "that not only does not proceed from our initiative, or respond to our expectations, and could never be reproduced [*in ne pourra jamais se reproduire*], but especially that gives *itself* to us starting from its *self*, to the point that it affects us, modifies us, almost produces us."⁹⁹

The prelinguistic goodness outlined in the previous chapter takes on some of the same characteristics that define the *self-givenness* of the lecture hall. Take for example a small-scale event in which I *enjoy* a cup of coffee in a café and uncritically welcome a quality (broadly defined as goodness) in the moment. Whether it is the complexity of the coffee or atmosphere of the café, my enjoyment discloses a certain goodness that seems to reflect on my surroundings. But like the lecture hall, my enjoyment here is dependent on phenomena that I cannot control. The coffee offers a unique (unrepeatable) taste that can never be fully replicated no matter how talented the barista or how consistent the farmer's yield. The next time I return to the café, not only will the coffee taste different, but the entire structure of the event will invariably change. I might be annoyed by another customer's noise, feel anxious about my work, or be distracted by a stiff neck—all of which can undermine my intention to return to a previous enjoyment. There is something that was inextricably given (it started from *itself* rather than me) within the moment of enjoyment, and there is no straightforward cause and effect that might allow me to guarantee another, similar experience. The contours of a prelinguistic goodness are defined by the same characteristics as any self-giving phenomenon, at least in the sense that its appearing is given and cannot always be controlled or predicted.

The overlap between a prelinguistic goodness and Marion's phenomenology of givenness takes on another degree of nuance if one considers what I have already referred to as a "descriptive distinction." I outlined this distinction within two phenomenological projects. First, I identified the difference between what is "initial" to experience and "secondary evidence" in Lacoste's phenomenology of liturgical experience. The prelinguistic goodness that appears in moments of joy and enjoyment is related to what is *initial* to experience; however, I located a more robust topology of creation's goodness within an interpretation that follows from *secondary evidence* such as the introduction of the Absolute. Second, I suggested that there is a related descriptive distinction in Claude Romano's analysis of the *gap* between "understanding" and "interpretation." I proposed that a prelinguistic goodness can be associated with the manifestation of what Romano designates as prelinguistic *understanding*, whereas the fullness of a concept like creation's goodness is an *interpretation* formed within an interpretative community that integrates this prelinguistic understanding into a broader horizon of place.[100] The distinction is drawn logically rather than chronologically, since one cannot freeze one moment as a "prelinguistic experience."

A similar way of distinguishing different contours of experience can be identified in Marion's account of the "gap" between what *gives itself* and *shows itself*—a gap that is fixed according to the *limits of the adonné*.[101] He explains, "For what gives itself shows itself only insofar as it is received by the gifted [*adonné*], whose proper function consists in giving in return that the given show itself" (one might recognize here the call-and-response structure noted earlier).[102] According to Marion, the one who *receives* what is given (the *adonné*) "remains, by definition, finite" and, as a result, "fixes the limit, each time variable, of the transfiguration of what is given into what shows itself."[103] What *gives itself* never appears immediately in its full phenomenality but only *shows itself* partially as it runs into the limits of the *adonné*. I cannot replicate the event in the coffee shop in part because what gives itself exceeds my capacity to fully receive it, objectify it, or recreate it. Similarly, *I never receive the pure manifestation of a prelinguistic goodness*, since it is part of what remains protected by the gap between what gives itself and shows itself to the *adonné*.

The complexity of Marion's analysis is clarified to some degree within concrete examples "of common-law phenomena" he offers in the following:

> We are always as if surrounded by the uninterrupted arising of the appearing that gives itself, but this appearing gives itself in the form and outlines of a signification: I do not perceive a pure sound, but the murmur of a mountain stream (even of *this* river), the sound of a motor (and of *this* automobile); I do not perceive the color yellow (which one, moreover?), but this small section of this wall, not this blue, but that of Klein or of Cézanne; I do not perceive the taste of wine, nor even of a varietal, but that of this burgundy or of this coast,

of this climate, of this producer, of this year, etc. In all cases, I perceive only if a signification opens the field to the mature appearing of pure sensations; and that is why the thing appears only ever as an outline—because the signification, straightaway achieved and visible for the spirit, must most of the time (at least in the case of common-law phenomena) wait for the *outlines*, always partial and to be completed, to come take their place there and little by little validate it.[104]

Similarly, I do not perceive a pure prelinguistic goodness but only its ambiguous play following "the mature appearing of pure sensations." I do not taste *the* goodness of beer at the end of the day but only an "always partial and to be completed" goodness within *this* lambic beer, brewed during a specific time at a particular Brussels location using a uniquely open-air fermentation process. A prelinguistic goodness, therefore, is not a ready-made object of perception but an active, capacious, enigmatic dynamic that shows itself only following the *adonné*'s response.

The limits of the *adonné* to receive what is given raise the necessity of a hermeneutical moment in Marion's account. Persistent questions regarding the role of hermeneutics in Marion's phenomenology have been raised over the years.[105] In *The Hermeneutics of Givenness*, however, he offers an extended response to these critiques and in the process clarifies the movement between the different kinds of description I have emphasized. Marion explains that what *gives itself* requires and in fact "awakens" a hermeneutical moment from within "the enigma of sense data by the discovery of their signification."[106] In other words, the *excess* of what gives itself opens the need for interpretation when it runs into the limits of what shows itself to the *adonné*. It is important to note that (like Romano) the structure of Marion's phenomenology endorses a "hermeneutic circle" rather than a "*vicious* circle" here.[107] While the initial field of the given does not have an immediate objectifiable presence, it still *initiates* the hermeneutical process (logically speaking): "The sense that hermeneutics (re-)finds for what it interprets does not come from the ego but from the thing itself awaiting interpretation; the ego less fixes a sense for that which awaits one than it receives a sense from that which awaits one."[108] This does not imply that a person has no room for choice or lacks interpretative capacities in Marion's account. His point of emphasis falls on the sense in which interpretation continually requires one to consider the appearance of a phenomenon in order to verify, nuance, or adjust the accuracy of one's interpretation. Similarly, the phenomenological description of a prelinguistic goodness also requires continually referring back to phenomena (or things themselves) in order to outline what appears and question one's interpretation.

Marion's phenomenology of givenness, then, clarifies the sense in which a prelinguistic experience of "goodness" is not constructed solely by the power of the *adonné* to interpret or project a meaning onto phenomena. As noted earlier, he contends that the phenomenology of givenness has a "factual character" and does not require reference to a Giver or Creator. This factual character of givenness is one of the central reasons why the prelinguistic play of goodness encountered in an enjoyable taste (coffee, curry, garlic) transgresses cultures and is not reducible to a confessional stance. At the same time, there is no reason for a *theology* of culture to separate this play of goodness from a Creator. Norman Wirzba offers an example of what this might look like in his reflections on the theology of food:

> Whenever people come to the table they demonstrate with the unmistakable evidence of their stomachs that they are not self-subsisting gods. They are finite and mortal creatures dependent on God's many good gifts: sunlight, photosynthesis, decomposition, soil fertility, water, bees and butterflies, chickens, sheep, cows, gardeners, farmers, cooks, strangers, and friends (the list goes on and on). Eating reminds us that we participate in a grace-saturated world, a blessed creation worthy of attention, care, and celebration.[109]

The good gifts that define the growing, cooking, sharing, and tasting of food are integral to what it means to affirm creation's goodness—even if (as I will explain) the *relation* of these gifts to God can appear ambiguous (Chapter 3), inaccessible (Chapter 4), and incomplete (Chapter 5).

Conclusion: Theological Interpretations of Culture

The binary distinctions drawn along confessional lines that stem from Marion's hermeneutics of confession is undermined (to an extent) by the pervasive presence of goodness at a prelinguistic level. If there is a goodness that *gives itself* in what *shows itself* by means of the *adonné*, then this goodness is operative in our lives prior to the hermeneutical moment (it does not follow from the logic of values) regardless of the cultural moment. Whether or not we embody the language of praise or enter into the community of believers, this goodness would still be at play and remain open to a variety of interpretations. This is important because it is easy enough to let ever-emerging sociopolitical problems overwhelm our capacity to notice how nihilism is being challenged. Or, perhaps worse, it is easy to forget how those who confess a Christian faith and employ the language of praise also continually participate in a nihilistic logic of values. Greater attentiveness to the appearing of a prelinguistic goodness guards against the excessive burden that Marion places on the hermeneutics of confession and opens the door to a more accurate theological reading of culture. It provides a way of engaging with one's surroundings that is not fully dependent on a problem-context inherited from Heidegger's and Nietzsche's understanding of the West and instead accounts for people's participation (or struggle to participate) in that which is good.

As I noted in the Introduction to this book, identifying a prelinguistic goodness does not indicate anything like a "pure nature" that is separate from God, since it only reflects an aspect of what appears rather than anything like a complete description. Different kinds of description do not necessitate the separation of what is theologically linked: immanence and transcendence, the natural and supernatural, nature and grace. Theologically speaking, what shows itself in rough outline as a prelinguistic goodness may be inseparable from a relationality with God in a broader topology of creation. Critically, from this point of view, creation's goodness permeates the place in which we find ourselves whether or not one recognizes it as such. While the meaning of creation's goodness may be clarified in the context of *confessio*, its theological significance for defining the place in which we find ourselves is not limited to the hermeneutics of confession. The biblical account cannot be reduced to the idea that creation appears "good" when one enters into the modality of praise with the community of believers; instead, the text makes a comprehensive statement about the kind of place in which we find ourselves. This goodness is operative regardless of the cultural moment.

There are different ways in which one might develop further a theological understanding of this prelinguistic goodness. In a Reformed tradition, for instance, one might relate it to the *common grace* that extends from God's ongoing providence to creation.[110] Alternatively, one might explore how the movement from a prelinguistic goodness to a topology of creation corresponds with Aquinas's understanding of the natural world being endowed with a purpose that is "beyond nature."[111] But in the following chapter, I consider how identifying a prelinguistic goodness within a topology of creation implies living within theological tensions like nature and grace, activity and passivity, knowing and unknowing. I examine the relationship between the contours of experience and a broader theological horizon of place—focusing in particular on the role of God's initiative in the process of adopting an explicitly Christian topology of creation.

3

Transfigured Goodness

Up to this point, I have maintained the tension between a prelinguistic goodness and its integration into a topology of creation by employing a descriptive distinction. Focusing on the prelinguistic contours of experience allowed for a description of "goodness" that is accessible regardless of confessional stance, while also maintaining that it can be integrated into a specifically Christian understanding of place. I have not yet examined the *movement* toward a particularly Christian experience of creation's goodness in detail. It is one thing to describe the prelinguistic play of goodness that remains open to a wide variety of legitimate interpretations, but as noted in the first chapter, another degree of hermeneutical complexity is introduced when this more general sense of goodness is integrated into something resembling a Christian understanding of place. The purpose of this chapter, then, is to articulate credibly what it means to adopt a topology of creation that integrates (and even transfigures) a prelinguistic play of goodness. This requires paying attention to some of the complications that stem from experiencing one's place as a "creation" that remains in relation to God, while at the same time outlining particular forms of theological knowledge that have the potential to address these complications.

While several authors play an important role in this chapter, the work of Emmanuel Falque is given particular focus because he emphasizes experiential difficulties that are related to encountering the world as a good creation. These difficulties stem from the widespread existence of pain and suffering (which I examine in the following chapter) as well as the *limits* of being human. These limits are of particular interest here, since they suggest that adopting a topology of creation's goodness is not primarily engendered from a person's particular experience of the world. In fact, Falque argues that what is first given to experience is a "blocked horizon of existence" (finitude) in which there seems to be no immediate experiential reference to God. If his account of finitude is accurate, further explanation is needed regarding both the philosophical and theological issues involved in a person's decision to adopt an explicitly Christian topology of creation (my focus in the latter half of this chapter).

Another reason to examine Falque's work is that it allows me to continue developing one of the ongoing arguments in this book—namely, that the appearance of phenomena associated with creation's goodness challenges some of the conclusions presented by the phenomenologists I examine. As suggested in the Introduction to this study, too often continental philosophy is characterized by an "obsessive negativity," which seems to overlook phenomena that might be considered life-giving or positive.[1] At times, Falque falls into this temptation through his prioritization of finitude as the decisive category for understanding what is held in common between people. While the concept helpfully identifies the limits of experience, his claim (following Heidegger) that finitude is what appears first and is most ordinary in experience is questionable. Using the insights of feminist phenomenologies, I argue that a more diverse range of phenomena is at play in what is initial to experience by critiquing aspects of Falque's approach to the *event of birth* in relation to finitude. Specifically, there is a prelinguistic goodness at work within the event that complicates the valueless horizon that supposedly makes up what is first given and most ordinary. Although questioning aspects of Falque's account of finitude may seem like a detour, my analysis further nuances Falque's attempt to identify what is held in common between people and the existential concerns that define contemporary culture. Since both of these issues are crucial to arguments I have developed so far, they require some attention in a chapter that engages his work.

As already noted, however, the central purpose of this chapter is to address some of the experiential issues that arise within an explicitly Christian topology. If, as Falque contends, finitude constitutes a "blocked horizon of existence" without any obvious reference to God, it necessarily leads to questions regarding how people might come to understand themselves to be living in a good creation that is defined by a relation to God. In the latter half of the chapter I propose that addressing these questions requires attending to a series of theological tensions starting with God's initiative and a person's freedom, as well as tensions such as nature and grace, activity and passivity, knowing and unknowing. These theological tensions are never resolved within a topology of creation but demand ongoing reflection and discernment. A Christian horizon of place does not require one to identify where nature ends and grace begins; instead, it is precisely because God's initiative is *noncoercive* that a substantial amount of experiential ambiguity remains within these theological tensions. This indicates some coherence between phenomenology and theology—which does not prove God's presence in the world—but perhaps offers some depth and credibility to what it means to inhabit one's place in light of such a possibility.

In the concluding sections of this chapter I return to the central theme in this study—the phenomenology of creation's goodness. I provide an initial sketch of how God's ongoing relation to creation may *transfigure* what one recognizes as "good" about one's place. Without diminishing the significance of personal experience or a prelinguistic goodness, I submit that a transfigured goodness is less reducible to my shifting perceptions and instead indicates that all of creation has intrinsic value in relation to God. The centrality of this enlarged concept of goodness will be critically important for the arguments I develop in the following chapters, when I examine phenomena that more directly challenge the affirmation of creation's goodness and therefore require a rendering that is more complex than its appearing within prelinguistic experience.

Finitude: A Grammar in Common

It is hard to overstate the significance of finitude in the development of Falque's philosophical and theological project. Not only is it a definitive concept in the first two books of his *Triduum philosophique*, but Falque also uses finitude as a starting point for thinking about contemporary culture and common human experiences.[2] One reason it is helpful to consider Falque's account of finitude is that it offers insight into why God's presence may no longer be a shared cultural assumption—without immediately calling this into question. His approach to finitude productively avoids reigniting old cultural battles drawn along confessional lines, while emphasizing the importance of dialogue and encounter between people who think differently. Of course, as I will explain, not everyone finds Falque's understanding of finitude in relation to Christianity and culture helpful. Joseph O'Leary criticizes what he perceives to be Falque's "triumphalist" approach to Christianity and culture, and Emmanuel Gabellieri suggests that Falque forgets Henri de Lubac's insights into the natural desire for the supernatural. However, as I will explain, Falque's account of finitude identifies (without condemning) ordinary ways in which human beings commonly experience the world without God. Not only does such an approach correspond well with the arguments I developed in the previous chapter, but it also forms a critical context in which to examine a more explicitly Christian topology that affirms God's relation to creation in the latter half of the chapter.

To begin, then, it is helpful to note that Falque's approach to finitude corresponds with his self-conscious association with a new generation of French phenomenologists who have been formed by a particular set of historical and cultural circumstances. According to Falque, a previous generation of Catholic phenomenologists, such as Jean-Luc Marion, Jean-Yves Lacoste, Jean-Louis Chrétien, and Didier Franck, established a "real relation to the history of philosophy" and renewed "French philosophy and philosophical research more generally." However, they began their work "in a time of crisis, or at least opposition," in which a Christian minority developed a "secret resistance" to their culture, while relying heavily on the idea of overcoming metaphysics.[3] In contrast, Falque submits that the current generation is defined by a different set of experiences. Less concerned with the cultural dividing lines of the 1960s (for example, the student riots, the "death of God," or the crisis of the human sciences), Falque suggests that their intellectual formation occurred in a context defined by a "new mode of tolerance and a certain type of relativism."[4] As Bradley Onishi explains, "Rather than asserting that all moral, philosophical and political authority and logic rests on the presence of God, whether or not all humans recognize it as such, Falque maintains that all logic—including his own theo-logic—is situated and provisional." This implies that the "catholicity of thought pertains to its ineluctable personal and cultural situatedness, not the prevailing universality and legitimacy of God's rule."[5] And this newfound tolerance, according to Falque, permits increased interaction between philosophy and theology—allowing Christian philosophers to be explicit about how theology interacts with philosophical research and nonconfessional philosophers to explore theological concepts.[6]

Nowhere is Falque's interest in dialogue and encounter demonstrated more clearly than in his assessment of the public debate between Jean-Luc Marion (his former doctoral supervisor) and Jocelyn Benoist. On the one hand, he observes Benoist's comments to Marion:

> I am an *atheist*: you are not.... There is nothing particularly *legitimate* in this interpretation of things, given what you believe you see—that is to say, given the *belief* in which your seeing is rooted and that

orientates your *seeing*. It simply remains a fact (enigmatic, incomprehensible—we shall come back to that) that one can *see differently*, that I and others do see *differently*. . . . That is so for me, to whom atheism has always simply been an obvious fact . . . for whom it has been an *existential attitude* and not a *theoretical certitude*.[7]

On the other hand, Falque observes Marion's argument that "atheism cannot any more be taken as the special privilege of atheists, just as theism cannot be taken as the special privilege of believers. The claims of the first are no less excessive than the affirmations of the second."[8] Falque then summarizes the dispute by stating: "The supposed certitude of Christianity as a stance of belief for many Christians corresponds then to the no less striking obviousness of atheism, as an existential stance, for many of our contemporaries. The legitimacy of one (the believer) cannot be said to hold the field at the price of a condemnation of the other (the atheist)."[9] The debate is defined by an atheist who *sees* the world one way (without God) and a believer who *sees* the world another way (in relation to God). Beyond these different existential stances, however, Falque pursues a dialogue wherein each person productively changes from the encounter.

As I indicated earlier, not everyone agrees that Falque's desire for greater exchange between philosophy and theology produces a constructive dialogue between those who think differently. Joseph O'Leary, for instance, argues that Marion's decision to separate meticulously his philosophy and theology allows him to offer a less "triumphalist" rendering of theology's relationship with philosophy than Falque.[10] O'Leary proposes that Falque opens up the "old battle against laïcité" by adopting "a tone of military triumphalism which throws caution to the winds."[11] As evidence of this triumphalism, he cites Falque's frequent use of "combat" language and the idea that crossing the Rubicon connotes entering "another territory as a conqueror."[12] While O'Leary may identify an important tension that stems from Falque's emphasis on encounter, it is important to keep in mind the nuances of the French terms Falque uses. For instance, *Le combat amoureux* (translated as *The Loving Struggle*) does not necessarily suggest a violent battle (that is, the death of his interlocutor's ideas) so much as the difficulty of working through differences. Lucas McCracken clarifies this in the translator's preface to the English translation:

> In its everyday usage, the French word *combat* carries a more sportive or athletic connotation than the English "combat," which is more uniquely militaristic. Hence, the obvious translation of *combat* by its cognate does not suffice to relay the images the French word evokes of wrestling, fencing or even jousting—all of which appear in the

text. With our choice of "struggle," we meant to capture the confrontational sense of *combat* without implying—as "combat" might—that such a combat consists in vanquishing foes, in victory and defeat, in hoisting one's flag while lowering another's.[13]

Falque's "struggle," therefore, is properly characterized as a modern form of *disputatio*, wherein he finds his own philosophical path by struggling to separate himself from those who have gone before.[14] And to this end, Falque often seeks to integrate the insights of nonconfessional philosophers (Derrida, Merleau-Ponty, Romano, Heidegger) while taking a more critical approach to his fellow Roman Catholic phenomenologists (Marion, Chrétien, Lacoste).[15] He explains, "Today it is less a question of confronting and combating atheism than of allowing ourselves to be questioned by it . . . the contemporary believer does not erect his faith into the sole norm of all truth and instead, like other human beings, reaches into the depths of his own existence."[16] This approach does not abdicate Christian claims about what is true but aims to account for the legitimacy of experiences that encounter the world without reference to God.

While Falque develops a variety of concepts through his engagement with "philosophical atheism" (bodily suffering, meaninglessness, the nothing), *finitude* offers the clearest illustration of how his concerns about *common experience* and *dialogue* with those who think differently converge. For example, finitude suggests a common human experience, since nobody can overcome the "blocked horizon of existence" on their own. By definition, it is "the impassable limit" for everyone who remains caught simply "between birth and death."[17] Even Christians, who place their hope in life after death, must face finitude as an integral aspect of being human.[18] At the same time, Falque's interest in finitude also underscores his prioritization of dialogue with those who think differently, given the genuinely diverse ways individuals might interpret their finitude, since "the *value* of the horizon of my finitude is thus paradoxically that I find myself always without value: not in the sense that, being valueless, the horizon would go beyond the limits of my finitude; far from it. It is simply that no other criterion apart from my own way of regarding the horizon could precisely give it a value."[19] There is not one kind of finitude for "believers" and a different one for "nonbelievers," but every individual must relate to (or evaluate) being between birth and death on their own. The inescapable horizon of finitude can be apprehended in diverse ways and leaves substantial space for open dialogue between those who think differently.

Falque's prioritization of finitude borrows from Lacoste's method of doing philosophy and theology.[20] As I explained in the first chapter, Lacoste emphasizes the *immanence* of Heidegger's being-in-the-world and its legitimacy (or "integrity") within the contours of human experience.[21] Falque explicitly adopts this insight in his analysis of finitude, proposing "at least from a heuristic point of view, that we come to picture for ourselves first of all simply the incarnation of a man rather than the image of a God."[22] He argues then, following Heidegger, that finitude is what "appears to us at 'first sight'" and is "most ordinary" about being human.[23] In fact, he even goes so far as to suggest that there are benefits from imagining that finitude is a kind of "pure nature," although "it is absolutely invalid from a dogmatic point of view."[24] Falque's point here is not that people are "created without grace," but that "all the same we find ourselves first in nature (or better in finitude)—that is to say, independent of the evidence that will be the revelation of God."[25] Finitude, then, underscores the legitimacy of experiencing the world without God within the first givens of experience, but it does not imply that this kind of experience is most important or definitive for what is true.

Falque's description of finitude alludes to important twentieth-century theological debates regarding *nature* and *grace*. And Emmanuel Gabellieri specifically questions whether the influence of Heidegger has led Falque to forget the tradition that affirms humanity's natural desire for God, particularly emphasized in the work of Henri de Lubac.[26] Along with other figures associated with *la nouvelle théologie*, de Lubac was concerned with "the average textbook-conception of the relationship between nature and grace" presented by the early twentieth-century manualist tradition.[27] He argued that a concept of pure nature would imply that "grace" was a "mere superstructure" added onto nature.[28] And moreover, de Lubac believed that the division contributed to the rise of atheism in the twentieth century, since it implies that there is a layer of reality that one can experience that is "sufficient unto itself," which in turn promotes the possibility that "the second, supernatural layer" of reality is superfluous and can be set aside.[29] In response, de Lubac insisted that it "was necessary to hold together two paradoxical notions: on the one hand, human beings had an innate natural desire for God; on the other hand, this natural desire was unable of itself to attain the beatific vision, so that the human interior aptitude in no way obliged God to give sanctifying grace."[30]

The possibility of a "natural desire for God" raises an important tension within Falque's emphasis on the "blocked horizon of existence," and it is not always clear how (or even if) this tension can be resolved (I will return to this issue shortly). But to his credit, Falque is aware of the problems raised by de Lubac, and he insists that he is not questioning "the supernatural at the heart of the natural" or the "image of God" in humanity.[31]

Instead, following Lacoste, he simply acknowledges that people today can live relatively content lives without finding rest in the eternal or the Absolute. Falque's emphasis on finitude does not contradict de Lubac's account of grace so much as it responds to a different kind of atheism. As Matthew Farley notes, Falque is interested in the kind of atheist who "is our colleague at the water cooler: she gives gifts at Christmas, she regards Richard Dawkins as quizzically as Ken Ham; she regrets all theological contretemps."[32] De Lubac was responding to a culture that was still scandalized by atheism, and as such, the possibility of a natural desire for God had a certain amount of cultural currency. In contrast, Falque seeks to address the relative contentment of many people who live their lives without a reference to God. This requires acknowledging the lack of "drama" that the question of God engenders today as opposed to the drama of twentieth-century atheist humanism.

In summary, then, Falque's approach by means of finitude is helpful because it recognizes the legitimacy to an experience of the world without God. If everyone starts with the blocked horizon of existence, even those who affirm God's presence to creation likely are familiar with the difficulties that follow from discerning this presence. A culture that operates as if God is not present does not necessarily require condemnation by Christians; instead, there is renewed space for a dialogue regarding our shared encounter with the limits of experience. From this point of view, Falque's emphasis on finitude helps produce a "*grammar in common* with those who see *differently*."[33] And as I indicated, such a position has the additional benefit of corresponding with (and likely influencing) several of the arguments I developed in the previous chapters. For instance, an "emphasis on commonality" underscores what I sought to outline by means of a prelinguistic goodness that appears regardless of confessional stance—which indicates various points of connection between those who confess a Christian faith and those who do not. Moreover, an emphasis on commonality reinforces my critique of Marion's overly binary rendering of the relationship between "believers" and "nonbelievers." While there are aspects of Falque's account of finitude that I put into question in the following section, my point for now is that the concept offers a helpful starting point for thinking about the challenges of adopting a topology of creation's goodness that I hope to address in the latter half of this chapter.

Birth and the First Givens of Experience

The aspects of Falque's analysis of finitude that I want to question relate to his claim that it is first given (or first to appear) in experience and the *extent* to which it defines contemporary culture. To explain my concerns, it is helpful to return to one of the central arguments in this book—namely, that phenomena associated with creation's goodness can challenge and nuance the conclusions presented by the French phenomenologists I examine. In the first two chapters, I made this argument based on the development of a prelinguistic goodness that appears in experience regardless of confessional stance. Emphasizing the presence of a prelinguistic goodness allowed me to argue for a degree of immanence in the goodness of creation, which complicated Lacoste's account of the differences between notions of "sacrality" and a Christian understanding of "creation." Then, in the context of Marion's work, the presence of a prelinguistic goodness helped me critique his overly negative interpretation of Western culture as one solely defined by nihilism. Along similar lines now, I will explain how a prelinguistic goodness also pushes back on Falque's conclusion that finitude is first given and the extent to which he argues that it defines contemporary culture.

The aspect of Falque's analysis of finitude that is most relevant is the role of *birth*. While the theme of death is most commonly associated with finitude, Falque proposes that we are always sent "back to 'another ending,' probably more originary even though never analyzed as such, the first of all the beginnings—the 'birth.'"[34] Birth, therefore, constitutes one end of the "blocked horizon of existence" (being "between" birth and death). Falque's account of birth borrows heavily from Claude Romano's "evential" hermeneutic in at least three significant ways.[35]

(1) Falque adopts Romano's understanding of the event as an *impersonal happening*: "To come into the world, or to be given birth, is not then to inscribe myself in a world, but literally, according to the French expression, to be '*mis au* monde' (put in the world), or to '*bring* a world *into being.*'"[36] There is no choice involved with whether or not I am born; I simply find myself already brought into existence.

(2) Similar to Romano, Falque also asserts that the event of birth has no specific cause, suggesting that not even the mother can "*give reasons for* my flesh or, even less, for my existence."[37] While there is the physical process of conception, pregnancy, and childbirth, these biological developments do not explain the event itself—which implies being brought into a world with possibilities and meanings unique to each person without any immediately satisfying answer as to *why* this has occurred.[38]

(3) Falque borrows from Romano's emphasis on the fact that I cannot relate to birth "except in terms of the past" (we are not "contempo-

raries" of its "actualization").[39] This implies that the event is forever hidden from memory and, by extension, that it never has a self-evident meaning. The meaning of one's birth requires ongoing interpretation over the course of one's life.

Each of these features of the "event" of birth underscore Falque's assertion that we begin with a blocked horizon of existence that is "independent of the evidence that will be the revelation of God" in the first givens of experience.

Now, in order to argue for a more complex understanding of what is first given in experience, I want to raise an issue that Falque generally overlooks (along with much of the history of phenomenology), namely, *the role of the mother* in the event of birth.[40] Whether speaking of Heidegger's emphasis on *thrownness* into the world "from no specific position or person," Merleau-Ponty's description of pregnancy as "'more an anonymous process which happens through [the mother] and of which she is only the seat,'" or "Sartre's account of being responsible for one's own birth"—there is a consistent tendency to ignore the mother in phenomenological accounts of birth.[41] Although Falque does allude to the mother's position as a privileged "witness" in the event of birth, as I will explain, there are important aspects of her presence in the "event" that go unnoticed because of the privileged status of finitude in his account.[42] In contrast to the "valueless horizon of finitude," I propose that accounting for the role of the mother in the event birth indicates that it is a *value-laden* event that opens the possibility of a prelinguistic goodness at play in experience.

My aim here is not to critique Falque's (and by extension Romano's) approach to the "event of birth" with a superficial reference to the *personal* presence of a mother. In fact, I would acknowledge that her involvement does not contradict the *impersonal* structure of the event that Romano outlines. For example, one might identify the way in which childbirth also "happens" to the mother in Louis Levesque-Lopman's phenomenology of childbirth. She submits: "My body seemed to take over in a tremendous sweep of physical energy. . . . As I tuned into the rhythm of my body, I had no doubt and my husband could only be in awe as I surrendered to the power of my body."[43] Or, as Iris Marion Young writes in her account of pregnancy and childbirth:

> As the months and weeks progress, increasingly I feel my insides, strained and pressed, and increasingly feel the movement of a body inside me. Through pain and blood and water this inside thing emerges between my legs, for a short while both inside and outside me. Later I look with wonder at my mushy middle and at my child,

amazed that this yowling, flailing thing, so completely different from me, was there inside, part of me.[44]

Just as birth "happens" to the one being born, there also is a sense in which it "happens" to the mother. Even if a woman has made a conscious decision to pursue pregnancy and childbirth, the process itself remains largely out of her natural control (for example, the date of the child's birth or the health of the fetus).[45] In many ways it is an experience that the mother "undergoes" (*faire, Erlebnis*), rather than an experience that she "has" (*avoir, Erlebnisse*).[46] By emphasizing the mother's role in the event, therefore, I am not questioning the evential hermeneutic of birth, as such; instead, I am seeking to identify how the event introduces *value-laden* relational dynamics that expand what might be considered first given.

In order to articulate these relational dynamics, it is instructive to note the way in which a newborn's body is completely *dependent* on the mother. As Allison Stone explains, "Because our brains are so undeveloped at birth, we encounter the world outside the maternal womb while most of our practical and mental capacities are still nascent."[47] As such:

> A weeks-old baby cannot sit or hold up her own head unaided, crawl or walk, stand, eat solid food, or hold objects, and has almost no voluntary control over her bodily movements. At a year old, most babies have gained some mastery of these things, but they still lack many basic abilities, including the abilities to speak and regulate their bowel and bladder movements. Babies depend on their care-givers—often their parents, especially their mothers—for all they cannot yet do themselves; for sleep regulation, food provision, cleaning, comfort when injured, care when sick, and more.[48]

Stone points out that the infant's attachment to her caregivers (especially their mothers) "becomes immensely affectively charged."[49] While the newborn may not yet distinguish her flesh from her surroundings, this dependency suggests the first signs of what Richard Kearney describes as a flesh that is "shot through with all kinds of values and desires, withholdings and yieldings."[50] As such, what is first given in the event of birth is not necessarily a "valueless" horizon of existence but rather an inextricably *value-laden* relationship between a mother and a newborn taking place in prelinguistic experience. The newborn's understanding here does not rise to a level of consciousness associated with Husserl's concept of "double sensation," in his well-known example of the left hand touching the right, but the child's radical dependency is at the very least "shot through" with various qualities or values.

Critically, associating "value" within the structure of dependency here does not imply an essentialist understanding of pregnancy, labor, motherhood, or childbirth, since these experiences are variegated and certainly are not limited to a category like "goodness."[51] But the diversity of experiences does not exclude the possibility that something like a prelinguistic goodness is put into play by the event of birth. A helpful way to explain what I mean here is by considering Marion's phenomenology of *givenness* explored in the previous chapter. Therein, I argued that a prelinguistic goodness *shows itself* from within the response of the *adonné* following what *gives itself* (there is a "gap"). It was important to highlight that the "goodness" I identified was not engendered primarily from a person's way of regarding the horizon but rather arose from within the field of *givenness*. Marion's phenomenology, then, leaves open the possibility that the first *givens* of experience may be more accurately understood in terms of a horizon *saturated with value* rather than one that is valueless.[52] Marion explicitly clarifies this possibility within his own phenomenology of the event of birth (also largely building on Romano's work):

> There is none among the living who did not first have to be born, that is to say, arise belatedly from his parents in the attentive circle of waiting for words that summoned him before he could understand them or guess their meaning. This observation is not at all trivial since it inscribes before and more essentially than mortality the gifted in his gap from the call. My birth, which fixes my most singular identity even more than my existence, nevertheless happens without and before me—without my having to know about it or say a word, without my knowing or foreseeing anything. All my slow coming to consciousness, stubborn about rising to the $I = I$ of "I think (myself)," has no other ambition than to absorb my delay in responding to my birth (call) and to contain the initial excess with the fragile poverty of solipsism.[53]

In the last line, Marion identifies the *saturated* or *excessive* horizon in which one might locate the value-laden dynamics (like goodness) in the event of birth. While there is no way for a person to recall explicitly that which was initially given, following a "slow coming to consciousness," she might still find herself affirming an *enigmatic goodness* at play in the event itself.[54] In other words, the event was value-laden rather than valueless and by extension complicates the idea that finitude accurately defines that which is first given or most ordinary to experience.

Emphasizing a prelinguistic goodness at play in the relationship between mother and child is important, in part, because it has the capacity to expand the range of common experiences between people who think differently. If, as Falque submits, there are heuristic reasons for considering the concept of "pure nature" wherein "we come to picture for ourselves first of all simply the incarnation of a man rather than the image of a God," then it is also important to come to an accurate understanding of "man." To this end, one might nuance Falque's conclusion near the end of *The Metamorphosis of Finitude* when he submits that what "makes mankind in modernity is . . . the anxiety that human beings undergo, and sometimes the absurdity of our 'being in the world,' of being thrown into existence, fully responsible for a 'situation' that we have not, however, chosen."[55] While the feelings of anxiety and thoughts of absurdity that often accompany reflection on finitude are important, Falque's appraisal of what is first given should be counterbalanced by the genuine enjoyment and happiness of "modern man."[56] This requires paying attention to phenomena that suggest life may be saturated with a given "value" rather than being valueless from the beginning, which in turn includes the possibility of the prelinguistic goodness I have developed over the course of this study.

To be fair, it is unlikely that Falque would challenge the idea that people today are also defined by happiness and enjoyment, even if he does not include this as part of his description of what is first given and most ordinary.[57] My point is that his prioritization of finitude establishes a range of experiential content in the first givens of experience that is too narrow. One does not violate the "blocked horizon of existence" by acknowledging value-laden phenomena that appear across confessional divides and do not require reference to God in order to be identified. This is important because the "heuristic value" that follows from picturing ourselves as "the incarnation of a man rather than the image of a God" only goes so far if it remains inattentive to a broader range of what is held in common between people. If existence is "shot through with all kinds of values and desires, withholdings and yieldings," then I propose that this includes a prelinguistic goodness at play in experience already from the start.

The Transformation of Finitude

The central difficulty remaining in this chapter is to explain credibly how a prelinguistic goodness is integrated and transfigured in an explicitly Christian topology. In the previous chapters I have made various connections between a prelinguistic level of experience and a theological understanding of creation; however, I have not examined in detail the experiential movement between what is first given to experience and the kind of

Christian topology that mediates one's encounter with this prelinguistic goodness. Because a category like creation's goodness necessarily includes a degree of theological or "propositional knowledge," it seems unlikely that people will come to understand the place in which they find themselves as a good creation exclusively through prelinguistic encounters with phenomena.[58] More needs to be said about the relationship between what is "initial" (prelinguistic) and how it interacts with a horizon of place that is mediated through theological knowledge.

In order to examine the movement toward a topology of creation in the following, I begin with Falque's analysis of the *transformation* of finitude (but will engage with a variety of sources). As I already alluded to in this chapter, the concept of finitude tends to emphasize the difficulties of moving from a concept of "world" to one of "creation" by emphasizing the "blocked horizon of existence" in which there is no immediate experiential access to God. Falque addresses this challenge by introducing the possibility of transforming or "metamorphosing" the "ontological structure of our Being-there" (finitude) following the resurrection of Christ.[59] In other words, he uses the concept of transformation in order to pivot from an experience of the world without God to an experience in which a person might confess a relation to God. In this section, I focus on the importance of *God's initiative* within that process, since it introduces important theological tensions and experiential ambiguities that are constitutive of a topology of creation. As I will explain, these "tensions" and "ambiguities" actually reinforce one another in a way that lends some credibility to what it means to understand one's place as "creation" without transcending the "blocked horizon of existence."

Falque's emphasis on God's *initiative* in the process of transformation was already intimated in his first book on Bonaventure, wherein he explores a *Trinitarian monadology*. The idea of a Trinitarian monadology implies that "nothing is produced in the human that is not first produced in God, apart from sin."[60] This "Trinitarian" principle defines transformation because the process begins with "the transfiguration of his [the Son's] finitude by the Father," which then enables "the transformation of our own finitude in Him (the Word), at the summons of the Father and under the force of the Holy Spirit."[61] Because finitude constitutes an inescapable limit to being human, according to Falque, no one can transform their own finitude. Any transformation of finitude must first take place in and by the Trinity following Christ's incarnation and resurrection.

Falque's emphasis on God's initiative, once again, raises issues related to the role of nature and grace. By prioritizing God's initiative in the process of transformation, he relinquishes the heuristic value of a "pure nature" associated with finitude. In fact, Falque argues that God's initiative in transformation frames the possibility of a person's *decision* to believe—submitting that the very possibility of a decision requires a situation in need of a decision: *"Deus est causa decidendi omnibus decidentibus*—God is the cause of the decision of all that decides."[62] One does not "decide" to welcome transformation without God initiating the very possibly of a decision. He explains:

> Inasmuch as "God works in us the willing and the doing of his good design" (Phil 2:13), God renders us not inoperative but capable of co-operating. God "operates in whatever is operating" (*Deum operari in quolibet operante*), in the words of a famous phrase from the *Summa theologia*. Thus, we are first the seat of his operation precisely in order that we operate. Far from operating "in our place" or causing us to succumb to the horizon of his operation or Providence, God "co-operates," strictly speaking, with our operation.[63]

The principle Falque alludes to here is similar to what Anthony Godzieba describes as "a simultaneous two-fold presupposed dependency," wherein "God's self-giving occurs in the midst of and through the conditions of human experience, while at the same time the very possibility of human experience is always grounded in God who gives it space to be."[64] Or, as Rowan Williams explains, "God makes the world to be itself, to have an integrity and completeness and goodness that is—by God's gift—its own."[65] Within the more existential language that Falque employs, therefore, the human "space to be" is protected by a "blocked horizon of existence" in the first givens to experience, while the resurrection of Christ "initiates" (or "enables") "co-operating" with God.

Falque's desire to affirm both God's initiative and a person's freedom to co-operate with transformation lends itself to a delicate and elusive rendering of the relationship between nature and grace. On the one hand, Falque attempts to avoid the image of a domineering God who chooses arbitrarily which submissive subject will be converted and transformed. To this end, he submits that it would be a mistake to depart from "the well-known Thomist adage, which underlies the strongest of Catholic traditions, that grace 'does not destroy nature but perfects it' (*cum enim gratia non tollat naturam sed perficiat*)."[66] On the other hand, Falque also aims to avoid basing transformation solely on the capacity of an individual to produce it autonomously.[67] As such, "it is 'by grace' that mankind is unified into and so incorporated into the Trinity" through "the *second person*—the Word incarnate."[68] Engendered from this tension, then, Falque identifies the concept of *co-operation* (or, perhaps, participation) in the Triune life of God.[69] Rather than a simplistic form of predestination wherein God controls all aspects of a person's life, the kind of initiative Falque seeks to describe is one that gives a person freedom to co-operate with God—a freedom that is initiated by the Triune life of God.

A good way to clarify how co-operating in the life of God may lead to transformation is to consider Jean-Louis Chrétien's reflections on Gregory the Great and the dynamics of activity and passivity. Chrétien identifies in Gregory's writings an acute awareness of the demands of Christian love—which include not only loving your neighbor but also your enemies. Chrétien explains that according to Gregory, "No one is able, spontaneously, to love his enemies. . . . God's love is what makes it possible for us to reach a high and dignified *statura*, a state that results from the way in which love dilates our actions."[70] Christian love (especially the love of your enemies) is not achieved through the power of one's ego or will but instead requires "the first loving dilation according to a vertical axis."[71] It becomes necessary, therefore, for God to *initiate* (or "dilate") the kind of love to which Christians are called to participate in.

In Chrétien's reading of Gregory, he clarifies that *waiting* for God's initiative does not imply that a person does nothing. There are practices (or activities) in which one might still cultivate openness to transformation in the life of God. For instance, Gregory connects interior transformation with the *activity* of caring for one's neighbor: "active life and care of one's neighbour are required as a preliminary expansion. . . . It is only by expanding through loving care of one's neighbour, with all that this implies of patience and focus, that one becomes strong enough to attempt to rise up toward God Himself."[72] The emphasis on "activity" here does not undermine the priority of God's initiative in transformation. Chrétien immediately adds that the Christian understanding of "rising" up to God should not be confused with a Neoplatonic *ascension*, since "the event of the Incarnation has transformed inner space and its dimensions."[73] Awaiting transformation can (and should) include activities that might help one prepare for "transformation from the one who 'is' *transformation itself*."[74] The effort to care for one's neighbor, according to Chrétien's reading of Gregory, is just one example of how individual effort works in concert (or co-operates) with what God has already done in the event of the incarnation.[75]

At the same time, it is helpful to note that both Falque and Chrétien propose that the experiential dynamics of transformation present challenges to the life of a believer by associating it with a phenomenology of the *event* (see Romano's evential hermeneutics, discussed earlier). For instance, Falque emphasizes that the process of transformation is not always self-evident to the one who goes through it (we are not the contemporaries of its actualization).[76] Like the event of birth, a spiritual rebirth may reconfigure (or transform) all my possibilities in the world, but it is not always clear to me while it is happening.[77] It is difficult to discern precisely what God has "initiated" and whether or not one is properly "co-operating" in the moment that it "happens." Similarly, Chrétien identifies overlap between Christian concepts of transformation and "contemporary phenomenologies 'of the event'" by noticing how it seems to "happen" in a way that remains beyond my control to produce.[78] He writes, "It is possible for God to come only when He actually comes, which is why there is no point in fretting about our wretchedly cramped selves. What we must prepare ourselves for is what is un-prepared."[79] Both from the standpoint of what *has happened* and what *will happen* it is not often easy to discern what kind of "initiative" God may be taking in one's life.

The idea that it is hard to determine what constitutes God's initiative introduces an essential *experiential ambiguity* within the context of transformation. Unlike the concept of a punctiliar conversion, in which everything changes in a moment (popularized in certain Protestant revivalist traditions), the effects of transformation are often unclear, ongoing, and unpredictable. As Karl Rahner writes, "The possibility of experiencing grace and the possibility of experiencing grace as grace are not the same thing."[80] Likewise, the experiential contours of transformation are more complex than simply choosing to co-operate with God's initiative. The process of transformation introduces one to ongoing theological tensions such as nature and grace and activity and passivity—but it does not resolve those tensions, and this subsequently results in a substantial degree of ambiguity. But a person who confesses a Christian faith is not left simply with unexplained ambiguity; instead, as I will explain, one might note how theological knowledge provides good reasons as to why these tensions lead to ambiguities in experience in the first place (which in turn will help explain what it means to adopt a topology of creation).

Theological Tension and Experiential Ambiguity

I propose several ways in which theological knowledge can help one understand the ambiguities in experience implicit to the process of transformation. There is substantial coherence between irresolvable theological tensions (like nature and grace) and the difficulty that follows from determining what might constitute God's initiative in my life (and more broadly God's initiative in creation). By using the language of "theological knowledge," I am again borrowing from the position outlined by Lacoste in his final essay in *The Appearing of God*. As I explain in Chapter 1, Lacoste describes two different kinds of theological knowledge: *propositional theological knowledge*, which is a conceptual discourse that stems from an engagement with Scripture, tradition, and history; and *intuitive theological knowledge*, which is attained through "affection, familiarity, and 'knowledge by acquaintance.'"[81] Both forms of knowledge "are two non-negotiable points of reference" that are not fully separable, since "there is a rhythm in the life of the self that links the two kinds without creating an opposition between them."[82] Now, by suggesting that a degree of "theological knowledge" can help make sense of the experiential ambiguities in the process of transformation, I am pointing toward an instance in which these "two non-negotiable points of reference" might come together. At the risk of oversimplifying my point, I will offer three examples of how theological knowledge works in concert with the experiential ambiguities intrinsic to the process of transformation.

First, experiential ambiguity follows from affirming God's initiative in transformation because of the association between *God* and *love* in the Christian tradition. Throughout *The Appearing of God* Lacoste argues that it is necessary for God to withhold presence at least in part because "God appears in presenting himself to be loved."[83] He acknowledges that a reference to "love" opens up the "major phenomenological problem of 'the loveable,'" but his central point is that certain phenomena need to be loved in order to be seen.[84] He proposes that a Bach prelude is a good analogue because its "value" can only "be seen" if it is loved. While not everyone will love a Bach prelude and therefore appreciate its value, this is to be expected with regards to phenomena disclosed through love, since they are "*proposed*, and not *imposed*" onto perception.[85] Pushing the point even further, Lacoste argues that it would go against the very "essence or intention" of love if it was forced onto a person.[86] This lack of imposition with respect to love is why "God does not appear like the Alps, huge and undeniable," but instead "appears in such a way that we can make up our mind about him, for or against."[87] God's noncoercive mode of appearing, therefore, necessarily implies some experiential ambiguity in order to be consistent with phenomena that appear when they are loved.

Second, it is helpful to note that a substantial amount of the experiential "ambiguity" I am referring to here is associated with how one *feels* about God.[88] While there may be "a long list of possible experiences that seem to meet the desire for first-hand-knowledge of God," Lacoste submits that these experiences often "create more ambiguity than they resolve."[89] The reason for this is that it is almost impossible to determine what "initiates" a particular feeling—it "may be no more than myself, my existence as being-in-the-world . . . affective tonalities that show me only how I am."[90] However, what is interesting about this ambiguity, I propose, is that it corresponds with the kind of propositional theological knowledge that affirms *God is known as unknown*. Lacoste writes:

> The tradition that has used the words "God known as unknown" acknowledges, before all else, God's unknowability. He is more than could lie within the compass of our feeling. But that leads on to speaking of his knowability, too. To say "unknowing exceeds knowledge" paradoxically focuses on the knowledge of God. In this context "I feel an absence of feeling" says something quite precise: the *unknown* cannot pass *unnoticed*. I know what it is I do not feel, though I would like to.[91]

Feelings may not be a reliable guide for understanding the precise dynamics of God's initiative (at least not on their own), since it is hard to distinguish what exactly gives rise to one's feelings. But the difficulties that follow from trying to discern whether or not the presence of God gives rise to a particular feeling corresponds to the idea that God is "more than could lie within the compass of our feeling." A person's feelings are not underappreciated here; however, understanding them in reference to God's presence requires a more complex theory of the interaction between intuitive and propositional knowledge.[92]

Third, it is important to note that theological knowledge does not just offer reasons for the ambiguity that follows from affirming God's initiative, but it also has the potential to provide guidance or direction related to this ambiguity (without overcoming it).[93] Chrétien's reflections on Gregory the Great are a good example in this respect, since Gregory is not waiting for transformation in a vacuum. Gregory waits for the kind of transformation that would be associated with loving one's enemies in the larger context of Christian charity. But even in this instance, theological knowledge does not eliminate the experiential ambiguities constitutive of transformation. To the extent that love is associated with feelings, one would still be left discerning whether my various interior dispositions are initiated by God or are another affective tonality that shows me "only how I am."[94] Moreover, it also would be difficult to distinguish *when* this "love" was actually initiated, since its beginning (like the beginning of any love) is "always already 'lost'" once it has occurred.[95] While there is clearly a long tradition in which theological knowledge informs spiritual experience, the ambiguities of experience that are integral to transformation continually invite (in a noncoercive way) one into an ongoing process of discernment.

I have outlined these different ways in which theological knowledge interacts with the experiential ambiguities that follow from affirming God's initiative because they help inform what it means to adopt a broader topology of creation. Following the experiential contours of transformation, it is possible to hold that God remains in consistent relationship to creation while also cautioning against a strong affirmation of one's capacity to trace the *precise* contours of that relationship. From this point of view, it is helpful to return to what I referred to in the Introduction to this book as a "world behind the scenes" in which God "remains hidden in the midst of self-revelation."[96] Understanding the relationship between God and creation here implies less a "specialist division of our professional philosophical language" than what Williams describes as "a *mode of conducting ourselves* in respect of finite reality."[97] In other words, it is a relationality that takes seriously a "swaying" back and forth between the inextricable limits and ambiguities of experience while remaining open to God's initiative and ongoing presence.[98] This is a relationality that affirms God's presence even if this presence does not appear "huge and undeniable," in part because that is the kind of presence that a nuanced theology would anticipate.

If adopting a topology of creation corresponds with the experiential contours of transformation (as I am suggesting), it also necessarily maintains theological tensions that require ongoing reflection in the life of a believer. As Williams submits, "Theological activity cannot escape tension and alternation between the poles of its reference, except at the price of subsuming God and creature under one heading, which would be the ultimate absurdity in thinking about God and about creatures, destroying the integrity and intelligibility of both terms."[99] Any unequivocal correspondence between creation and God is guarded against by unresolvable tensions that remain (at least to a certain extent) ambiguous in experience. In this regard, a phenomenological description of transformation and theological knowledge complement one another and even *cohere*. This coherence does not prove a Christian topology but offers some depth and credibility to what it means to inhabit one's place as a creation that remains in relation to God.[100] In other words, exploring theological reasons for why God does not appear "huge and undeniable" alongside the experiential ambiguities that are constitutive of transformation introduces the complexity that follows from adopting a topology of creation—rather than simply asserting God's presence in order to reestablish the battle lines between those who confess a Christian faith and those who do not.

In summary, the theological tensions that follow from affirming God's initiative have important consequences for a topology of creation. The one who undergoes transformation does not suddenly notice God everywhere in the world but instead is introduced to a more involved relationship between God and creation, since "those who find themselves attuned to God and understanding the world according to a relation with God must contend with an attunement and an understanding that are otherwise defined."[101] A topology of creation neither forecloses God's presence nor identifies it with anything that would betray God's noncoercive appearing and the freedom of a person to "co-operate." This introduces the mysteries of nature and grace, activity and passivity, God's appearing and hiddenness, knowing and unknowing. And it suggests that those who confess a Christian faith enter into a process of ongoing theological reflection that never resolves these tensions.

Conclusion: Transfigured Goodness

In conclusion, it is important to return to the central theme in this study—the phenomenology of creation's goodness. I submit that the experiential contours outlined in this chapter can clarify what it means to integrate and even *transfigure* a prelinguistic goodness within a topology of creation. At various times in the previous chapters I argued that a prelinguistic goodness is essential for understanding the Genesis affirmation of creation. I explained that one does not need to confess a Christian faith in order to recognize this goodness (particularly in moments of joy and enjoyment); however, it plays an important role in the appearance of phenomena that might be associated with the Genesis affirmation. While this use of the term "goodness" produces a general category, it has the benefit of being accessible to people who use diverse frameworks (or topologies) in order to understand their surroundings. What I have outlined in the latter half of this chapter, however, is a more specifically Christian horizon of place that mediates one's encounter with this goodness. And critically, within this "horizon" (or topology), creation's goodness becomes a more expansive category than it would be if it was limited to an association with a prelinguistic goodness.

The central reason the concept of "goodness" is transfigured within a topology of creation is that "goodness" is no longer reducible to what is initial to experience but instead finds its first meaning in relation to the One who "is before all things" and in whom "all things hold together" (Col 1:17). While I remain grounded by all the limits and ambiguities of experience noted previously, the place in which I find myself might still be defined by a relationality that has the potential to "enlarge and transfigure the created order without destroying it."[102] The *kind* of relationship that is implied here is crucial, since God and creation "are not two items that could conceivably be partnered in any list, added to each other, but a relational complex in which one cannot be spoken of without the other."[103] In other words, the relationship between God and creation's goodness is not "something that tears apart but stably anchors a rhythm like that of breathing or heartbeat. It is a contradiction only if we seek to arrest the rhythm, and 'freeze' one moment of it."[104] While the dynamics of this relationality require ongoing reflection (like the dynamics of transformation), it also has the potential to sustain the status of creation's goodness beyond my own precarious perception. Or, more specifically, it suggests the possibility that God "anchors" the worth of creation (its goodness) even when it no longer appears as such within the contours of my own experience.

It is important to keep in mind that although a reference to anchoring or stabilizing here stems from God's relation to creation, it does not undermine or contradict the importance of a prelinguistic goodness. The language of transfiguring is appropriate because it connotes an expansion or elevation of the importance of goodness rather than opposing its prelinguistic appearance. I will expand on the implications of this transfigured goodness in the following chapter, but for now it may be helpful to note that a good example of it is presented in *Laudato si'* when Francis proposes that Christians "are called to recognize that other living beings have a value of their own in God's eyes: 'by their mere existence they bless him and give him glory,' and indeed, 'the Lord rejoices in all his works' (Ps 104:31)."[105] Elizabeth Johnson provides another constructive example in *Ask the Beasts* when she argues that "the intrinsically worthy quality of what has been created" is a "key corollary" to the doctrine of creation.[106] Both Francis and Johnson emphasize how the intrinsic value of creation challenges tendencies toward anthropocentricism and the idea that the "natural world was simply there as something God created for human use."[107] The kind of experiences that introduce a prelinguistic play of "goodness" remain integral to affirming what is good about creation because they disclose a kind of initial encounter with the meaning of "goodness." It would be hard to imagine anything like an intrinsic value that "the Lord rejoices in" without something like a prelinguistic experience of goodness. At the same time, within a Christian topology of creation this goodness is enlarged with reference to God in a way that goes beyond the particularity of these experiences.

The reason this transfigured understanding of goodness is so important becomes evident in the following chapter, wherein I examine more closely how much of life seems to challenge the status of a good creation. I will argue that a transfigured goodness is essential for a topology of creation's credibility, since it does not overlook or diminish the often-tragic circumstances of life but rather underscores the necessity of compassion and care for all suffering life.

4

Obscured Goodness

If a prelinguistic experience of goodness has the potential to be transfigured in relation to God, this raises questions regarding how such a goodness might appear (or disappear) given the immense amount of pain and suffering in the world. There is an abundance of reasons to question a straightforward affirmation of a good creation. As Brian Treanor submits, all the "traditional reasons for despair" remain today: "loneliness, fallibility, impotence, loss, tragedy, senselessness, death, and the like," not to mention "the heart-wrenching plight of refugees, and the callous indifference of many governments and people to their plight; diseases both novel and resurgent . . . xenophobia, misogyny, racism, anti-Semitism, homophobia . . . increasing anthropogenic climate chaos; and more."[1] If creation's goodness is to remain credible, then it cannot depend on an argument that the balance of self-evidently "good" phenomena outweighs the "bad," nor can it diminish the significance of negative phenomena. The concept of creation's goodness would need to *legitimize* rather than contradict the reasons for despair. And so, in what follows I explain that this is often the consequence of a transfigured goodness that affirms the intrinsic value of all creation.

Given the wide range of tragedies and injustices one might consider, there is no way to address adequately all the philosophical and theological questions they will engender. This chapter necessarily takes a limited approach by focusing on issues that arise from the *materiality* of creation. In particular, I examine the biological limits of the body (death) and physical suffering (particularly associated with chronic and terminal illness). As I explained in the Introduction, one of the distinctive features of the Genesis text is that the material or physical world is integral to the affirmation of creation's goodness. This feature of creation's goodness has been an important resource for theologies that resist various forms of Gnosticism (for example, Irenaeus responding to Valentinus and Marcion). At the same time, however, affirming the materiality of creation raises questions about the extensive suffering and death that seems to be intrinsic to it.[2] Christians have used a variety of strategies to address the existence of evil and suffering, but there are hardly straightforward answers as to why an "omniscient, omnipotent, perfectly good God" would create a world full of suffering.[3] In what follows, then, I do not attempt to justify people's often tragic circumstances or investigate the problem of evil as it is classically formulated. While this may be disappointing given the legitimacy and urgency of questions related to why there is so much suffering, following the basic principles of phenomenology I continue to examine *how* things appear more so than *why* they appear. This approach resists saying too much about the meaning of suffering and may even accentuate the urgency of the problem.

In the first part of this chapter I outline various ways in which the phenomenology of creation's goodness might be rendered inaccessible or obfuscated in experience. I consider Emmanuel Falque's account of the body's ongoing biological "struggle for life," particularly because it raises issues related to the phenomenology of creation's goodness—as well as controversial theological issues such as the relative value of chaos to order, *creatio ex nihilo*, and the doctrine of original sin. While I do not provide a comprehensive analysis of the debates surrounding these issues, I argue that theological disagreements demonstrate how an ongoing bodily struggle for life (ending in death) can obscure and restrict the appearing of creation's goodness. I then consider an important corollary to the struggle for life— namely, the physical pain and suffering that is often intrinsic to being a body. Using the work of Claude Romano, I expand on the way instances of chronic pain or terminal illness are capable of reconfiguring a person's entire world and their place within it. The purpose behind reflecting on suffering and death is to show that affirming creation's goodness requires a complexity that goes beyond how a person might feel in a particular moment, if it is to remain a credible topological category.

The latter half of the chapter describes why one might credibly affirm the intrinsic value of creation with a particular Christological reading. Specifically, I examine a connection between the bodily suffering of Jesus and creation's groaning (Romans 8). If the Word has an indissoluble link with creation from "the beginning" (John 1) that is embodied in the life and suffering of Jesus, then this Word underscores the idea that *all* of suffering life is worthy of compassion—rendering the questions raised by pain and suffering in a less anthropocentric light. I then conclude by proposing that affirming creation's goodness does not require one to overlook or diminish the burden of suffering and death but only underscores its significance. The intrinsic value of all creation (a transfigured goodness) legitimizes a range of affectivity (joy and sorrow, thanksgiving and lament) and provides a helpful topological signpost.

The Struggle for Life

Falque's account of a bodily struggle for life provides a constructive context in which to consider how creation's goodness often seems unclear or obfuscated in experience. His understanding of "struggle" does not imply a dialogue between evolutionary biology and theology; instead, the concept stems from being a body that is at once full of life, as well as decaying and on its way to death. Falque proposes that this bodily struggle is a microcosm of a broader presence of chaos in the created order that is depicted in the first chapter of Genesis. His analysis leads to important questions related to the place of biological death in a good creation—which, as I will explain—helps clarify how the appearance of creation's goodness is complicated by an ongoing bodily struggle that inevitably ends in death.

It is important to distinguish Falque's account of the "struggle for life" from the language of "struggle" I outlined in the previous chapter with respect to Falque's *Le combat amoureux* (*The Loving Struggle*). Therein, I explained that he articulates an account of struggle related to the development of philosophical concepts—connoting something like a wrestling or fencing match that does not involve vanquishing one's enemies.[4] However, in the present context, the *bodily* struggle for life is derived from the materiality of the body. Falque contends that the "biological" or "organic" body is underexamined in the history of phenomenology because of a tendency to focus on the flesh (*Leib*) or the auto-affective dimensions of being a body.[5] Most phenomenologists, according to Falque, see the material body "as an obstacle to the body's subjectivity" or the "ideal of lived experience."[6] However, the so-called *struggle for life* (*combat pour la vie*) avoids this tendency, since it is "an internal struggle with our own corporality (viruses, microbes, infections, secretions, digestion, and so on)."[7] And because Falque suggests that this bodily struggle is neither straightforwardly positive nor negative, it forms a helpful context in which to examine how the appearing of creation's goodness can be obscured.

Two opposing examples within Falque's reflections on the body clarify the struggle for life. On the one hand, he proposes that being a body involves "a surge or impetus, something both alive and vast: intoxication (or rapture) as 'the feeling of plenitude and increased energy,' a dionysiac dimension of the Life."[8] Falque associates this feeling with an "innate" drive or "inclination to continue to exist (*conatus*)."[9] While some may call into question aspects of this "surge or impetus" (for instance, its association with intoxication), the important point here is that it is a "physiological condition" that lends itself toward the affirmation of life (it is *vast* and *alive*).[10] On the other hand, Falque also offers extensive reflection on how the body bends in the opposite direction. He spends considerable time describing how the body appears as a kind of *meat* on its way to being a cadaver. Borrowing from Gilles Deleuze's interpretation of Francis Bacon's paintings of butchers' shops, Falque argues that the images present a "unity" between people and animals through the category of meat.[11] In Bacon's *Painting*, in particular, Falque proposes that "the carcass of an animal" offers the image of a "limit-zone" intrinsic to being a body.[12] This account of biological decay is substantially different from Heidegger's existential interest in death, since Falque is primarily interested in the body's material struggle, which in fact, he argues, is the root of the existential concern.[13]

As Falque points out, this biological struggle raises issues related to creation theology. He suggests our corporeal struggle is explicitly related to the biblical theme of *chaos*, what he describes as the "Tohu-Bohu."[14] The Tohu-Bohu is a concept Falque develops based on a reading of the Hebrew terminology in the opening verses of Genesis 1: "In the beginning when God created the heavens and the earth, the earth was a formless void [*tohu wabohu*] and darkness covered the face of the deep (Gen. 1:1–2)."[15] Falque describes this "formless void" in relation to a variety of other ancient myths, which he proposes also indicate the presence of a "formless void." For instance, he relates the Tohu-Bohu to the ancient Greek concept of "Chaos," which implies a "fissure, or gap, in the abyss of all existence," as well as other myths that explore themes he describes as a "'jumble,' 'confusion,' 'disorder' . . . the 'wide open,' the 'yawning gap.'"[16] One might also note that the concept is related to the influential Babylonian-Assyrian myth of *Enuma Elish*, which portrays a cosmic battle against *chaos* that scholars argue influences the Old Testament texts in a variety of ways.[17] Falque identifies the Tohu-Bohu with a wide range of references because he does not want to "assimilate" a meaning preemptively at the expense of "negating it."[18] But what is particularly important in this context is that he asserts this "chaos" remains intrinsic to bodily life today as part of an innate biological struggle for life.

The connection between a primordial chaos and the body can be extended even further by looking at additional biblical passages that directly illustrate how chaos (and by extension our bodily struggle for life) complicates the Genesis affirmation of creation's goodness. Specifically, there is a relationship between *chaos* and the *vulnerability* of creation represented in Psalms 74 and 89. In both psalms, chaos is a threat to the cosmos, and it is unclear why YHWH would allow this, given the defeat of a primeval chaos in the first creation narrative.[19] In the book of Job, God points toward the Leviathan's "fearsome teeth," whose "snorting throws out flashes of light; its eyes are like the rays of dawn" (Job 41:18).[20] While this image of a fierce and untamed beast may suggest a feeling of "plenitude and increased energy" in life, it also alludes to the danger that follows from this "energy." And finally, the flood narrative depicts "profound anxiety" about the ongoing threat of chaos in creation. YHWH promises to sustain the created order, but this promise follows his expression of regret for creation and the destructive chaos of the flood.[21] In each case, chaos *threatens* those who are vulnerable to death and decay, which in turn raises questions about why chaos seems intrinsic to a creation that has been called "good" in Genesis 1.

Two important related theological issues illuminate why the threat of chaos makes it difficult to affirm creation's goodness. First, as I noted in the Introduction, some scholars associate the goodness of creation with an image of God "as a craftsman fashioning initially shapeless material into something pleasing that evokes his delight in his handiwork—hence the repeated pronouncement that what has been made is 'good,' and indeed, when taken as a whole, 'very good' (Gen 1:31)."[22] This interpretation suggests that creation's goodness is associated with *order* far more than chaos and relies on the idea that YHWH only declares creation to be "good" after organizing it and working with it.[23] It is an interpretation that has been reinforced, historically, by the doctrine of *creatio ex nihilo*, which tends to emphasize God's "sovereignty" and "divine transcendence" over creation.[24] In contrast to this position, some scholars question the extent to which creation's goodness is defined by "order" in opposition to chaos. Jon Levenson points out that the biblical text never claims that the forces of chaos are fully extinguished, even following the affirmation of its goodness.[25] Catherine Keller goes so far as to argue that an emphasis on *creatio ex nihilo* and the ordering process leads to a denigration of creation's materiality (despite the best intentions of those subscribing to the doctrine).[26] And while Falque does not go as far as Keller with respect to the doctrine of *creatio ex nihilo*, he does submit that interpreters of Genesis too often overlook the importance of chaos in the text for its opposite features such as "the world, order, beauty."[27] These differing evaluations of order and chaos demonstrate the difficulty of assessing the relative value of chaos in relation to creation's goodness. Chaos seems to be an intrinsic and even powerful part of creation, but it also threatens those who are vulnerable to decaying and death amid an ongoing biological struggle for life.

The danger of chaos, therefore, raises another contentious issue related to the status of creation's goodness—namely, whether the doctrine of original sin is a plausible explanation for biological vulnerability and death. Already in early Christianity people sought to draw a link between sin and biological death, engendered from concerns over theodicy.[28] If God is fully the source of a good creation, then Christians are left to account for evil, suffering, and death in a way "that doesn't jeopardize the goodness of God or human responsibility," and the doctrine of original sin has been used to rationalize how this is possible.[29] And yet, the doctrine's reception in the history of Christianity is mixed. Aquinas proposed that death is a natural part of our (good) bodily condition—although there is some disagreement among scholars regarding whether or not he maintained that God originally created people with an additional gift of immortality that was lost because of sin.[30] In contemporary theology, original sin is commonly contested in part because of questions related to how an "original sin" or the "Fall" interacts with evolutionary biology.[31] It is unclear how a supposedly historical "punctiliar event" involving an "original couple" interacts with current theories "for the evolution of anatomically modern *Homo sapiens*," which locate their origin two million years ago with a population of at least two to ten thousand.[32] Moreover, the traditional Augustinian teaching that Adam's guilt is transmitted through the male seed seems highly unlikely today. And there are questions that follow from whether it is justified to believe that all people are condemned to carry the burden of suffering and death because of a supposed original transgression.[33]

Further complicating debates related to original sin are varying interpretations of the meaning of Genesis 2:17: "but you must not eat from the tree of the knowledge of good and evil, for when you eat from it you will certainly die." For theologians skeptical of traditional readings of original sin, the reference to *death* in the passage does not imply that mortality was suddenly introduced to human beings after Adam and Eve ate from the tree. Falque, for instance, argues for a more "literal" translation of the passage: "On the day you eat from it [the tree of the knowledge of good and evil], suffer to die of death" (*Du jour où tu en mangeras [de l'arbre de la connaissance du bien et du mal], souffre de mourir dans ta mort*).[34] Rather than implying biological death, Falque submits that the text implies "suffering death (spiritual death)," which "refers above all to a 'mode of being of life' rather than just 'being-at-the-end-of life.'"[35] And J. Richard Middleton provides a comparable interpretation when he argues that the Genesis reference to "death" should be understood in relation to its counterpoint in the story—the tree of *life*—a symbol of *flourishing* (one of the primary definitions of creation's goodness I noted in the Introduction).[36] Middleton's interpretation suggests a contrast between "a life that conforms to wisdom, rooted in reverence for God, which results in blessing and shalom, and a life of folly, characterized by rejecting God's ways, which is thereby deformed and plagued by corruption and calamity."[37] What is important in both examples is that Genesis 2:17 does not imply that Adam and Eve fell from an original state of immortality (or "perfection," for that matter).[38]

Now, without oversimplifying these theological debates, I propose that they illustrate (if nothing else) the ongoing difficulty Christians have with how the reality of death (or the biological struggle for life) interacts with the affirmation of creation's goodness in Genesis 1. And this is important for a phenomenology of creation's goodness, since it would need to account for the ways that material bodies subject to decay and death do not always appear straightforwardly good. The lack of clarity regarding what is "good" about the material body does not *necessarily* denigrate materiality or lead to Gnosticism, but at the very least, the struggle for life is capable of obfuscating that which is "good" about creation—which is why it is not surprising Christians have sought to exclude biological death from what was initially declared "good" in the first chapter of Genesis.[39]

At the same time, if one is willing to admit that creation's goodness is not entirely "limited to some past golden age in Eden," then the pressing question for this study is not whether original sin is the cause of biological death or whether *creatio ex nihilo* historically produced matter-nihilating theologies; instead, the primary question is how our ongoing bodily struggle for life challenges what it means for creation's goodness to appear within the contours of experience.[40] Of course, this is a possibility I have argued for in the previous chapters by outlining the appearance of a prelinguistic goodness in various ways. But it is also worth noting that Falque intimates a way forward specifically within the context of the body's struggle—submitting that it can be understood as both "good" and "beautiful."[41] He references Paul's struggle in the letter to Timothy: "I have fought the good fight, I have finished the race, I have kept the faith" (2 Tim 4:7).[42] From this point of view, the concept of struggle forms a condition upon which one comes to value something more broadly—like working through a difficult project or becoming wiser after dealing with past emotional wounds. One might even identify this positive evaluation of struggle already following the "tumultuous, dramatic, and difficult" passage from womb to world, when a newborn finally lets out a vast and alive cry for the first time.⁴³ As such, the struggle for life would be both capable of obfuscating the appearing of creation's goodness and being a condition on which the affirmation of creation's goodness might take place.

In any case, however, theological debates related to order and chaos, *creatio ex nihilo*, and original sin indicate how the struggle for life obscures the appearing of creation's goodness and presents legitimate reasons to question its topological significance today. While one might still find ways to affirm the goodness of creation, this may not be a source of comfort for those who are immediately facing their own biological limits: "One considers the meaning of suffering only when one is not actually suffering."⁴⁴ As I indicated earlier in this chapter, then, the credibility of creation's goodness cannot depend on overlooking or diminishing the reality of suffering and death but instead needs to integrate and even legitimize the significance of the problem—an issue I further address in the latter half of this chapter.

The Suffering Body

If a bodily struggle that ends in death renders the appearing of creation's goodness unclear, then this is only deepened if one considers the extensive pain and suffering that is a corollary of the struggle. Physical pain challenges the phenomenology of creation's goodness through sharply contrasting phenomena that demand one's attention to the point where a more diverse horizon of place seems inaccessible. In instances of terminal illness, in particular, suffering upends one's entire world and often removes ordinary ways in which one might encounter creation's goodness. Yet, as I will explain, the phenomenology of creation's goodness is not reducible to bodily well-being or the relative privilege of a person's circumstances. The appearing of creation's goodness in the midst of pain and suffering indicates the need for a complex accounting of its persistence within a broader horizon of place.

First, to explain how suffering deepens the obfuscation of creation's goodness engendered by the struggle for life, it is helpful to consider Falque's account of the *nonverbal* significance of bodily suffering. His interest in the nonverbal aspects of the body can be identified across a range of texts, but in "Towards an Ethics of the Spread Body" he specifically relates this theme to physical suffering. The essay engages with images of a body "splayed" or "spread" out on a hospital operating table following Falque's time spent volunteering at the Palliative Care Unit of Luynes-CHU in Tours.⁴⁵ One of the principal positions in the essay is that a certain amount of silence is called for during surgical procedures. Falque writes, "By talking too much or too technically one runs the risk of smothering the pain that nevertheless tries to make itself heard."[46] The importance of silence does not imply that Falque gives up on the search for signification with respect to suffering. He proposes, "Certainly, we must both 'tend' and 'think' and have 'words' of speech in order to describe the 'woes' of the body."[47] But his starting point is that verbalization itself has the potential to obscure the *nonsensical* reality of suffering. Similar to his reflections on chaos and the "Tohu-Bohu," Falque seeks to allow the fullness of nonsensical, nonverbal, phenomena to show themselves—at least to the extent that it is possible.

Within the history of phenomenology Falque identifies a precursor (and inspiration) for his emphasis on the nonverbal significance of suffering in Maurice Merleau-Ponty's later work on "brute or wild being."[48] He argues that Merleau-Ponty probes the "pre-reflexive" and "ante-predicative" aspects of bodily life that often function in the obscurity of "silent experience."[49] Falque submits that his account of the body is similar because it seeks to gather "silent experience" and search "underneath *logos* and reason, or even narrative as well, for the action of 'binding sheaves' or 'gathering together' (*legein*) this 'scattered body' having such a hard time existing."[50] Physical suffering, according to Falque, is an exemplary instance in which we become aware of this silent (or nonverbal) experience of the body. In fact, the nonverbal dimensions of suffering are capable of demanding attention to the point where one's entire horizon of place finds its point of reference in the body's pain.

This narrowing horizon is represented most effectively in Falque's account of the *invasive* characteristics of suffering from illness. Describing the experience of a cancer patient, Falque proposes that a tumor is not something that simply grows; "it also begins to 'invade,' 'dissect,' 'putrefy,' or 'decompose,' in such a way that the person him-or-herself becomes 'disfigured' by it."[51] On the one hand, these tumors "are not me," but on the other, they "progressively invade me; they flood me in invasive fashion and soon become me *entirely*."[52] Falque relates the invasive characteristics of physical suffering to Levinas's reflections on "hyper-materiality" and the "horror of Being" following World War II.[53] Falque submits, "The camps and the anguish over surviving when the majority of his family had been exterminated at Auschwitz *eats into* Levinas with the pain of suffering that he can still continue 'to exist' yet 'without existing.'"[54] According to Falque, a body that undergoes invasive physical suffering similarly exists without existing—an interpretation confirmed by Christian Wiman's first-person description of undergoing cancer: "It's hard to describe extreme pain, and the pain of cancer has an otherworldly intimacy that makes it almost impervious to words. It feels like existence itself is eating you."[55] While it is ordinarily possible to ignore the "silent experience" of the body, the kind of invasive physical suffering Falque describes overtakes conscious thought and is capable of cutting off access to a more diverse range of phenomena.

One way to clarify this constricting horizon is by reflecting on the idea that we rarely pay attention to our bodies when things are going well.[56] So, for instance (borrowing from Heidegger's well-known analysis of tools in *Being and Time*), if a carpenter is framing a wall and uses a hammer (or more likely today, a nail gun), then she is not focusing on the tool but is instead engaged in a larger project: She uses the tool to frame a wall for a room, in a house, that may be for herself or others within personal, economic, and time constraints. But if the nail gun breaks or goes missing, then suddenly the tool becomes "present-to-hand," which is to say, it appears to be "standing in the way," and she needs to "take explicit account of it."[57] Drawing on his experience as a physician, Drew Leder proposes that the suffering body is similar when a normally "unproblematic unity with the self" is interrupted by the "alien presence" of pain.[58] This interruptive (or invasive) characteristic helps explain why medical patients often refer to their pain as an "it" that is separate from the "I."[59] Describing a man suffering from acute heart disease, Leder writes: "'It' is what stops him from going to the kitchen. 'It' stands between him and all aspects of a normal life."[60] The pain discloses what is "normally" hidden in the recesses of bodily life and forces one to account for the physical body as its pain becomes almost omnipresent.

It is important to note that I spent considerably less time examining the body in chapters focused on a prelinguistic goodness at play in experience. This lack of attention to corporeality is not because the body is uninvolved or insignificant with respect to the kind of understanding one might draw from a prelinguistic goodness. Instead, the moments in which one encounters this goodness are often defined by what Leder describes as the "unproblematic unity" of the body. So, for instance, I argued that enjoyment (joy *of* a particular thing) discloses a prelinguistic goodness that Christians might relate to the Genesis affirmation of creation (enjoyment here was distinguished from *existential joy*, which is related to Heidegger's account of *Befindlichkeit*).[61] I proposed that even something as banal as a pleasant smell or cup of coffee can be a significant source for understanding a "meaningful order" of prelinguistic experience that includes a general quality of goodness.[62] Given the analysis of suffering, however, it is instructive to note how the body becomes fully immersed with a particular phenomenon in moments of enjoyment. When I enjoy a cup of coffee in a favorite café, the tasting notes and smell of a single-origin roast temporally become the focal point of perception. As my attention is drawn to the pleasant aroma and taste, my body recedes to the background of my perception even though it is essential to experience. Rather than undermine the body's importance, its withdrawal from my perceptual field underscores its absorption in the place in which I find myself and its importance in the disclosure of a meaningful order of prelinguistic experience.

Critically, however, the obfuscation of various qualities of goodness in moments of suffering goes beyond the invasive experience of pain and the narrowing of one's perceptual field. There also are larger topological consequences that often follow from a suffering body that further obscure the appearance of creation's goodness. These topological consequences are identified and developed in detail in Romano's account of the *event of suffering*. In the previous chapter, I noted that Romano's approach to the "event" implies impersonal, large-scale "happenings" that do not have a singular cause or origin.[63] This last feature (no singular cause) is particularly significant with respect to understanding the topological implications of suffering from a terminal illness. While one might say that the "event" of undergoing cancer is caused by the fact that cancer is growing in new areas of the body, within the broader phenomenology of an event, this fact isolates one physiological cause from the context that defines the *event* itself.[64] The suffering that follows from cancer takes place in a wider network of significations that have an endless variety of causes and factors (or "inner-worldly" facts, to use Romano's terminology).[65] For instance, there is the patient's relationship with the physician, the patient's age, social context, economic status, support system—all these factors and more contribute to the meaning of the event. Romano explains: "An encounter does not have its character as *event* conferred on it simply by happening as a fact: it becomes an event by radically transcending its own actualization, reconfiguring my possibilities articulated in the world, and introducing into my adventure a radically new meaning that shakes it, upends it from top to bottom, and thus modifies all my previous projections."[66] The event of suffering from a terminal illness is not just a physical change in one's body—it transforms one's entire world.

Romano uses Leo Tolstoy's story of *The Death of Ivan Ilyich* to illustrate how the event of suffering can transform a person's world. He writes:

> Thus, in Tolstoy's novel, the brilliant official Ivan Ilyich, struck by the event of an incurable illness and increasing suffering, progressively becomes a nobody, unrecognizable, not only externally, for others, due to bodily changes following his illness, but also for himself. . . . With suffering's intrusion into an existence that is entirely motivated

by ambition, Tolstoy describes an emptiness and chill that are always greater, which invade not only the character but also his world, all that surrounds him, and even the dazzling sun, which lacerates him, scrapes him to the bone, and pierces his flesh by gathering all the joys that have not been accomplished and all the promises that have not been fulfilled by his life itself.[67]

Everything flattens in the midst of Ilyich's suffering—his career success, the perceptions of others, "even the dazzling sun." His world begins to shrink, and pain obscures not only the formerly experienced "joys" but also his self-conception and involvement in meaningful projects. The suffering body not only restricts one's horizon of place but also puts into question where *I* fit within the world. As Romano explains, suffering "renders me unable to recognize myself by equating me to all others, in their extreme banality, in *making* me *banal*: not only because of the truism that we are all equal before suffering, but more profoundly because intimately endured suffering ends up erasing everything that belongs to my social and public persona, everything that makes me externally recognizable and identifiable by others."[68] In other words, not only does extreme suffering make it impossible for me to perform ordinary tasks or enjoy various aspects of life, but it also renders my place within a broader community or "world" no longer relevant.

Of course, not everyone suffers from a terminal illness, but the "struggle for life" often ends with the invasive and transformative physical suffering described here. For many people, suffering unfolds relatively slowly at the end of life and is a less clearly distinguished event. In Iris Marion Young's reflections on her stepfather growing old in the years following her mother's death, she describes the slow, world-changing results of his aging body in a way that illustrates this progressive change. Her stepfather's shifting topology began when kidney failure "circumscribed" his life considerably at the age of seventy-three; however, Young recounts that his small, cluttered cottage helped him preserve his world despite the significant setbacks to his health. The cottage "contained the history of his life" and helped him recall the various projects and relationships he once actively participated in because it contained numerous paintings, letters, photographs, and records from his life.[69] A stroke at age eighty-six, however, rendered him unable to live on his own and forced him to move into an extended-care facility. Young describes how his entire world slowly receded without his small cottage. There was no room for him (or his roommates) to "arrange things around them in an individualized dwelling space that reflected their habit memories."[70] The world he knew and his place within it slowly became less accessible—including his accomplishments as a painter, meaningful relationships, and the significant stories of his past.[71]

Physical suffering, then, is capable of transforming one's world and introducing an entirely different meaning to life. A potentially open and diverse world can become inaccessible, and the various rhythms of life that have been cultivated in order to encounter phenomena broadly considered "good" become restricted. This may include intimacy with others, social status, involvement in a religious community, meaningful projects or work, access to beautiful spaces, music, or enjoyable food. Suffering not only demands one's attention and forms the focal point of perception but often changes "who I am" in the world and cuts off access to various avenues one might have used in order to encounter "good" phenomena.

However, much like the "struggle for life," it is critical to note that a phenomenology of suffering does not imply that the appearing of creation's goodness is exclusively associated with a healthy functioning body. People regularly recognize various manifestations of "goodness" in surprising circumstances. I alluded to this in the first chapter when I noted that a tired person with little money on a crowded subway may find herself in joy, while the wealthy first-class airline passenger may be continuously irritated and unable to find any sense of contentment. Joy, in this example, is the *existential joy* I have alluded to—implying "the condition of affective familiarity with a given context of meaning and its contents" that "is the primordial way that a world of meaning is opened up to us."[72] This kind of affectivity is noteworthy because it suggests that a prelinguistic goodness (disclosed in a moment of joy) is capable of appearing regardless of whether *enjoyable things* are accessible or not. This point, of course, becomes even more clear if one considers instances in which people find themselves experiencing joy despite prolonged suffering. As Jack Gilbert writes, "There is laughter / every day in the terrible streets of Calcutta, / and the women laugh in the cages of Bombay."[73] James Cone also explains how the tradition of Black spirituals embodies joy in the face of injustice and suffering: "The Spirit sometimes makes you run and clap your hands; at other times you just want to sit still and perhaps tap your feet, wave your hands, and hum the melody of a song."[74] Perhaps one is less likely to experience joy in the midst of immense suffering, but joy is not reducible to circumstances that are overtly positive—and by extension, neither is the manifestation of a prelinguistic goodness.

Because the appearing of a prelinguistic goodness is not exclusively reducible to one's bodily well-being or circumstances (despite the importance of these factors), any evaluation of the role this "goodness" plays within a broader horizon of place (like creation) requires a more complex explanation.

Accounting for the surprising manifestation of goodness despite the abundance of suffering in the world requires one to consider ways in which goodness does not contradict experiences like suffering and death but rather integrates and even legitimizes those experiences. Now, I hope to outline such an account in the following sections by returning to a specifically Christian understanding of creation's goodness. My intention is not to argue that Christians are the only ones who might provide a more complex accounting of the manifestation of goodness in relation to pain and suffering. But understanding how a prelinguistic goodness is *transfigured* in relation to God may help clarify the ongoing topological significance of goodness across a variety of experiences.

In the previous chapter, I submitted that a helpful example of this transfigured goodness can be found in *Laudato si'*, when Francis proposes that Christians "are called to recognize that other living beings have a value of their own in God's eyes: 'by their mere existence they bless him and give him glory,' and indeed, 'the Lord rejoices in all his works' (Ps 104:31)."[75] From this point of view, the value of creation (its goodness) is not located primarily in apprehending it within a meaningful prelinguistic order but within its *relation* to God. I also outlined significant caveats regarding the difficulty of determining the precise dynamics of God's "relation" to creation in the previous chapter. This included emphasizing the experiential ambiguities engendered from irresolvable theological tensions such as nature and grace, God's initiative and one's response, knowing and unknowing (among others)—tensions that define a topology of creation. Without fully reiterating these caveats, however, I intend to add significantly more detail regarding what I mean by God's *relationship* to creation. Specifically, I examine a Christological reading of creation that reinforces the idea that creation has intrinsic value (goodness), while also clarifying how such an idea integrates the realities of suffering and death. As I will explain, Christ's compassion for everything that suffers implies a transfigured goodness that does not diminish the pain and sorrow of suffering and death but instead confirms that it is worthy of care.

Christ's Compassion

In *The Guide to Gethsemane*, Falque's reflections on the tears of Jesus offer a helpful starting point for developing a Christological reading of creation that emphasizes compassion for suffering. The text was written in response to the unexpected death of two close friends and demonstrates an acute sensitivity to the difficulty (even meaninglessness) of suffering.[76] He identifies a crucial connection between Jesus's tears of sorrow in the Garden and creation's groaning described in Paul's letter to the Romans—although he does not develop its implications in detail. I seek to build on his insight by turning to the work of Elizabeth Johnson, who expands on the meaning of creation's groaning by explicitly paying attention to nonhuman suffering while also strengthening the Christological reasons for why this is significant. Johnson provides a less anthropocentric approach to suffering than Falque, which, in turn, helps accentuate the idea that *all* of creation has intrinsic value.[77] And more importantly, reading Falque and Johnson alongside each other opens the way for me to articulate what it can look like to affirm creation's goodness even in light of the extensive reality of pain and suffering.

Falque begins his analysis of Christ's tears in the Garden by distinguishing them from the tears shed over the death of Lazarus. He suggests that Christ's tears for his friend represent "suffering with the sufferer," which "arise, like fear, when faced with the suffering or demise of a particular being."[78] According to Falque, however, Christ's tears in the Garden are more like the "sobbing" that takes place when one "'breaks down' and 'opens up' all his or her person" (Mt 26:37).[79] This sobbing indicates the overwhelming prospect of Christ's own "incarnate suffering" that seems to have no immediate justification and achieves "nothing other than accepting an entry into the Nothing."[80] While it is possible to submit reasons for Christ's suffering (for instance, by pointing to the history of salvation), in Falque's account these reasons are either obscured by fear or seem too difficult for Jesus to bear in the Garden ("Father, if you are willing, take this cup from me," Lk 22:42).

Falque identifies Christ's tears with a childlike *vulnerability* associated with intense sorrow that overwhelms articulate discourse, similar to a wounded child who cannot explain why he or she is crying while gasping for breath: "When words are silent, the flesh speaks, and what springs up is the 'infantile shaking and sobbing,' that of the child without-speech (*infans*)."[81] But according to Falque, Christ's childlike crying does not imply regression or immaturity but acknowledges that Christ fully assumes the vulnerability of being human. Falque proposes that Jesus "is no longer at home with the image of himself as a God so powerful that he can work through signs [or miracles] and exercise his power to reestablish some kind of lost integrity in the world."[82] And it is without "shame or resignation" that Christ displays "the total non-mastery of the self that follows from incarnate anxiety."[83] Falque imagines Jesus giving himself over to the Father with his tears like a child who cries out for his parents.

Falque then identifies the connection between Christ's tears and a groaning creation in the moments following Christ's appeal to his disciples to stay awake and pray even though the "flesh [*sarx*] is weak (Mark 14:38)."[84] The reference to "flesh" is important in this context, since Falque argues that it represents Christ's nonsinful vulnerability and weakness: "The first experience of sobs, or of the gaping and indeterminate opening of his being in flesh, can be read in the avowal by Christ himself of the weakness of his own flesh. . . . This is neither the consequence of sin . . . nor even the scolding of a teacher."[85] But when the burden of being "flesh" is too much, Jesus throws himself to the ground to pray ("*epi tes gês*") in the midst of intense isolation.[86] Falque writes:

> The embedding in the flesh at Gethsemane is thus furtively anticipated, in a fall that is a kind of burial in the *earth*, in the *humus* of the garden of the Mount of Olives (Luke 22:44), and then again at the depths of a "tomb which was hewn in stone" (Luke 23:53 JB), but that will be found to be empty (Luke 24:3).[87]

The imagery Falque uses here (the "humus of the garden") knits together Christ's flesh and the earth. With the loneliness that comes with facing his own suffering and death, Jesus falls to the ground and lets his tears merge with creation so that his sorrow reverberates through it—displaying an embodied (or nonverbal) intimacy with a suffering creation. According to Falque, then, Jesus enters into the "same movement and into the same shipwreck, of the whole creation subject to futility (Rom 8:20)."[88] He connects Christ's mourning to the "the entire creation," which has been groaning "in one great act of giving birth" since the beginning (Rom 8:22 JB).[89]

Falque's reflections on Christ's tears in the Garden allude to notable positions on atonement theology and Trinitarian theology. For instance, he argues that the reason for Christ's entrance into the "flesh" is not to appease God's wrath, and he consistently opposes any theology of penal substitutionary atonement that suggests the Father is vengeful.[90] Alternatively, Falque proposes a "non-substitutable substitution" that implies "Christ suffers and dies *for* me and *with* me: he does not suffer and die in my place."[91] As such, Christ does not lift the burden of facing suffering and death: "The true 'place' of suffering for the Christian comes down first of all to accepting that one take *one's* place—not instead of [*à la place de*] Christ, but *with* Christ, who is suffering and resurrected with me, and not *without* me."[92] According to Falque, then, because Christ suffers with us he *passes* each person's suffering to the Father—implying a uniquely "Trinitarian communication" between the Father and the Son wherein Christ will "teach" the Father "not because of his ignorance, but through a total communion with the Son's suffering."[93] This communication (or passage) is not heroically accomplished by stoically facing death for the sake of a larger cause.[94] Instead, Falque stresses Christ's incorporation of weakness and vulnerability as he breaks down sobbing over the difficulty of the road he faces and his complete dependence on the Father.

Falque's positions on atonement theology and the Trinity clearly raise important issues for systematic theology. Some readers may have questions related to the impassibility of God or present versions of penal substitutionary atonement less likely to depict the Father as vengeful.[95] Furthermore, one might examine Falque's description of "Trinitarian communication" by exploring its differences with Jürgen Moltmann's account of the Trinity in the Easter events. Whereas Moltmann argued for a "deep conformity" or "community" in the separation between the Father and the Son at Gethsemane, Falque criticizes Moltmann and proposes that the Son delivers "his being as a gift, even literally abandoning it" to the Father through "the state of supreme irresponsibility" intimated with his tears and finally consummated with his death on the cross.[96] All of these issues are important in their own right and have the potential to influence one's understanding of Christ's relation to creation within a broader theological framework. In the context of this chapter, however, it is the connection between Christ's sorrow and creation's groaning that is particularly important. This connection suggests the unique possibility that Jesus suffers not only "with" and "for" human beings *but with and for all of creation*. And as I will explain with the help of Johnson, this possibility is part of what enlarges (or transfigures) the meaning of creation's goodness so that all of life might be understood to have intrinsic value and be worthy of compassion and care. This Christological frame has the potential to go beyond twentieth-century existential (and anthropocentric) preoccupations with anxiety and fear over death.

Johnson's recent book *Ask the Beasts* helps clarify the full extent of what it means for creation to be groaning. For instance, she identifies the continual presence of death over hundreds of millions of years of evolutionary history:

> An average life lasts a few hours for a mayfly, a few days for a daisy, ten years for a dog, hundreds of years for some trees, three score and ten for human beings, but however long the time span the biological life of the individual comes to an end either by accident, predation, or internal collapse.[97]

She also elucidates the intense pain and suffering that often accompanies the constant threat of death:

> Orcas chase a sea lion through the waves, flipping it playfully in the air before devouring it; a lioness snags a wildebeest, knocking it down

and biting its throat to cause asphyxiation; a hawk plummets to hook a scampering rodent with its sharp talons.[98]

But perhaps Johnson's most acute example of creation's groaning follows from her account of two white pelican chicks. She explains that the two chicks are typically born only days apart, but the first chick to hatch grows quickly and "tends to act aggressively toward the second-born, grabbing most of the food from the parents' pouch and often nudging the smaller bird out of the nest." The younger chick is ignored by the parents and "normally suffers starvation and dies despite its struggle to rejoin the family."[99] Johnson goes on to explain that "the ostracized chick's pinched face, small cries, desperate attempts to regain the nest, and collapse from weakness to become food for the gulls is a scene of such distress as to call for an account of this suffering in a created world considered good, the more so as the anguish of this one little creature is continuously repeated on a grand scale."[100] While she acknowledges that there are debates regarding the extent to which animals can suffer, Johnson argues that it is increasingly the consensus that as "species evolve, nervous systems and brains grow more complex, allowing for heightened alertness, all the way to levels of consciousness typical of sentient animals. At this point, physiological hurt triggers not only basic avoidance behavior but also emotional distress such as fear, anger, and grief stemming from the sense that something awful is happening."[101] Her attentiveness to the suffering of animals, therefore, reinvigorates the meaning of a groaning creation and subsequently opens the possibility that all suffering is worthy of our compassion.

Johnson then further develops the Christological relation to a suffering creation by drawing on the first chapter of John's gospel: "In the beginning was the Word, and the Word was with God, and the Word was God. He was with God in the beginning. Through him all things were made; without him nothing was made that has been made. In him was life, and that life was the light of all mankind" (Jn 1:1–4). And then a few verses later, "The Word became flesh and made his dwelling among us. We have seen his glory, the glory of the one and only Son, who came from the Father, full of grace and truth" (Jn 1:14). Johnson particularly focuses on the importance of *flesh* in these verses—noting that "the prologue does not say that the Word who existed before creation became a human being (Greek *anthropos*), or a man (Gr. *aner*), but flesh (Gr. *sarx*), a broader reality."[102] While she notes that *sarx* can have negative connotations in the biblical text, in the context of the prologue, the emphasis falls on the Word's entry into the "sphere of the material" and the "mortal realm of earthly existence."[103] The becoming flesh of the Word assumes a vulnerability that reinforces the indivisible relationship between a creation that suffers and Christ.

There are important connections to be drawn between Johnson's understanding of the Word made flesh and Falque's understanding of the tears of Christ.[104] As I noted earlier, Falque proposes that Christ's tears represent the flesh (*sarx*) anticipating its future burial and incorporation with the earth. Both this sense of flesh intimated in the Garden and the Word made flesh identified by Johnson are not related to sinfulness but instead to a Christological entry into "the sphere of the material." And for this reason, one might suggest that the tears of Christ "gather in themselves the sadness or the joy of that which cannot weep," so that within those tears it is the "world that shines in their ephemeral crystal."[105] Within a broader Christological reading of creation, Christ mourns for *all* suffering in the moment that he is "overwhelmed with sorrow to the point of death" (Mk 14:33–34). In other words, Jesus cries for the shipwreck that his own life has become while also crying for the shipwreck of all creation. And while it may not be necessary to refer to Christology in order to express this kind of compassion for suffering, a topology of creation that is defined by the Word's ongoing relationship to creation necessarily implies it.

The connection between Christ's tears and a groaning creation clarifies what it means to affirm the goodness of creation in light of the extensive pain, suffering, and death in this world. The tears of Christ are the reverse side of Francis's statement that "other living beings have a value of their own in God's eyes: 'by their mere existence they bless him and give him glory,' and indeed, 'the Lord rejoices in all his works' (Ps 104:31)." Christ *mourns* for a suffering creation that also brings him joy because that which is worth rejoicing over is also worthy of compassion. From this point of view, affirming creation's goodness does not require one to face affliction stoically or to downplay the significance of suffering in the world; instead it legitimizes both rejoicing and mourning—thanksgiving and lament. The intrinsic value of creation suggests: "There is no (true) joy without suffering and there is no (meaningful) suffering without joy. . . . The burn of being I feel in my bones, which makes life seem so joyful, and the burn of unbeing that rages right alongside, which makes that joy so tragic, seem, ultimately, one thing."[106] If the intrinsic value of creation helps define this "one thing," then its status as "good" might be sustained amid the fluidity of affective experience. Less reducible to how I feel in a particular moment, a transfigured goodness is a value engendered from creation's relationship to God. It accommodates and even legitimizes a wide spectrum of affectivity and ultimately affirms that what happens in the place in which we find ourselves somehow matters.

Finally, it is important to caution against any misleading connotations that follow from the image of Jesus crying in the Garden. While his tears are an exemplary instance of compassion (especially when read in light of a broader Christology), one cannot reduce compassion or care to displays of emotion or mourning. Within the context of the gospels, this would become clear if one considered other instances in which Jesus displays compassion by simply caring for the sick, oppressed, and vulnerable. One also might intuit this principle from personal experiences in which "compassion may involve or even require overt kindness or concern," while at other times "emotional display may be disabling."[107] As Jan Zwicky explains, "The goal of compassion is the alleviation of suffering. This is sometimes achieved by offering companionship in suffering. Often, though, what helps the most is empowerment, disinterested assistance towards clear understanding, courage, and self-control."[108] Similarly, the compassion of Christ is not reducible to an affective state. It implies the hard work of *resisting* suffering through concrete action in the world and goes further than the capacity to outwardly emote.[109] This concrete action alludes to broader sociopolitical considerations that extend from the phenomenology of creation's goodness. I will touch on some of these considerations in the conclusion of this book. But for now, it is important to see that an explicitly Christian horizon of place interweaves the appearing of a good creation with one's response to a suffering creation.

Conclusion: Suffering in Creation

In the first part of this chapter, I proposed that if one is willing to acknowledge that creation's goodness is not "limited to some past golden age in Eden," then it is important to let negative phenomena challenge what it means for creation to be good today. Following this principle, I sought to explore how the realities of suffering and death often render the appearing of creation's goodness unclear or even inaccessible to experience. Our bodily struggle for life that leads to decaying and death obscures a straightforward affirmation of the physical world. Likewise, the experience of intense physical pain and suffering challenges the phenomenology of creation's goodness by reconfiguring one's world so that the ordinary ways in which one encounters "goodness" become distant or even inaccessible. While death and suffering do not make it impossible to identify the appearing of goodness in one's life, they suggest that the topological significance of creation's goodness depends on accounting for negative phenomena in a way that does not diminish or overlook their presence.

In response to the different ways in which negative phenomena challenge the status of creation's goodness, I proposed that one consider how a *transfigured goodness* integrates realities like suffering and death. I developed a Christological reading of creation that emphasizes compassion for all of suffering life precisely because creation is worthy of our care. In this context, the value of creation is not based on my encounter with things that are enjoyable or my particular mood (even though these remain critically important for being able to conceive of goodness at all); instead, the *value* of creation follows from Christ's relation to creation. It is worth noting that Treanor outlines a similar perspective in *Melancholic Joy* without using explicitly theological concepts. He argues that a proper understanding of "reality" must fully acknowledge "the reasons for joy and the reasons for sorrow, without minimizing or disparaging either—a bittersweet appreciation of the mystery of being."[110] In his account, life is "shot through with meaning, mysterious to be sure, but saturated with value and significance."[111] The latter half of this chapter shows how a Christological reading of creation affirms this "value and significance" with reference to Jesus's sorrow in Gethsemane. This Christology builds on the conclusions offered in the previous chapter, in which I examined what it means to adopt a topology of creation wherein God's ongoing and active presence becomes constitutive of one's horizon of place.

Throughout this chapter I continued to employ the distinction between a prelinguistic appearing of goodness and its integration into a topology of creation at various times. Some readers may question whether my explicitly Christological language ultimately *imposes* a Christian meaning onto the ambiguous prelinguistic appearing of goodness. My description of a prelinguistic goodness in the previous chapters depicted a general quality of goodness disclosed in certain moods and does not require any confessional stance. At first glance, this kind of goodness may seem very different from affirming the intrinsic goodness of all creation based on Christology. From the beginning of this study, however, I have maintained that the distinction between a prelinguistic goodness and its integration into a topology of creation is not oppositional but reflects different dimensions of what might appear (or that which is "real"). I employ a *descriptive distinction* that follows from reflection on the contours of experience—but this distinction does not imply that prelinguistic experience and a broader horizon of place are noticeably demarcated within the flux of experience.

Another way of thinking the difference between a prelinguistic experience and its integration into a Christian horizon of place is by associating it with layers (or a depth) of experience. I have alluded to these layers at various times by examining Romano's account of the difference between *understanding* (prelinguistic meaning) and *interpretation* (one's response it), Marion's description of the gap between what *gives itself* and what *shows itself* within the response of the *adonné*, and Lacoste's account of what is *initial* to experience and *secondary evidence* that may arise from something like a reference to the Absolute. While there are nuanced differences between these various accounts, they all suggest some differentiation between what initially appears within prelinguistic experience and the language, concepts, and assumptions one uses in order to make sense of our ordinary engagement with things. Critically, this differentiation would be present in any effort to understand the meaning of prelinguistic experience within a broader horizon of place, and it is part of what gives way to the diversity of interpretations roughly outlined in the first chapter.

Adopting a topology of creation is distinguished, in part, because it implies that one's horizon of place is defined by its relation to God. What counts in this situation is less my capacity to perceive creation's goodness and integrate it into a broader horizon of place than the Word who "stably anchors" creation even as this stability is experienced with ambiguity.[112] While Christians clearly hold diverse views on what precisely constitutes the relationship between God and creation, I have outlined a particular theological understanding by advocating for a noncoercive relationality that opens up a series of theological tensions that are never fully resolved over the course of one's life; I have also described a specifically Christological understanding of this relationality that follows from Christ's compassion for a suffering creation. For people living in secular contexts, some of the overt theological language may seem substantially distant from a prelinguistic appearing of goodness. But to the extent that a transfigured goodness intrinsically values a diverse range of experiences, it also is capable of affirming and enriching one's horizon of place without doing violence to that which initially appears. Christian faith does not need to put into question the naïve acceptance of appearances but in fact has the potential to cohere with it in many instances.

If the affirmation of creation's goodness can enrich the world I inhabit, this does not imply that it lessens the burden of suffering and death. Affirming the intrinsic value of all creation may only expose one to more disappointment and pain. On top of gratuitous human suffering, one is left caring for the dragonfly nymph that starves and dies when its legs get stuck in algae strands, the frog that is slowly eaten by a giant water bug, or the bobwhite quail who cries on a cliff side waiting for a mate that never arrives.[113] This burden is one of the reasons why it is appropriate in the Christian tradition to maintain that creation's goodness, in itself, often remains unsatisfying. And so, in the final chapter, I explore the importance of relating creation's goodness to the nonexperience of a liturgical topology within the Christian life. The *goodness* of the first six days of creation leads to the *holiness* of the seventh day, in which one anticipates a further transfiguration of that which is good.

5

Not Good Enough

As I concluded in the previous chapter, affirming the integrity and goodness of creation, on its own, often remains unsatisfying. Not only does it expose one to the burden of caring for a suffering creation, but it does little to address why so much pain and suffering remains in the world. While it brings into focus life's often-tragic circumstances, this can leave people still seeking more of what makes the place in which they find themselves good. Within the Christian tradition, this persistent sense that creation remains incomplete points toward the eschatological structure of God's relation to creation. Even following the Easter events, creation is not fully reconciled with God.[1] No matter how "good" one's life may seem, it remains at a distance from the promises of the resurrection. Creation, in a sense, appears not good enough.

Turning to eschatology cannot justify ongoing tragedies and suffering by alluding to a distant reward that finally tips the scales in a "quasi-economic sense in which we receive 'twice as much' as we lose."[2] In the context of this book, eschatology's relevance stems from the way anticipating the future is interwoven with an understanding one's place. Specifically, I propose that eschatology has the potential both to *qualify* and further *transfigure* the significance of creation's goodness. While it will take the length of this chapter to clarify what I mean by "qualify" and "transfigure," broadly speaking, these terms imply that the eschatological structure of God's relation to creation clarifies the sense in which the gifts of creation are not always central to the Christian life. At the same time, this eschatological relation exposes one to the possibility that the significance of creation's goodness is enlarged by a temporal duration not defined by the apprehension of finitude. Continuing a pattern set in the previous two chapters, I am focused on the interaction between a particular kind of theological knowledge (eschatology) and contours of experience (phenomenology).

The possibility of a temporal duration not defined by how I apprehend finitude is contested within the context of existential phenomenology. The idea directly challenges Heidegger's classic account of *Dasein* in which a person's most important possibilities are defined in relation to the ever-present possibility of death.[3] And so, in order to introduce the possibility of authentic Christian eschatological anticipation, I return to the work of Jean-Yves Lacoste. His critique of Heidegger's account of temporality shows that it is possible to accommodate a variety of eschatological dispositions without rendering the experience inauthentic (particularly through an account of being-at-peace). I build on Lacoste's work to argue that eschatological anticipation might lean toward the *far end* of a topology of creation, where sight becomes nonsight and the limits of experience are laid bare—essentially, a liturgical *nonplace*.

Then, in order to clarify how this kind of eschatological anticipation has the potential to *qualify* the significance of creation's goodness, I reflect on Christ's instructions to "consider the lilies" and "look at the birds" in Matthew 6:24–35. There is a sense in which this text might be read as an amplification of creation's goodness, since the aesthetic qualities of birds and flowers conceivably offer some inspiration not to worry; however, given the previous chapter's emphasis on creation's groaning, the relative comfort that follows from contemplating the aesthetic qualities of the birds and flowers may not account for the full implications of the text. The passage necessitates being read in light of the eschatological structure of God's relation to creation. Søren Kierkegaard provides a good example of this approach by arguing that it is because God is unlike creation that one finds reasons not to worry. This emphasis on the transcendence of God from creation reinforces the centrality of eschatology for understanding creation in a way that corresponds well with Lacoste's work. But more importantly, attending to the eschatological context of the passage qualifies creation's goodness and clarifies a sense in which concrete gifts (or blessings) are not always most important within a topology of creation.

At the same time, the eschatological structure of God's relation to creation *transfigures* the appearing of a good creation in ways that are yet to be identified in this study. To explain what I mean by "transfigure," I will consider the relationship between the "goodness" associated with first six days of creation and the "holiness" of the seventh day in the Genesis account. Abraham Joshua Heschel's *The Sabbath* provides an exemplary examination of these themes in the context of Jewish creation theology, philosophy, and liturgy. It is not my intention to appropriate or sublate Heschel's work with Christian concepts but rather to show how Heschel's work can critically inform a Christian horizon of creation. Heschel's account of the Sabbath offers a remarkable account of the temporal (eschatological) dimensions of the Sabbath—describing it as a *palace in time* that exposes one to a temporal duration that encircles and *reinvigorates* creation's goodness while dissipating in the holiness of God. Deliberate participation in the Sabbath safeguards against the danger of associating God too closely with any "thing" in creation (such as its goodness).

Being-at-Peace: Phenomenology and Eschatology

As noted earlier, eschatology is an important theme in phenomenology starting with Heidegger. As a young student he attempts to develop a theological method that accounts for "lived experience" by examining early Christian eschatology; however, an important shift takes place in his thought and comes to fruition in *Being and Time*.[4] While the early Heidegger views Christian eschatological experience as the "instantiation *par excellence* of authentic religious existence," he eventually interprets it "as fundamentally inimical" to understanding the human situation.[5] At the center of Heidegger's shift is a conviction that philosophy ought to describe the human situation "solely from within," which includes abandoning interest in things like the "objects" of Christian hope (for instance, "the coming Kingdom of God").[6] As Judith Wolfe explains, Heidegger becomes convinced that "phenomenology is logically prior to theology because it lays bare the existential structures of which specifically Christian experiences or concepts are only particular *existentiell* outworkings."[7] By the publication of *Being and Time* (1927), Heidegger associates Christian eschatology with religious sentiment that is engendered from more primordial "existential structures." Moreover, he goes so far as to suggest that Christian eschatological experience is inauthentic because it "projects an end" to a fundamental "unrest" that he believes is essential to understanding the human situation.[8]

One of the central reasons I think it is instructive to consider Lacoste's account of being-at-peace is that he meets Heidegger on his own terms—at least to an extent.[9] Lacoste concedes that there is a degree of theological knowledge (for example, the coming of the Kingdom) that is not explicit in the first givens of experience; however, he does not go so far as to acknowledge that Christian concepts are simply "existentiell outworkings" of a more primordial existential structure. Instead, Lacoste argues for a better understanding of what it means to anticipate the future from within the context of Heidegger's account of disclosing moods (*Befindlichkeit*).[10] Specifically, he proposes that there are a range of moods that leave open eschatological possibilities otherwise circumscribed by Heidegger's account of time. As I will explain, within Lacoste's account, Christian eschatological experience does not obscure what is most basic to the human situation but instead fits within a more diverse and open account of what it means to project various possibilities into the future.

In Chapter 1, I touched on several elements of Lacoste's engagement with "disclosing moods," and in particular I noted that Lacoste challenges Heidegger's prioritization of *anxiety* as *the* fundamental disclosing mood (*Grundstimmung*). But for the purposes of this chapter, it is important to note more precisely why Heidegger argues that anxiety is so fundamental to *Dasein*.[11] Throughout *Being and Time* he describes *Dasein* as always being "ahead-of-itself" and comporting itself toward different possibilities right up to death.[12] According to Heidegger, anxiety is the mood that best discloses the precariousness of this situation, since *Dasein* is never fully in control of its future (in particular, its death), and anxiety attunes *Dasein* to this uncertain future because it has *no proper object*—it discloses the "threat of the indefinite."[13] Jeffrey Bloechl explains the implications of this position for Christianity well:

> According to *Being and Time*, death approaches, singles me out, from before and beyond my relation with anything else. Anxiety thus qualifies as the originary affection (*Grundstimmung*), the one in which anything else affects me, and from which they receive their meaning. And if this means that the givenness of things is a function of our mortality, one still cannot expect that the givenness proper to the things of faith will get their meaning from wholly elsewhere—as if from the relation with God, and not at all with our own death—for the simple reason that those who believe in God are nonetheless mortal.[14]

Because Christian eschatological expectation implies a definitive object of hope that does not stem from how I apprehend my own finitude, Heidegger contends that it covers up the more primordial (and authentic) sense of being-in-the-world that anxiety discloses.

Lacoste challenges Heidegger's account of anxiety by first showing that one might relate to the uncertainty of the future in a variety of ways. Specifically, Lacoste explains that being-at-peace does not require one to forget about the ever-present possibility of death but instead discloses a particular way of relating to finitude. He explains:

Understood in a non-theological sense (distinct as such from the *quies* and the monastic *hèsykhia*) as well as a non-political sense, peace, being-at-peace, is the name that we will agree to give to a non-"vulgar" presence of the present, in which the present is not lived as *"ständige Anwesenheit"* ["persisting presence"] but as a happy moment always renewed, or as a duration that is never troubled by an unhappy memory or a fearful future.[15]

This "happy moment" should not be associated with Heidegger's critique of a "present" that "abolishes what it receives from the future."[16] In fact, Lacoste questions whether Heidegger's concept of such a "present" is even possible, since "we exist within a 'living present,' in the perpetual synthesis of the past, the present and the future, and if this synthesis was bracketed (which is purely and simply impossible), all consciousness would collapse."[17] Being-at-peace, then, is a mood that has a duration (like all affective attunement), but it reveals something important about the meaning(s) of being by presenting an authentic way of anticipating the future. This future may remain uncertain and unknown, but being-at-peace suggests that one might experience the unknown with a sense of contentment.

In order to clarify his position, Lacoste associates being-at-peace with a variety of ordinary circumstances and activities—we "live, love, work, leisure, and so on, in peace."[18] As such, being-at-peace functions as a background attunement that orients the self in relation to the world (a kind of "fundamental tonality").[19] He writes, "When peace reigns in me, and thus concerning everything and everyone, it becomes secondary (secondary to the intelligence of the phenomenon) whether I am occupied or not with others."[20] For example, the prospect of completing a large project does not need to be anxiety inducing, since one might look forward to a sense of accomplishment. Or one might remain at peace while caring for a friend who is struggling with a personal problem.[21] According to Lacoste, being-at-peace is possible with a range of experiences and accommodates various ways of engaging with the future. It demonstrates that one might relate to the future from within a "living present" that does not exclude the sense in which the future remains uncertain.

Within the phenomenological contours of peace, then, Lacoste creates space for the possibility of authentic eschatological anticipation (or hope)—although, in a highly qualified sense. He describes peace as a *microeschatology*—which is a term borrowed from Richard Kearney but developed within the specificity of Lacoste's own phenomenological project.[22] Lacoste's central argument is that being-at-peace does not imply that all *desire* has been fulfilled in the here and now. So, for example, a person might be waiting to acquire a book or anticipating the arrival of a friend, and in these instances it remains normal to be happy "even though we suffer some lack."[23] According to Lacoste, there is an "infinite horizon" of desire that is unlikely to be forgotten when a person is at peace; however, one might embody and acknowledge this desire without becoming discontented or unsettled.[24] These mundane examples help clarify that being-at-peace is not a uniquely religious sentiment but part of the flux of affectivity that defines ordinary experience.

Only after offering commonplace examples of the integration of desire and peace does Lacoste relate its phenomenological structure to situations more specific to Christianity—and specifically the *desire* for God. He submits that although the desire for God may be moved by fear and trembling (*tremendum*), it also can be initiated when a person peacefully contemplates the mystery of God (*mysterium*).[25] In both cases the desire for God is never fully satisfied: "Whether expressed in Latin theology as *visio Dei* or in Greek as *theôsis*, any idea of satiation is not included in an eschatological experience that corresponds to divine infinity."[26] While there is a long Christian tradition following Augustine that locates the desire for God in a rest*less* heart (this was the early Heidegger's preoccupation), Lacoste underscores the importance of a tradition wherein desire for God is accommodated in a rest*ful* heart. There is *always more* of God to be desired (a principle that corresponds well to the assertion that it is impossible to satisfy desire more generally), and Lacoste maintains that *one's desire* for God can be accommodated and integrated in peaceful contemplation.

Included within the infinite range of desires, then, are specifically Christian objects of hope and desire. Lacoste makes this point explicit when he describes the feeling of ease (*l'aise*) or "peaceful joy" that he feels during a moment of solitude while drinking tea in his office (an example already considered in Chapter 1).[27] While earlier in this study I noted how Lacoste relates this moment to the affirmation in Genesis of a good creation, Lacoste also relates it to a "*sabbatical* experience" that "restores creation to us" and "anticipates the Kingdom."[28] It is important to note, however, that when Lacoste draws this connection to "the Kingdom" his argument is not that peace is an affectivity particular to Christianity. Almost two decades later in *Thèses sur le vrai*, Lacoste clarifies this point by proposing that one may *secularize* the meaning of the biblical text with a phenomenology of being-at-ease (*l'aise*) or peace.[29] Finding oneself at peace does not require a particular confession of faith or a Christian object of hope, yet it certainly may accommodate these within the range of future possibilities.

Lacoste remains cautious and does not overextend the eschatological consequences that follow from a phenomenology of peace. While peace "manifests to us what no other phenomenon can manifest, not even joy or innocence: a present that mirrors the *eschaton*," he is quick to point out that mirroring the eschaton does not imply "the realization of the eschaton."[30] Consistent with the qualified claims characteristic of Lacoste's approach to phenomenology, being-at-peace does not provide definitive insight into the future. He concludes, "It is a categorical reality, that we find ourselves in the dark about the last word. Whatever certainties we may have formed about ourselves, as revealed through the life of the affections, we never reach more than penultimate words."[31] Being-at-peace does not cover up the ineluctable uncertainty of that future, but it does provide space for a more diverse spectrum of possibilities within the human situation than Heidegger allows in *Being and Time*. In other words, Lacoste's account of being-at-peace leaves open the door to an "elsewhere" that is not determinable according to the strict logic of being-in-the-world.[32] In contrast to Heidegger, this means that one might authentically enact distinctively Christian eschatological anticipation that begins by *placing oneself before God*.

A Liturgical Nonplace

While Lacoste's phenomenology of peace is helpful because it leaves room for Christian eschatological anticipation that is otherwise excluded by Heidegger, his account of liturgy examines the implications of enacting it for understanding one's place. In his reflections on liturgy Lacoste is not concerned with various forms of affective attunement that disclose the diverse meanings of being; instead, he articulates the way in which liturgy (defined as "being-before-God") specifically *subverts* the logic of Heideggerian topology.[33] Some scholars question this emphasis. As noted in the first chapter, Emmanuel Falque and Joeri Schrijvers submit that Lacoste has an overly negative evaluation of Heidegger's "world." And as I will explain shortly, Christina Gschwandtner contends that Lacoste introduces too much "rupture" between liturgy and topology. However, I propose his description of a liturgical *nonplace* also leaves open the possibility of integration with topology (rather than exclusively rupture). This possible integration is particularly evident if one employs a concept of topology that is not strictly associated with Heidegger's thought.

To this end, it is crucial to understand why Lacoste's description of liturgy (as a nonplace) is developed in contrast to Heidegger's account of "world" and "earth." Lacoste submits that the Heideggerian topologies are defined by a "logic of inherence"; this implies that the place in which we find ourselves holds a certain "sovereignty" over us.[34] So, for instance, we do not possess a "world," since the world "precedes us as something for which we have not wished, as that which preexists and outlives us, and where the mode of our presence in it must be understood as that of a house arrest."[35] Within Heidegger's analysis of place, we find ourselves in a world that coordinates our existence prior to any conscious awareness it. By comparison, Lacoste describes liturgy as "the resolute deliberate gesture made by those who ordain their being-in-the-world a being-before-God."[36] Coming before God is characterized by an "act of freedom" rather than "house arrest."[37] One is thrown into the world in Heidegger's topology, whereas entrance into a liturgical nonplace requires a degree of intentionality and decision.

Lacoste submits that *eschatological anticipation* is essential to the decision to come before God. Rather than starting with "being-there" in the world, liturgy is initiated by "being-toward" the Absolute.[38] He outlines this shift by explaining how liturgy subverts Heideggerian concepts of historiality and being-in-the-world:

> The liturgical subversion of the topological cannot thus be thought here (nor anywhere) except in terms of the *eschaton* or, in any case, in terms of eschatological anticipation. Historiality and being-in-the-world are inextricably linked. When man releases himself (whether symbolically, actually, or both) from his relation of inherence to the world, the horizon of history finds itself exceeded. What bearing does the historial have on the relation between man and the Absolute? We are not questioning the historical prevalence of religions; one does not doubt that they have indeed shaped history. We are asking, rather, whether he who encounters the Absolute exists within historical time, and is faithful to the logic of this time.[39]

Entering the nonplace of liturgy implies taking reprieve from the "world" and its "history" in order to expose oneself to a temporality (the *eschaton*) that follows from being-before-God. It is helpful to note that Lacoste uses a variety of terms in order to describe the effects that follow from this eschatological anticipation. He submits that liturgy "overdetermines," "thwarts," "suspends," "plays," "dances," or "transgresses" one's inherence in the world. In each case, the language he uses implies a different way of seeing the world "as if from outside the world" (albeit for a short period of time).[40] Lacoste consistently acknowledges that one can never be fully abstracted from the world or history; however, by adopting a mode of eschatological anticipation one might set aside its topology (momentarily) and expose oneself to the possibility of that which is not defined by the world as such.

A good way to clarify what is at stake in Lacoste's account of liturgy is by returning to the example of being-at-peace in *Être en danger*. Therein, Lacoste notes that the kind of "peace" offered in the context of liturgy is substantially different from his description of peace as a microeschatology. He explains that the sacrament (the bread and wine) constitutes a "rupture" that offers "a possible enjoyment of the end here and now."[41] He refers to the following statement in the liturgy: "In this bodily life we know the daily operations of your mercy, yet even now possess the tokens of eternity."[42] The "eternity" named in this statement is not organized by the infinite play of finite possibility; instead, he describes the sacrament as *metahistorical*. Lacoste writes, "The 'thing,' the *res*, of the sacrament, though present here and now, is comparably present at every moment of history and therefore has no history of its own."[43] The one who recognizes the "sacramental character" of the bread and wine is therefore presented with the possibility of being "included in a temporal duration not defined as being-towards-death."[44] While his phenomenology of peace indicates one possible future among many (as noted earlier), the sacrament exposes a person to an entirely different set of claims within the nonplace of liturgy.

The distinction between liturgy and topology is further clarified by accounting for Lacoste's subtle understanding of the relationship between philosophy and theology. He submits that any reference to eternity beyond finitude is where "we reach the limits of description" (phenomenology), even if it is not "the limits of all thought," since the sacramental site offers what "history has no place for."[45] By exploring the "limits" here, Lacoste is indicating what Bloechl characterizes as an "*eschaton* of reason," which implies that human beings are capable of thinking beyond the conditions of facticity and history.[46] The bread and wine offer this "beyond" for "thought," since they "are inscribed in history without submitting to claims that they be understood as the expression of a meaning that is finally and only historical."[47] Critically, Lacoste is not implying that liturgy is ahistorical or lacking philosophical rationality; in fact, it may very well be of interest to philosophy that people continually expose themselves to this "beyond."[48] Lacoste is searching for a way to describe accurately what it means to suspend momentarily (not cover up) one's being-unto-death and expose oneself to the limits of thought.

The precise language and concepts Lacoste uses are important, since, as noted, Gschwandtner contends that Lacoste places too much emphasis on a liturgical "rupture" with topology. She argues that Lacoste's focus on "being-before-God" overlooks the significance of concrete embodied practices and rituals that are essential to contemporary sociological understandings of religion—practices that in turn bind liturgy to a particular place far more than Lacoste acknowledges.⁴⁹ She submits, "The phenomenological experience of liturgy is one of bodies bent toward the altar or toward each other, not to some invisible non-place."⁵⁰ Then, following her careful descriptions of Orthodox liturgical practices, she writes (in contrast to Lacoste): "Liturgy functions not as a suspension of either world or earth, but instead as a particular 'arrangement' or 'experience' of the world, which is possible because liturgy 'opens a world' through orientation and directionality."⁵¹ It should be clear that Gschwandtner's analysis appropriately identifies Lacoste's emphasis on liturgy's "rupture" with topology. However, as I will explain, it also is important to recall that this rupture is developed specifically in contrast to Heideggerian topology (rather than topology, as such).⁵² There may be room for the integration of Lacoste's liturgical nonplace and topology if one entertains a concept of "place" beyond its strictly Heideggerian conception.

This integration is particularly important given the sense in which I have described creation as a topology throughout this study. If there is some confusion here, it likely is the result of Lacoste using the term "topology" as a shorthand for Heidegger's world and earth. A topology of creation (as I have described it) clearly does not follow the laws of inherence; instead, like liturgy, there is a sense in which the concept of creation "escapes the *initial* conditions bestowed upon it."⁵³ In the third chapter I describe this "escape" as part of a person's *decision* (in conjunction with God's initiative) to adopt a topology of creation. A degree of freedom is central to understanding a Christian horizon of place.

At the same time, from the beginning of this study I have argued that creation's *goodness* is integral to the place in which we find ourselves. The prelinguistic appearing of "goodness" discloses aspects of creation that are part of a "publicly accessible reality" and not just "the mind's inward reflection on its own contents, in short introspection."⁵⁴ In Chapter 1, I acknowledge that not everyone will associate this goodness with a Christian concept of creation (its prelinguistic appearing—including its appearing as *creation*—remains open to a variety of interpretations and is not reducible to a confessional stance). But I also sought to show how this prelinguistic goodness *entangles* creation with other topologies—including Heidegger's concepts of world and earth. This entanglement does not mean that creation corresponds with "world" or "earth," but it suggests that the category of topology (as a shorthand for horizon of place) might extend beyond its strictly Heideggerian sense.

In the following sections, then, I will explore the interaction between liturgy and a topology of creation in more detail. Specifically, I show how the *nonplace* of liturgy allows one to take reprieve from (or suspend) ordinary engagement with the gifts of creation. Being-before-God qualifies the topological significance of creation's goodness in light of the eschatological structure of God's relation to creation. However, I also will examine how liturgy exposes one to a temporal duration that is not defined by how I apprehend my own finitude. This has the potential to transfigure the goodness of creation so that its value remains long after I have perceived it within my own experience. This transfiguration of creation's goodness suggests that beyond producing a rupture with topology, the nonplace of liturgy also presents the possibility (or mystery) of an ongoing intimacy between God and creation.

Consider the Lilies and the Birds

Christ's instruction in Matthew 6:25–34 offers a good illustration of how a liturgical nonplace qualifies the goodness of creation. The passage both underscores the importance of eschatological anticipation and raises questions about the significance of a good creation within this anticipation. The text is part of a cluster of teachings in the Sermon on the Mount that begin at 6:19, following instructions about fasting, piety, and "the most mundane issues of daily life" (in particular, money).[55] I am interested in verses 25–34 primarily because of the four imperatives: do not "be concerned/anxious," "look at" the birds, "consider" the lilies, and "seek" first the kingdom of God and his righteousness.[56] The passage states:

> [25] "Therefore I tell you, do not worry about your life, what you will eat or what you will drink, or about your body, what you will wear. Is not life more than food, and the body more than clothing? [26] Look at the birds of the air; they neither sow nor reap nor gather into barns, and yet your heavenly Father feeds them. Are you not of more value than they? [27] And can any of you by worrying add a single hour to your span of life? [28] And why do you worry about clothing? Consider the lilies of the field, how they grow; they neither toil nor spin, [29] yet I tell you, even Solomon in all his glory was not clothed like one of these. [30] But if God so clothes the grass of the field, which is alive today and tomorrow is thrown into the oven, will he not much more clothe you—you of little faith? [31] Therefore do not worry, saying, 'What will we eat?' or 'What will we drink?' or 'What will we wear?' [32] For it is the Gentiles who strive for all these things; and indeed your heavenly Father knows that you need all these things. [33] But strive first for the kingdom of God and his righteousness, and all these things will be given to you as well.

[34] "So do not worry about tomorrow, for tomorrow will bring worries of its own. Today's trouble is enough for today."

As I will explain, the imperatives raise several issues related to the interaction between creation's goodness and the eschatological anticipation that defines "being-before-God" in the nonplace of liturgy.

There are two different types of interpretations that I will consider. First, I examine literary readings of the text that use Christ's instruction as an invitation to contemplate what might broadly be understood as the goodness of creation. The birds and flowers display qualities that have the potential to teach one about the kingdom of God and offer reasons not to worry. These examples illustrate how creation's goodness might help cultivate a relation to the future that is not defined primarily by anxiety over death—they are good examples of a microeschatology. However, as I already indicated, the goodness of creation often seems to provide insufficient reasons "not to worry." While I consider these literary examples because they offer important insight into creation's goodness, a broader theological perspective helpfully contextualizes the text within the eschatological structure of God's relation to creation to a greater degree. To this end, Søren Kierkegaard's interpretation of the birds and the lilies identifies the importance of a liturgical overdetermination of the topological (including the goodness of creation). He deliberately calls into question poetic interpretations of the birds and flowers that focus on aesthetics, and his reading of the text corresponds remarkably well with Lacoste's account of liturgy (this produces the added benefit of further elucidating the influence of Kierkegaard on Lacoste).[57] While I do not fully endorse Kierkegaard's criticisms of poetic readings of the text, his interpretation of the passage shows how the nonplace of liturgy qualifies creation's goodness in light of the eschatological structure of God's relation to creation.

In order to outline the insights offered by two literary responses to Christ's teaching, it is helpful to associate them with what Paul Ricoeur describes as "poetic discourse" that "brings to language a pre-objective world in which we find ourselves already rooted, but in which we also project our innermost possibilities."[58] Rather than start from a historical-critical exegesis of Matthew 6, these literary responses are initiated by the various qualities of birds and flowers, which stimulate the author to imagine new ways (or "impertinent" ways) of encountering that which appears in one's place.[59] These authors do not subvert or overdetermine topology but instead recall something like the originary blessing described in the first chapter of Genesis. The literary approaches may also be considered examples of what Kevin Hart describes as the "phenomenological realism" intrinsic to certain poems, as the authors lead us "back to the phenomena that manifest themselves to us in the world about us and to see them freshly, as though for the first time."[60] The authors discover reasons "not to worry" based on their encounters with what is good about the place in which they find themselves.

In the first example, Mary Oliver's "Consider other kingdoms" reflects on Christ's imperative to meditate on nonhuman life and in doing so intimates a life-giving sense of well-being. She writes:

> Consider other kingdoms. The
> Trees, for example, with their mellow-sounding
> titles: oak, aspen, willow.
> Or the snow, for which the peoples of the north
> have dozens of words to describe its
> different arrivals. Or the creatures, with their
> thick fur, their shy and wordless gaze. Their
> infallible sense of what their lives
> are meant to be. Thus the world
> grows rich, grows wild, and you too,
> grow rich, grow sweetly wild, as you too
> were born to be.[61]

By considering "other kingdoms," Oliver identifies various qualities that permeate the world and teach her something about herself and others. She asks her readers to let themselves be affected by the "mellow-sounding" oak and those creatures who have an "infallible sense of what their lives are meant to be." Observing what is "good" (to put it bluntly) in other kingdoms infuses Oliver's "living present" to the point where she is untroubled by the past and future—finding rest in the idea that "you too, / grow rich, grow sweetly wild, as you too / were born to be."

A related example is found in Margaret Renkl's "After the Fall." Therein, she indicates how the birds and the flowers seem to reorient her relationship to time even as she notices herself getting older. Her engagement with Matthew 6 more explicitly involves a back and forth of creation's goodness and eschatology. She writes:

> Time claims you: your belly softens, your hair grays, the skin on the top of your hand goes loose as a grandmother's, and the skin of your grief, too, will loosen, soften, forgive your sharp edges, drape your hard bones.
>   You are waking into a new shape. You are waking into an old self. What I mean is, time offers your old self a new shape.

What I mean is, you are the old, ungrieving you, and you are also the new, ruined you.

You are both, and you will always be both.

There is nothing to fear. There is nothing to fear. Walk out into the springtime, and look: the birds welcome you with a chorus. The flowers turn their faces to your face. The last of last year's leaves, still damp in the shadows, smell ripe and faintly fall.[62]

In Renkl's text, the goodness of creation forms a context in which she contemplates the possibility that all will be well. The birds and flowers are creation's welcome sign that life continues to flourish even as she ages, and this becomes a genuinely meaningful context in which to consider her own life. Similar to Oliver, Renkl demonstrates an awareness of how the various qualities of creation define the meaning of one's place and have the potential to teach us something about ourselves and our future.[63] Both authors seem to respond to what Ellen Davis argues is the aesthetic purpose of the Genesis text—to teach readers to "stand 'in mute awe before the wonder of being.'"[64] They describe authentic moments of peace (microeschatologies) that follow from Jesus's imperative to consider the birds and flowers. These literary responses make no claim to being a definitive interpretation of Matthew 6, but they model an attunement to that which is good about creation that may be implicit to Christ's teaching.

However, as indicated earlier, any approach to the text that focuses on the various qualities of creation raises problems. In fact, interpretations that focus on the beauty of creation have been heavily criticized in the historical reception of the text—since "every 'starving sparrow'" seems to contradict Jesus.[65] One might recall the example of the second white pelican chick to hatch noted in the previous chapter. It is unclear how a chick desperately trying to rejoin its family after being pushed out of the nest by a sibling provides assurance that "your heavenly Father knows" what it is that you need. Reflecting on the beauty of birds and flowers does not seem to disclose enough "goodness" to address the reasons one might have to worry. And so, it is important to consider an interpretation of Matthew 6 that accounts for the broader liturgical and eschatological dimensions of the text.[66] This provides a theological context in which the significance of creation's goodness is qualified in relation to God.

Søren Kierkegaard's interpretation of the passage in the *Edifying Discourses* illustrates what it means to read Christ's teaching with attention to liturgical and eschatological themes. Lacoste submits that Kierkegaard's *Edifying Discourses* provides "one of the best examples" of theology seeking to speak "*to* God" rather than "*of* God."[67] In other words, they are liturgical in the sense that Kierkegaard places himself before God in order to speak about God.[68] But what is particularly interesting about Kierkegaard's understanding of Christ's teaching in Matthew 6 is that he argues that the birds and flowers demonstrate what it means to enact such a liturgical stance. He submits that the birds and flowers show "that *you are before God*" in an exemplary fashion.[69] Critically, the similarity in language to Lacoste's description of liturgy (being-before-God) is not just coincidental—there is substantial conceptual overlap between the two thinkers.

George Pattison provides helpful clarification with respect to Kierkegaard's use of the phrase "you are before God." He explains that it is "not so much a matter of direct experience (as if we might, one day, feel the eyes of God boring through us)."[70] Instead, Kierkegaard's account of being before God implies a "critical self-relation in which we actively adopt and take upon ourselves a certain understanding of life, a matter of actively and deliberately sustaining a certain kind of awareness, of learning to take note of how our own thoughts might be bearing witness against us."[71] Pattison's description of Kierkegaard's position largely resembles Lacoste's account of liturgy in *Experience and the Absolute*, when he argues that liturgy is "the exemplary case of a decentering or marginalization of the ego," since God bears "witness against us" and clarifies our incapacity to "take measure" of the Absolute.[72] Essential to Lacoste's understanding of liturgy is the idea that the "aims of consciousness" meet their limits when one comes before God, since they "are without power and have no rights before God" (this is related to what Bloechl identifies as the "eschaton of reason").[73] For both Lacoste and Kierkegaard, then, placing oneself before God subverts the ego much in the same way it subverts topology, since the Absolute does not simply condescend or appear because the "I" intends it.

Now, the idea that "you are before God" is essential to Kierkegaard's interpretation of the passage because (as indicated earlier) he argues that the "lily and the bird" exemplify this liturgical situation. Rather than being aesthetic objects that demand the attention of a poet, he submits that the bird and lily communicate a sense of "worship" and "respect for God."[74] The bird and lily are not concerned with themselves (or us); instead, they "signify to you that you are before God, so that you remember that you are before God—so that you also might earnestly and in truth become silent before God."[75] In Kierkegaard's account, the silence and stillness of the bird put into question the significance of our daily concerns and anxieties.[76] He writes, "Even if what you want to accomplish in the world were the most amazing feat: you shall acknowledge the lily and the bird as your teachers and before God you are not to become more important to yourself than the lily and the bird."[77] Moreover:

And even if the entire world were not large enough to contain all your plans when you unfold them, with the lily and the bird as teachers, you shall learn before God to be able simply to fold all your plans together into something that occupies less space than a point, and makes less noise than the most insignificant trifle: in silence.[78]

The silence of the lily and the bird models the importance of putting aside your daily activities and preoccupations in order to attend to the reality that "you are before God."

One of the underlying issues in Kierkegaard's reading of the text is that (again, like Lacoste) he is concerned with distinguishing a Christian concept of creation from notions of the sacred or pantheistic notions of God's immanence. As Bruce Kirmmse explains, Kierkegaard made use of the natural world for reasons "precisely the opposite of the pantheistic religion of nature so common among his contemporaries and our own. Kierkegaard insisted on the absolute transcendence of God, and he held that human beings, unlike other beings, are not only capable of relating to the radically transcendent God, but are fragmentary, incompletely realized, beings, unless they do so."[79] While this position is in danger of being a simplistic dismissal of religious and spiritual traditions not associated with Christianity (a sentiment I do not share),[80] its significance in this context underscores the essential role of *divine transcendence* within the nonplace of liturgy. If there are reasons not to worry in the face of the harsh and often fragile realities of living in creation, it is because God is *unlike* creation.

Introducing a concept like divine transcendence here has the potential to be misleading given the variety of complex philosophical and theological frameworks in which a concept like "transcendence" is used. But Lacoste offers some context in this regard by distancing himself (and Kierkegaard, for that matter) from an overly "abstract concept of otherness or transcendence" (he associates the early Barth and Rudolf Otto with this problem).[81] He also attempts to provide some clarity for the concept of divine transcendence by turning to a basic phenomenological insight: "We perceive a cube, not merely the surface of the cube, and if we admit that it is the cube we perceive, though perception is not 'adequate' (a synthesis of present sense-data and no more), we are forced to add that what we 'perceive' includes what is not seen."[82] The example of the cube shows that every perception of a thing includes both visible and invisible aspects to some degree. "Transcendence," according to Lacoste, is the "right word" for describing this play between the visible and invisible.[83] While there are manifold ways in which the lines between the visible and invisible are ambiguous (especially with respect to my perception of God's relation to creation), in its simplest form, divine transcendence implies that there is more to God than what I feel, know, or experience.

The principle of divine transcendence responds to the idea that nothing in creation (no matter how "good") can "save" me from the ineluctable eventuality of suffering and death.[84] This is why Lacoste emphasizes that one might feel "at home" in the liturgy only by *anticipating the kingdom* and not by the "luminous treasures of the earth."[85] Within the context of eschatological anticipation that is constitutive of being-before-God, one finds rest in the sense that God cannot be identified with any "thing" in creation. I would note, however, that divine transcendence should not imply that God is "outside" or "other than" creation, since this would imply "that there is something more than—something in addition to—God."[86] In other words, God and creation are not "two mutually delimiting objects," but, instead, God is (somehow) still understood to be the source and sustainer of creation.[87] Theologically speaking, there has to be a way of discussing how "the creature and the Creator are both enacting the creature's life though in different ways and at different depths."[88] The affirmation of divine transcendence is part of what opens the possibility of this mutual enactment—giving conceptual space to the idea that God is not only "present here and now" but "comparably present at every moment of history and therefore has no history of its own."

Of course, underscoring the importance of divine transcendence does not address the complicated debates in twentieth-century theology over the precise language and concepts used in order to describe it.[89] But my central point, here, is simply to observe how divine transcendence (as understood by Lacoste and Kierkegaard) is part of what *qualifies* the goodness of creation within a broader liturgical situation. Deliberately enacting a mode of eschatological anticipation by "being-before-God" implicitly acknowledges that the integrity and goodness of creation in-itself may finally not be good enough. And the language of divine transcendence is part of what introduces one to the possibility of something more—which in turn, reinforces the eschatological structure of God's relation to creation.

The Holiness of Sabbath

The nonplace of liturgy not only qualifies the goodness of creation; it also uniquely points toward its transfiguration in relation to God. And in order to articulate what I mean by transfiguration, it is helpful to return to the creation hymn in Genesis and consider the significance of the seventh day of creation. The Sabbath exemplifies a liturgical situation in which one puts aside ordinary engagement with the world in order to be exposed to a temporal duration that is not defined by one's "existential" situation. Without collapsing the Jewish and Christian liturgy then, it is possible to relate a Sabbath temporality to the "metahistory" Lacoste associates with the sacrament of the Eucharist. In both cases there is a sense in which one is confronted with the presence of God in eternity (of course, without leaving behind the inextricable limits of my own temporality). Such a presence further transfigures creation's goodness so that its value has the potential to be maintained (or anchored) despite its ever-changing appearance over one's experience of time.

The primary source I use in order to articulate the meaning of the Sabbath is Abraham Joshua Heschel's classic 1951 text *The Sabbath*. He provides a distinctively Jewish approach to the seventh day while also remaining sensitive to the trends of twentieth-century philosophy. As a recent immigrant to the United States, Heschel was sensitive to a "new reality" for Jews following World War II—one that was "far more suburban than urban, less anti-Semitic in the wake of the Holocaust, but one still driven by consumerist pressures and technological advances. Jews were wealthier too, now living with their Christian neighbors, and middle-class choices awaited them."[90] Throughout the text, Heschel confronts this new context by reflecting on "the grandeur of time in contrast to the entrapments of space, advancing a phenomenology of being to help deflect the technology of acquisition."[91] Heschel does not denigrate the good gifts of creation that often accompany relative safety and wealth but pursues categories for thinking about God that are not grounded in spatial images. As I will explain, his reflections on the temporal dynamics of the Jewish liturgy integrate creation's *goodness* into the *holiness* of the Sabbath, which, in turn, elucidates the transfiguration of a good creation in relation to God.

To begin, then, Heschel argues that it is often tempting to associate God with spatial images because that is typically how people imagine "presence." He writes, "There is much enthusiasm for the idea that God is present in the universe, but that idea is taken to mean His presence in space rather than in time, in nature rather than in history; as if He were a thing, not a spirit."[92] Alternatively, Heschel submits that focusing on the *time* of the Sabbath suggests a different kind of presence: "It is a day on which we are called upon to share in what is eternal in time, to turn from the results of creation to the mystery of creation; from the world of creation to the creation of the world."[93] And he submits that this understanding of God's presence in time stems from a biblical perspective on history:

> Unlike the space-minded man to whom time is unvaried, iterative, homogeneous, to whom all hours are alike, qualitiless, empty shells,

the Bible senses the diversified character of time. There are no two hours alike. Every hour is unique and the only one given at the moment, exclusive and endlessly precious.[94]

Heschel associates this diversified, qualitative time with a God who is "the Redeemer from slavery, the Revealer of the Torah, manifesting Himself in events of history rather than in things or places."[95] He is not implying that space and time are separable.[96] Instead, his point is that there is a presence in time that is not reducible to the kind of presence typically associated with things, places, or objects.

Heschel associates God's action in history with a philosophy of *events*—which is an approach that one might identify as a precursor to Claude Romano's account of the event. As I noted in previous chapters, Romano defines the event as a *happening* that has no clear cause and produces a lasting and transformative effect. Similarly, Heschel proposes that events are "*happenings* in the world" that are not reducible to simple causal explanations yet remain significant over a long period of time.[97] Unlike Romano, however, Heschel describes the event as something that happens "suddenly, intermittently, occasionally," and he identifies a spiritual significance in it that Romano does not consider.[98] The *event* of the Sabbath manifests a particular spiritual *quality* in time that implores deliberate attention.

Heschel associates the quality of time specific to the Sabbath with metaphors such as *Palace*, *Queen*, and *Bride* in the rabbinic tradition. He explains, "Such metaphorical exemplification does not state a fact; it expresses a value, putting into words the preciousness of the Sabbath as Sabbath."[99] The reference to images (like a queen or bride) does not relocate the value of the Sabbath in the world of space but leads Heschel to emphasize the apophatic use of metaphors and images:

> The idea of the Sabbath as a queen or a bride did not represent a mental image, something that could be imagined. There was no picture in the mind that corresponded to the metaphor. Nor was it ever crystallized as a definite concept, from which logical consequences could be drawn, or raised to a dogma, an object of belief.[100]

The *value* of the Sabbath that is relayed through the metaphor stems from "more than what minds could visualize or words could say."[101] As Edward Kapin explains, Heschel's use of metaphor "actualizes the vertical dimension of language."[102] The image dissipates the further it travels up the vertical axis because its value is not derived from a thing in space (like a literal queen or a bride). And so, the quality of the Sabbath is its *holiness*, which Heschel notes "is not in the grain of matter" but "is a preciousness bestowed upon things by an act of consecration and persisting in relation to God."[103] The holiness of the Sabbath exemplifies the persistence of things in "relation to God," precisely because it is defined less by "things" than by the holiness that encircles creation in time.

It is important to note that the language of holiness corresponds with the French distinction between the sacred and the holy (*sacré* and *saint*) identified in Chapter 1. As Levinas explains in *Nine Talmudic Readings*, the *holy* reflects the "purity" and "separation" to which "the Jewish tradition aspires," whereas the *sacred* reflects a "half-light" that Revelation refuses to entertain.[104] This distinction is also adopted by Lacoste in *Experience and the Absolute*, who argues that the "holy fool" demonstrates a radical subversion of the sacred or the "numinous treasures" of the earth. As such, holiness is not grounded in the appearing of things in creation (including its goodness) but emphasizes the significance of divine transcendence noted in the previous section. As Heschel explains, "One of the most distinguished words in the Bible is the word *qadosh*, holy; a word which more than any other is representative of the mystery and majesty of the divine."[105] The holiness of God is not associated with any sacred place or object like a mountain, spring, or temple—as such, the Sabbath is a *nonplace* that does not depend on a particular location or space.[106]

Critically, however, the holiness of the Sabbath does not necessarily produce a rupture with topology but instead provides a time in which one recalls the original Genesis blessing. Heschel explains that the Sabbath "is a day in which we abandon our plebeian pursuits and reclaim our authentic state, in which we may partake of a blessedness in which we are what we are, regardless of whether we learned or not, of whether our career is a success or a failure; it is a day of independence of social conditions."[107] In a sense, then, the Sabbath recontextualizes the first six days of creation by requiring one to set aside the ordinary ways of engaging with one's place. Heschel writes:

> He who wants to enter the holiness of the day must first lay down the profanity of clattering commerce, of being yoked to toil. He must go away from the screech of dissonant days, from the nervousness and fury of acquisitiveness and the betrayal in embezzling his own life. He must say farewell to manual work and learn to understand that the world has already been created and will survive without the help of man. Six days a week we wrestle with the world, wringing profit from the earth; on the Sabbath we especially care for the seed of eternity planted in the soul.[108]

The liturgical rhythm of the Sabbath reframes the gifts of creation and helps safeguard them from the ideologies of a particular time and context.[109] As noted earlier, Heschel was particularly concerned with the "consumerist pressures and technological advances" in midcentury suburban America, but the enduring relevance of the Sabbath is that whatever tendencies there are toward the misuse of a good creation in a culture, they are countered by the deliberate enactment of rest and exposure to the holiness of God in time.

Heschel makes a point of not diminishing the goodness of creation in contrast to the holiness of the Sabbath. He writes, "To disparage space and the blessing of things of space, is to disparage the works of creation, the works which God beheld and saw 'it was good.'"[110] Instead, the Sabbath indicates "a profound conscious harmony of man and the world, a sympathy for all things and a participation in the spirit that unites what is below and what is above."[111] By setting aside one's preoccupation with that which is "good," entrance into the Sabbath implies recalling the relationship (or unity) between the good and the holy that animates creation. The holiness of the Sabbath, therefore, reinvigorates and transfigures creation's goodness rather than disparages it.

This transfiguration of a good creation is clarified further if one accounts for the eschatological dimensions of the Sabbath. Heschel's reflections on the Hebrew term for rest (*menuha*) illuminate this aspect of the seventh day. He writes:

> To the biblical mind *menuha* is the same as happiness and stillness, as peace and harmony. The word with which Job described the state after life he was longing for is derived from the same root as *menuha*. It is the state wherein man lies still, wherein the wicked cease from troubling and the weary are at rest. It is the state in which there is no strife and no fighting, no fear and no distrust. The essence of good life is *menuha*. "The Lord is my shepherd, I shall not want, He maketh me to lie down in green pastures; He leadeth me beside the still waters" (the waters of *menuhot*).[112]

Within the liturgical context of the Sabbath, the green pastures and still waters foreshadow a world to come. And while Heschel notes that "the Jewish tradition offers us no definition of the concept of eternity," he submits there is a "taste of eternity or eternal life within time."[113] *Menuha* is a "synonym for the life in the world to come, for eternal life."[114] If one were to use the language of Lacoste, the "rest" that is identified with green pastures and still waters is a microeschatology that is transfigured in relation to the *eternity* encountered in the nonplace of liturgy. While the language of eternity (similar to "transcendence") can be misleading, it has the benefit of distinguishing the liturgical time of the Sabbath from anything like

Heidegger's existential time identified in the first section of this chapter. A reference to eternity does not deny the reality of being-unto-death, but it is engendered from a completely different starting point. As Heschel explains, the holiness of the Sabbath is not dependent on the "grace of man" (let alone the *existential* situation of *Dasein*), but instead, "It was God who sanctified the seventh day."[115] Of course, stating this distinction is not an argument for its truth, but similar to the logic of "God's initiative" explored in the third chapter, it is important to note that God's involvement is a condition on which one is exposed to the possibility.

The language of "exposure" here implicitly acknowledges that not everyone will seek to enact a liturgical "being-before-God." But as Heschel and Lacoste both indicate, the decision to place oneself before God has the potential to reconfigure one's understanding of "place." It is helpful to associate this "reconfigured" topology as part of what Lacoste describes as a "secondary immediacy."[116] He submits that liturgy's "greatest success would be for it to become so implicit that we would believe ourselves to be living in a theophanic world—indeed, it is essential to liturgy that it simulate the joy we anticipate in the Parousia."[117] In language closer to Heschel, one might describe this liturgical "success" as recognizing the holiness of the Sabbath more fully within the first six days of creation. Any recognition of "holiness" (or a "theophantic world") remains subject to all the experiential ambiguities I have emphasized throughout this book. There is nothing inevitable about "seeing" one's place in relation to eternity, and any affirmation of such a vision remains defined by a sense in which "our sight is at the same time and inescapably non-sight."[118] By definition, holiness in time can only be intimated through nonsight and dissipates in reference to God.

In summary, Heschel's vision of the Sabbath depicts a nonplace that reinvigorates and transfigures the goodness of creation by intimating a "profound conscious harmony" between God and creation. Within the time of the Sabbath, eschatological anticipation exposes one to a sense in which creation participates in a temporal duration that is not defined by my apprehension of finitude. It offers a transfigured sense of the goodness of creation through "a sympathy for all things and a participation in the spirit that unites what is below and what is above." While it is understandable if this "harmony" is difficult to discern over the course of daily life, the seventh day is a regular invitation to participate deliberately in such a vision.

Conclusion: Eschatology and Creation's Goodness

At the beginning of this chapter, I suggested that an eschatological structure defines the relationship between God and creation. I submitted that explicitly exposing oneself to this structure within a liturgical nonplace has the potential both to qualify and transfigure the topological significance of creation's goodness. Creation's goodness is *qualified* by setting aside our ordinary engagement with things in order to acknowledge that the gifts of creation may not be most important all the time. And creation's goodness is *transfigured* when it is understood in relation to a temporal duration that is not defined by my being-unto-death. This transfigured goodness implies that the value of creation may endure long after its appearance within the contours of experience.

By examining the eschatological structure of God's relation to creation in the context of liturgy, this chapter also sketched various ways that a liturgical *nonplace* is integral to a topology of creation. In the previous two chapters I described this topology as being defined in relation to God, which in turn introduces irresolvable tensions between nature and grace, activity and passivity, knowing and unknowing—and, one might now add, God's intimacy with and transcendence from creation. The centrality of eschatological anticipation to liturgy ensures that these irresolvable theological tensions remain suspended within a topology of creation and safeguards against the danger of associating God too closely with any "thing" (especially, creation's goodness).

The nonplace of liturgy recoordinates one's horizon of place. It marks the far end of a topology of creation, where sight becomes nonsight and the limits of experience are exposed. From this point of view, one might affirm with Lacoste that "it is perhaps by transgressing it that liturgy is integrated into topology."[119] This transgression follows from a decision to set aside the gifts of creation (if only momentarily) in order to attend to an eschatological vision that suggests there is always more to see within the place in which we find ourselves. But rather than result in the devaluation of creation's goodness, liturgy intimates a harmony between God and creation so that the still waters of rest might also be seen as a taste of eternity. Liturgy leans into the eschatological dimensions of creation—giving space to acknowledge when creation does not seem to be good enough, while still allowing those gifts to inspire eschatological anticipation.

Conclusion
The Credibility of Creation's Goodness

This book began with the conviction that if there is something good about creation that is ongoing and definitive, then it will appear in experience and be describable to some degree. There is a sense in which this description had the potential to be straightforward, since it is relatively common to encounter "real sensible qualities out there in the world" that are reducible to a concept of goodness—the bread is good, the wine is good.[1] But explaining how this general quality is integrated into a topology of creation introduces substantial complexity. Not only does this integration include examining a possible relation between small-scale encounters with goodness and God, but it also requires outlining how this relation might appear in experience and potentially affect the meaning of goodness.

In order to describe creation's goodness in a meaningful fashion, I first sought to outline the reduction to a *prelinguistic* goodness that is widely accessible regardless of confessional stance. It makes sense for Christians to relate this goodness to a primordial Genesis blessing; however, I argued that it remains open to a wide range of legitimate interpretations. Without falling into a simplistic relativism or foreclosing the diversity of interpretations, I sought to articulate how a prelinguistic goodness is integrated and transfigured within a specifically Christian horizon of place. When the goodness of creation is defined in relation to the One who "is before all things" and in whom "all things hold together" (Col 1:17), it is less reducible to its often-precarious appearing in my experience. It finds its primary meaning in the sense that "other living beings have a value of their own in God's eyes."[2] This transfigured goodness is not a theological imposition onto what initially appears as a general play of goodness, since affirming it can only take place as an act of freedom. A transfigured goodness appears within the context of irresolvable tensions such as nature and grace, activity and passivity, knowing and unknowing (which I propose to be integral to a topology of creation). Intentionally living within these tensions never overcomes the limits or ambiguities of experience but instead opens up a lifelong process of discernment and reflection.

In the Introduction to this book I presented three potential contributions that follow from the arguments in this study. First, following Brian Treanor, I noted a tendency in continental philosophy to use melancholic dispositions as "a watermark of sorts for serious continental philosophy, which is concerned with otherness, alienation, inauthenticity, angst, anxiety, dread, melancholy, finitude, mourning, and death."[3] A full accounting of reality, however, requires one to acknowledge both "the reasons for joy and the reasons for sorrow, without minimizing or disparaging either—a bittersweet appreciation of the mystery of being."[4] Without discounting the abundant reasons for despair, then, I proposed that identifying phenomena related to creation's goodness has the potential to help counterbalance a certain negative tendency in continental philosophy. To this end, I outlined the appearing of a prelinguistic goodness within diverse horizons of place. The description of this broadly defined "goodness" was not presented as a solution to the problem of evil or the burden of being human; instead, it outlines an integral part of the place in which we find ourselves—as such, it deserves to be a noteworthy theme for philosophical discourse.

Second, I proposed that a phenomenology of creation's goodness nuances and even challenges some of the conclusions presented by important figures in French philosophy. This aspect of the project was first evident in the issues I raised regarding Jean-Yves Lacoste's understanding of the "sacred." While Lacoste focuses on how a Christian theology of creation is distinct from atheistic or agnostic understandings of the sacred, I complicated his account by identifying how various horizons of place are entangled around a prelinguistic appearing of goodness (including atheistic approaches to sacrality). Similarly, I questioned Jean-Luc Marion's understanding of the binary differences between those who confess a Christian faith and those who do not. Not only do the differences he outlines fail to correspond with the mixed history of Christian praxis, but they also contradict several of Marion's own broader philosophical and theological positions—specifically, a prelinguistic goodness *gives itself* to the *adonné* regardless of one's confession of faith. And finally, with respect to Emmanuel Falque, I questioned his assertion that finitude is an adequate summary of what is first given and most ordinary to experience by outlining how a prelinguistic goodness is at play in the "event of birth" through feminist accounts of the mother's relationship to the child—an aspect of birth too often forgotten in the history of phenomenology.

Third, I suggested that developing a phenomenology of creation's goodness contributes to theological interpretations of culture. Part of this argument relates to the critiques outlined in the previous paragraph. For both Lacoste and Marion, I noted a tendency to place Christianity in opposition to contemporary Western cultures (perhaps an issue that is related to their experience as students in Paris during the 1960s and 1970s). While Lacoste helpfully explains how atheistic topologies (like the "world") are integral to being human, he overlooks how these horizons of place might also enlarge a Christian understanding of what is good about creation. With respect to Marion's work, I submitted that his assertion that the current "era" (in the West) is solely defined by nihilism is especially problematic. I outlined a theological reading of culture that integrates the ongoing presence of a prelinguistic goodness in a way that pushes back on the threat of nihilism. Creation's goodness is an integral point of reference for theological interpretations of culture because of its expansive appearing within a variety of cultures (I will return to this point shortly).

Falque's approach to Christianity and culture differs from those of Marion and Lacoste, since he explicitly seeks to avoid cultural battles drawn along confessional lines. In fact, his effort to identify common human experiences influences this study's emphasis on shared encounters with a quality of goodness. However, I raised concerns over Falque's tendency to focus on negative phenomena when describing what "makes mankind in modernity" (anxiety, suffering, death, absurdity).[5] By arguing for the appearing of goodness in that which is "initial" in experience, I sought to expand the range of phenomena one might emphasize in order to understand contemporary life. A prelinguistic goodness provides another productive starting point for thinking about what is held in common between people.

The effort to provide a nuanced reading of culture alludes to the broader purpose of this study—namely, to explain how creation's goodness is a helpful category for understanding the place in which we find ourselves. This purpose goes beyond the specific outcomes noted here and opens up fundamental questions related to the credibility of understanding one's place as a good creation today. The language of credibility is worth emphasizing, since it alludes to the idea that affirming creation's goodness does not require an irrational leap of faith or a naïvely optimistic disposition. Instead, it is possible to outline reasons for affirming the goodness of creation, which in turn engages with important philosophical questions related to the dynamics of phenomenology and hermeneutics, reality and relativism, as well as commonalities and diversities in experience.

One of the primary reasons I argued it remains credible to affirm creation's goodness is that *aspects* of it are widely recognizable in varying circumstances. Creation is good (in part) because it appears at a prelinguistic level that is not reducible to a confession of faith or personal status. It has a capacious presence. The phenomenological contours of *joy* uniquely disclose this expansiveness, since joy often appears in surprising circumstances that are not reducible an immediate cause. Joy even has the capacity to appear in the midst of intense forms of struggle and suffering. The phenomenological contours of *enjoyment* (joy of particular things) also disclose a prelinguistic goodness. Mundane encounters with a simple slice of bread, a cup of coffee, or the way snow rests on the branches of a birch tree can reveal a quality of goodness at play in experience. Because this goodness appears across various cultures and socioeconomic conditions, it offers a productive starting point for thinking about commonalities and differences. There is prelinguistic goodness that *entangles* various horizons of place and operates beneath language. Perhaps, in hyperpolarized contexts, one may even find more in common with someone who thinks differently through shared encounters with a quality of goodness than through extended dialogue. While there is never a guarantee that "goodness" will appear with a degree of commonality, some of the most simple and accessible practices (sharing a meal or hiking a local trail together) have the potential to cultivate a shared sense of place and experience.

Going beyond the prelinguistic appearing of goodness, I also identified some reasons why a specifically Christian understanding of goodness is credible. To this end I sought to emphasize coherence between the ambiguities of experience and a nuanced theology of creation. This coherence underscores the idea that adopting a specifically Christian horizon of place does not imply indiscriminately interpreting one's life in a way that contradicts appearances; instead, confessing creation's goodness affirms a wide range of experiences and affectivities (it does not diminish or overlook them). Theological knowledge, of course, is variously capable of challenging assumptions about the definitive meaning of one's experience, but this function is different than putting into question the naïve acceptance of appearances. None of these arguments translate into an explicit argument for the existence of God, but they offer some "depth and substance to imagining what it is like to believe and what new connections and possibilities are opened up."[6] Encountering one's place as a good creation should enrich one's experience instead of delegitimizing or circumscribing it.

It is important to acknowledge that trying to speak of a Christian concept of creation's goodness in ways that are credible is complicated and challenging in Western contexts today (for understandable reasons).[7] Western Christians, in particular, have not always modeled what it means to affirm the goodness of creation. One of the underlying reasons for this situation likely relates to the misappropriation of creation theology. Christians have a long history of using biblical references to humans being made in the "image of God" and having "dominion" over the earth as excuses for "unbridled exploitation."[8] In my Canadian context, this exploitative theology is evident in the abuse of the Indigenous people who have been caring for creation long before the arrival of Christians in the Americas. The Catholic Church's historical endorsement of the "doctrine of discovery" upheld a racist legal framework that implied land (or creation) already inhabited can be claimed by European settlers.[9] Another obvious example of misappropriated creation theology is signified by the substantial guilt Western Christians carry for the ongoing climate and biodiversity crisis. The immediate credibility of a concept like creation's goodness in contemporary culture hinges on Christians taking concrete action to care for a suffering creation and to address their historical and ongoing sins.

There is a growing body of literature in theology that counters historically misappropriated understandings of creation—especially in the context of ecotheology.[10] I have outlined a phenomenology of creation's goodness that implicitly supports this theological trajectory without making an explicit argument in environmental or theological ethics. Describing the appearing of a good creation (I hope) accentuates vital rhythms which make *all* life worth caring about. In a beautiful and haunting essay, Jan Zwicky advocates for attending "to the real, physical world, its immense and intricate workings, its subtlety; its power, its harshness, and its enormous beauty," in the face of catastrophic ecological collapse.[11] She argues that paying attention to these rhythms helps make it possible to envision a wider context of community and land.[12] And when we see ourselves as part of a broader context, it has the potential to awaken a sense of remorse over "our addictions and self-deception about our addictions" contributing to "the crashing numbers of wild animals, shellfish, fish, pollinators . . . the coastal communities losing their supplies of fresh water and homes."[13] While it may be overly optimistic to say that describing the phenomenology of creation's goodness can awaken a sense of remorse, perhaps it orients one to the "immense and intricate workings" of the physical world and gives logic to the idea that all vulnerable life is worthy of compassion and care.

Acknowledging the troubled history of creation theology is one of the reasons I have not situated this study by contrasting a theological concept (creation) in opposition to something like secularity. Too often, confessional Christian theologians presume that the best way to engage with culture is to point out its idolatry, while appearing to overlook the continual failure of the church and those who profess to be members of it. My concern with this issue is best represented in the second chapter, when I criticize Marion's assertion that Christians are the only ones with resources to address the problem of nihilism. Christians urgently need to face their own historical and ongoing sins before these kinds of scholarly critiques are appropriate: "Idolatry critique is first and foremost self-critique."[14] This does not mean that there is no appropriate context for theological criticisms of culture or that one cannot find Christians who are exemplary sources for positive sociopolitical change. However, especially with respect to creation theology, the disciplines of not casting the first stone and confessing the sins of the church (sin in which I am complicit) are essential.

At the same time, I have not argued for a despondent form of Christianity. I maintained that creation's goodness is a helpful category for making sense of the place in which we find ourselves. I sought to offer reasons to affirm its capacious appearing and argued that it provides an integral point of contact between diverse horizons of place. My hope, then, is that this book may be an encouragement to attend to the ordinary yet often surprising appearing of creation's goodness. Noticing it with regularity has the potential to animate an abiding affection for one's place, accentuate our reasons to care for it, and confirm that what happens in the place in which we find ourselves is of genuine significance.

Acknowledgments

I am grateful to the Australian Catholic University (ACU), KU Leuven, and the University of St. Michael's College in the University of Toronto for the support needed to complete this project. Thank you to the series editor, John Caputo, for including this book in the series. And thank you to Tom Lay for guiding me through the publishing process and Rob Fellman for sharpening the text.

Stephan van Erp's guidance and friendship have been essential to writing this text over the years. When the initial idea for the project took shape he was quick to see its potential, encouraged me to make it my own, and provided the resources to support it. Robyn Horner has been a wonderful source of ongoing scholarly and personal support. During the initial stages of this manuscript she patiently read through many drafts, sharpened my understanding of phenomenology, and helped me write with greater clarity and rigor. I also want to thank Yves De Maeseneer for being a meticulous reader of various drafts and supporting my research at KU Leuven.

I am grateful to Emmanuel Falque and members of the International Network of Philosophy of Religion for inviting me to present my writing at various seminars and offering insight and encouragement. David Newheiser also deserves special thanks for cultivating space for my research at ACU and responding to various portions of this text. The roots of this project began at Regent College and McGill University. Loren Wilkinson and Craig Gay helped initiate my interest in creation theology and philosophy.

And Garth Green generously supported my interest in phenomenology while challenging me to become a more thorough researcher.

I want to thank Brian Treanor, Lieven Boeve, Christiaan Jacobs-Vandegeer, and James McEovy for reading an early draft of the manuscript and offering valuable feedback. The research for this book also was supported by Darren Dias, Daniel Minch, Anne Siebesma, Anthony Atansi, John Bosco, Derrick Witherington, Trevor Maine, Lydia Shahan, Wilson Espiritu, Thomas Aquinas Quaicoe, Sarah Clarke, Alda Balthrop-Lewis, Rachel Davies, and Lexi Eikelboom. My parents and family also have been a source of constant support and encouragement while I developed this project.

The most important acknowledgement belongs to my wife, Kristin. She is my most careful reader and a constant reminder of creation's goodness. Her patience, encouragement, and love helped make this project worth completing.

Notes

Introduction: It Is Good

1. Richard Kearney, "The Wager of Carnal Hermeneutics," in *Carnal Hermeneutics*, ed. Richard Kearney and Brian Treanor (New York: Fordham University Press, 2015), 27–28.
2. Kearney, "The Wager of Carnal Hermeneutics," 48. Emphasis is mine.
3. Paul Ricoeur, *Freedom and Nature: The Voluntary and Involuntary*, trans. Erizam V. Kohák (Evanston, IL: Northwestern University Press, 1996), 94.
4. Christina Gschwandtner, *Postmodern Apologetics? Arguments for God in Contemporary Philosophy* (New York: Fordham University Press, 2012), 14.
5. Jean-Yves Lacoste, *The Appearing of God*, trans. Oliver O'Donovan (Oxford: Oxford University Press, 2018), 85.
6. If this approach constitutes a form of natural theology or apologetics, it would be an apophatically inflected instance in which I attempt to articulate an aspect of Christianity with clarity and credibility. While a broadly conceived definition of natural theology might very well incorporate this kind of project, such a claim would require a longer discussion on the historical development and definition of natural theology—something that falls outside the focus of this book. One might, for example, suggest that I am using phenomenology in order to open up what Walter Kasper describes as a "natural 'access-point' of faith." Walter Kasper, *An Introduction to Christian Faith*, trans. V. Green (New York: Paulist, 1980), 20. Cf. Anthony J. Godzieba, *A Theology of the Presence and Absence of God* (Collegeville, MN: Liturgical Press Academic, 2018), 43. Christina Gschwandtner has explored the relationship between the phenomenology of religion and apologetics at length in *Postmodern Apologetics*. She argues that authors such as Jean-Yves Lacoste, Jean-Luc Marion, Paul Ricoeur, Jean-Louis

Chrétien, and Emmanuel Falque offer a kind of "quasi-apologetic argument in their respective works." Gschwandtner, *Postmodern Apologetics*, 287.

7. Gschwandtner includes Paul Ricoeur and Michel Henry in her summary of what is similar in contemporary French phenomenology of religion. Gschwandtner, *Postmodern Apologetics*, 209.

8. Gschwandtner, *Postmodern Apologetics*, 209.

9. Ellen Davis, *Scripture, Culture, Agriculture: An Agrarian Reading of the Bible* (New York: Cambridge University Press, 2009), 45. Cf. Paul Ricoeur, *Interpretation Theory: Discourse and the Surplus of Meaning* (Fort Worth: Texas Christian University Press, 1976).

10. R. W. L. Moberly, *The Theology of the Book of Genesis* (Cambridge: Cambridge University Press, 2009), 43.

11. Othmar Keel and Silvia Schroer, *Creation: Biblical Theologies in the Context of the Ancient Near East*, trans. Peter T. Daniels (Winona Lake, IN: Pennsylvania State University Press, 2015), 1.

12. Keel and Schroer, *Creation*, 1.

13. Keel and Schroer, *Creation*, 4.

14. Keel and Schroer, *Creation*, 3.

15. Walter Brueggemann, *Genesis: A Bible Commentary for Teaching and Preaching* (Atlanta: John Knox, 1982), 37. Moberly also argues that goodness is not an ethical description "depicting the sinless nature of creation prior to the Fall or the moral dimensions integral to creation." Moberly, *Book of Genesis*, 43.

16. Davis, *Scripture, Culture, Agriculture*, 43. Most scholars agree that Genesis 1 is understood to be written by a Priestly tradition that "worked within a long, multicultural tradition of creation stories" while also maintaining distinctly Israelite features and even innovating within that tradition. Davis, *Scripture, Culture, Agriculture*, 43. Cf. Gerhard von Rad, *Genesis: A Commentary* (Philadelphia: Westminster, 1973), 27.

17. Davis, *Scripture, Culture, Agriculture*, 43.

18. Westermann adds, "The goodness of creation is based solely on God's authority; what it is good for, such as it is, only God knows. But because it is good in God's sight, joy in God's creation (as it is expressed in the praise of creation in the Psalms) is set free in human beings." Claus Westermann, *Genesis*, trans. David E. Green (London: T&T Clark, 1987), 11–12.

19. Denis Edwards, *Christian Understandings of Creation: A Historical Trajectory* (Minneapolis: Fortress, 2017), 96. Cf. Barbara Newman, "St. Hildegard, Doctor of the Church, and the Fate of Feminist Theology," *Spiritus* 13 (2013): 50.

20. Edwards, *Christian Understandings of Creation*, 96. Cf. Hildegard of Bingen, *Book of Divine Works, with Letters and Songs*, ed. Matthew Fox, trans. Robert Cunningham (Santa Fe, NM: Bear & Company, 1987), 1.4.59.

21. Edwards, *Christian Understandings of Creation*, 183.

22. William A. Dyrness, *Reformed Theology and Visual Culture: The Protestant Imagination from Calvin to Edwards* (Cambridge: Cambridge University Press, 2004), 65. Cf. John Calvin's commentary on Ex. 20:4–6 in *Complete Old*

Testament Commentaries, trans. John King et al. (Grand Rapids, MI: Eerdmans, 1948).

23. Elizabeth Johnson, *Ask the Beasts: Darwin and the God of Love* (New York: Bloomsbury, 2014), 37.

24. Keel and Schroer, *Creation*, 133–34. Westermann also pays close attention to this theme: "As long as the earth exists, every single one of the millions of plants must belong to its species as part of the organized whole. The most unprepossessing piece of grass or strip of moss is part of God's coordinated world; each in its own species fits into the ordered whole." Claus Westermann, *Genesis 1–11: A Commentary* (Minneapolis, MN: Augsburg, 1984), 125.

25. Moberly, *Book of Genesis*, 43. John Walton argues that "goodness" should not be associated with "quality of workmanship" but instead refers to "functioning properly." Walton's argument is (I think questionably) based on the principle that the next nearest use of the term (Genesis 2) should be normative for its meaning in Genesis 1: "It is not good for the man to be alone." Because there is a surplus of meaning in the term good, however, "proper function" is another possible meaning. John C. Walton, *The Lost World of Genesis One: Ancient Cosmology and the Origins Debate* (Westmont, IL: Intervarsity Press Academic, 2009), 50–52.

26. Catherine Keller, *Face of the Deep: A Theology of Becoming* (New York: Routledge, 2003), 19–20. See also Vitor Westhelle, "Creation Motifs in the Search for a Vital Space: A Latin American Perspective," in *Lift Every Voice: Constructing Christian Theologies from the Underside*, ed. Susan B. Thistlethwaite and Mary Potter Engel (San Francisco: Harper, 1990), 131.

27. Keller, *Face of the Deep*, 28.

28. David Fergusson, "Creation," in *The Oxford Handbook of Systematic Theology*, ed. Kathryn Tanner, John Webster, and Iain Torrance (New York: Oxford University Press, 2007), 78.

29. Moberly, *Book of Genesis*, 48–49.

30. M. C. Steenberg explains: "Gustaf Wingren, whose 1947 *Man and the Incarnation* was perhaps the key monograph in the renewal of scholarly appreciation for Irenaeus during the past century, claimed in his opening paragraph that creation must be the starting-point for understanding the whole of Irenaeus' theological reflection. This approach has been followed by many, and it no longer falls within the realm of creative or original scholarship to find in the writings of Irenaeus a creation-based theology and thought." M. C. Steenberg, *Irenaeus on Creation: The Cosmic Christ and the Saga of Redemption* (Boston: Brill, 2008), 2. Cf. Gustaf Wingren, *Man and the Incarnation: A Study in the Biblical Theology of Irenaeus*, trans. Ross Mackenzie (Edinburgh: Oliver & Boyd, 1959), 3.

31. Edwards, *Christian Understandings of Creation*, 39.

32. Edwards, *Christian Understandings of Creation*, 39–40.

33. Scholars relate Augustine's struggle with affirming materiality to the Manichaeism of his youth. See Colin Gunton, *The Triune Creator: A Historical*

and Systematic Study (Edinburgh: Edinburgh University Press, 1998), 74. For more on the complicated rendering of the relationship between Augustine and Manichaeism, see Mathijs Lamberigts, "Was Augustine a Manichaean? The Assessment of Julian of Aeclanum," in *Augustine and Manichaeism in the Latin West: Proceedings of the Fribourg-Utrecht International Symposium of the International Association of Manichaean Studies (IAMS)*, ed. Johannes van Oort, Otto Wermelinger, and Gregor Wurst (Boston: Brill, 2001), 49:113–36.

34. Gunton, *The Triune Creator*, 78.

35. Edwards, *Christian Understandings of Creation*, 66. Cf. Augustine, *City of God*, trans. Marcus Dods, in *The Nicene and Post-Nicene Fathers*, series 1, vol. 2 (Edinburgh: T & T Clark, 1887), 504, http://www.ccel.org/ccel/schaff/npnf102.toc.html.

36. Charles Matthews, "A Worldly Augustinianism: Augustine's Sacramental Vision of Creation," *Augustinian Studies* 41 (2010): 335. Cf. Peter Brown, *The Body and Society: Men, Women, and Sexual Renunciation in Early Christianity* (New York: Columbia University Press, 1988), 425. Cf. Rowan Williams, "'Good for Nothing'? Augustine on Creation," *Augustinian Studies* 25 (1994): 9–24.

37. Johnson, *Ask the Beasts*, 2, 181.

38. Martin Heidegger, *Identity and Difference*, trans. Joan Stambaugh (New York: Harper & Row, 2002), 70–71.

39. Merold Westphal, "The Importance of Overcoming Metaphysics for the Life of Faith," *Modern Theology* 23, no. 2 (April, 2007): 261.

40. Westphal, "The Importance of Overcoming Metaphysics for the Life of Faith," 261.

41. Heidegger, *Identity and Difference*, 55.

42. Westphal, "The Importance of Overcoming Metaphysics for the Life of Faith," 263.

43. Heidegger, *Identify and Difference*, 56.

44. Westphal, "The Importance of Overcoming Metaphysics for the Life of Faith," 263. Martin Heidegger, *The Question Concerning Technology and Other Essays*, trans. William Lovitt (New York: Harper & Row, 1977), 26.

45. Heidegger, *Identity and Difference*, 72.

46. Richard Kearney, *Anatheism: Returning to God after God* (New York: Columbia University Press, 2010), 53.

47. Kearney, *Anatheism*, 58.

48. John D. Caputo, *The Weakness of God: A Theology of the Event* (Bloomington: Indiana University Press, 2006), 75.

49. Anthony Godzieba, "Adventures in Chiasmus and Sacramentality: Merleau-Ponty Saves the World," *Louvain Studies* 44, no. 3 (2021): 278.

50. Emmanuel Falque, *God, the Flesh, and the Other: From Irenaeus to Duns Scotus*, trans. W. C. Hackett (Evanston, IL: Northwestern University Press, 2015), 22.

51. W. C. Hackett explains that Falque argues that the concept is historically inaccessible and that the "sources are themselves much more complicated than

the 'Heideggerian' philosophical narrative told and retold today." W. C. Hackett, "Translator's Foreword," in *God, the Flesh, and the Other*, xiii.

52. Jean-Luc Marion, "Metaphysics and Phenomenology: Relief for Theology," *Critical Inquiry* 20, no. 4 (1998): 573–74. Cf. Christina M. Gschwandtner, *Reading Jean-Luc Marion: Exceeding Metaphysics* (Bloomington: Indiana University Press, 2007), 9.

53. Marion, "Metaphysics and Phenomenology," 576.

54. Bernard McGinn, *Thomas Aquinas's Summa Theologiae: A Biography* (Princeton, NJ: Princeton University Press, 2014), 87.

55. Jean-Yves Lacoste, *Note sur le temps: Essai sur les raison de la mémoire et de l'espérance* (Paris: Presses Universitaires de Frances, 1990), 88.

56. McGinn, *Thomas Aquinas's Summa Theologiae*, 84. As John Webster explains, "Creation out of nothing is ineffable, not simply because of the grandeur of the agent or the magnitude of the act, but because of its incommensurability as 'the introduction of being entirely.'" John Webster, "Love Is Also a Lover of Life: *Creatio Ex Nihilo* and Creaturely Goodness," *Modern Theology* 29, no. 2 (2013): 162.

57. Westphal, "The Importance of Overcoming Metaphysics for the Life of Faith," 264.

58. Jan A. Aertsen, "The Goodness of Being," *Recherches de Théologie et Philosophie Médiévales* 78, no. 2 (2011): 281–95. Denys Turner, *Thomas Aquinas: A Portrait* (New Haven, CT: Yale University Press, 2013), 53.

59. Francis, *Laudato si' of the Holy Father Francis: On Care for Our Common Home*, encyclical letter, May 24, 2015, 69, https://www.vatican.va/content/francesco/en/encyclicals/documents/papa-francesco_20150524_enciclica-laudato-si.html.

60. Maurice Merleau-Ponty, *Phenomenology of Perception*, trans. Donald A. Landes (London: Routledge, 2012), lxx. Cf. Claude Romano, *At the Heart of Reason*, trans. Michael B. Smith and Claude Romano (Evanston, IL: Northwestern University Press, 2015), 6.

61. Merleau-Ponty, *Phenomenology of Perception*, lxxi.

62. Merleau-Ponty, *Phenomenology of Perception*, lxxi.

63. Romano, *At the Heart of Reason*, 5. Romano adds, "The 'descriptive' watchword refers to a description sometimes focused on the psyche (the early Husserl), at other times on an 'I' having a transcendental status (the late Husserl); sometimes on Being in contrast with beings (Heidegger), or on the body-subject and its modalities of experience (Merleau-Ponty), and at other times on a supposedly 'absolute' life (Michel Henry), on a givenness that operates beyond Being (Jean-Luc Marion), or on the event as opposed to the fact, and so on." Romano, *Heart of Reason*, 6.

64. Romano, *At the Heart of Reason*, 232.

65. Romano, *At the Heart of Reason*, 232. Cf. Martin Heidegger, "Die Idee der Philosophie und das Weltanschauungsproblem (Auszug aus der Nachschrift Brecht)," *Heidegger Studies* 12 (1996): 10.

66. Romano, *At the Heart of Reason*, 487.

67. Kearney, "The Wager of Carnal Hermeneutics," 16–17.

68. Paul Ricoeur, "Experience and Language in Religious Discourse," in *Phenomenology and the "Theological Turn": The French Debate*, trans. Thomas A. Carlson (New York: Fordham University Press, 2000), 130. As Gschwandtner explains, "Henry is emphatic in *Words of Christ* that Christ's words do not require interpretation. They are self-validating and self-authenticating precisely because of their immediacy that requires no hermeneutics of any kind." Christina M. Gschwandtner, "The Truth of Christianity: Michel Henry's Words of Christ," *Journal of Scriptural Reasoning* 13, no. 1 (June, 2014), https://jsr.lib.virginia.edu/vol-13-no-1-june-2014-phenomenology-and-scripture/the-truth-of-christianity-michel-henrys-words-of-christ/. Cf. Michel Henry, *Words of Christ*, trans. Christina M. Gschwandtner (Grand Rapids, MI: Eerdmans, 2012), 115.

69. Romano, *At the Heart of Reason*, 485.

70. Emmanuel Falque, *Crossing the Rubicon: The Borderlands of Philosophy and Theology*, trans. Reuben Shank (New York: Fordham University Press, 2016), 47.

71. Romano, *At the Heart of Reason*, 497.

72. Romano, *At the Heart of Reason*, 498.

73. Romano, *At the Heart of Reason*, 232–33.

74. Romano, *At the Heart of Reason*, 4–15.

75. Romano, *At the Heart of Reason*, 87.

76. Jean-Yves Lacoste, *Experience and the Absolute: Disputed Questions on the Humanity of Man* (New York: Fordham University Press, 2004), 7–8.

77. Abraham Olivier, "Understanding Place," in *Place, Space, and Hermeneutics*, ed. Bruce B. Janz (Cham: Springer International, 2017), 10.

78. Olivier, "Understanding Place," 10. Cf. Dan Zahavi, *Subjectivity and Selfhood* (Cambridge, MA: MIT Press, 2005), 4, 5.

79. Within the context of phenomenology, the language of topology is often associated with Heidegger's sense of "finding oneself" always "already 'there,'" in the world, in 'place.'" Jeff Malpas, *Heidegger's Topology: Being, Place, World* (Cambridge, MA: MIT Press, 2006), 6. Malpas argues, "The idea of topology as such appears only quite late and rarely in Heidegger's thinking. Yet a topological approach can be seen to underlie much of Heidegger's work both early and late. In spite of the shifts in his thinking that occur between the 1910s and 1950s, all of his work can be seen as an attempt to articulate, that is to 'say,' the unitary place in which things come to presence and in which they come to be." Malpas, *Heidegger's Topology*, 305–6. In Chapters 1 and 5 I explain in detail how a topology of creation differs from Heidegger's topology.

80. Lacoste, *Experience and the Absolute*, 102–3.

81. Lacoste, *Experience and the Absolute*, 103.

82. Brian Treanor, "Joy and the Myopia of Finitude," *Comparative and Continental Philosophy* 8, no. 1 (March, 2016): 8.

83. Treanor, "Joy and the Myopia of Finitude," 10.

1. Entangled Topologies

1. *Erfahrung* is the term Heidegger uses to describe experience as an "encounter." See Robyn Horner, "The Experience of Joy: Saturation and Non-Experience," in *Routledge Handbook on Phenomenology and Theology*, ed. Joseph Rivera and Joseph O'Leary (London: Routledge, forthcoming).

2. Throughout this text I use the French title when the book is untranslated. The English translations provided are my own. Jean-Yves Lacoste, *Être en danger* (Paris: Les Éditions du Cerf, 2011), 197. Cf. Horner, "The Experience of Joy."

3. Lacoste, *Être en danger*, 199.

4. Robyn Horner, "Is Anxiety Fundamental? Lacoste's Reading of Heidegger," in *Heidegger and Contemporary French Philosophy: New Yearbook for Phenomenology and Phenomenological Philosophy* (London: Routledge, 2022). Cf. Joeri Schrijvers, *An Introduction to Jean-Yves Lacoste* (New York: Ashgate, 2012), 158.

5. Thomas Sheehan, *Making Sense of Heidegger: A Paradigm Shift* (New York: Roman & Littlefield, 2015), 161.

6. Sheehan, *Making Sense of Heidegger*, 161.

7. Horner, "Experience of Joy." Cf. Claude Romano, *Event and World*, trans. Shane Mackinlay (New York: Fordham University Press, 2009), 148.

8. Lacoste, *Être en danger*, 198.

9. Lacoste, *Être en danger*, 198.

10. Lacoste writes, "*Mais lorsqu'il [joie] apporte son témoignage, celui-ci est sans ambiguïté: être-dans-le-monde peut s'entendre comme un 'bien-être' dans le monde.*" Lacoste, *Être en danger*, 199.

11. Lacoste, *Être en danger*, 199.

12. Lacoste, *Être en danger*, 200.

13. Lacoste, *Être en danger*, 200.

14. Lacoste, *Être en danger*, 209.

15. Lacoste, *Être en danger*, 253.

16. Claude Romano, *At the Heart of Reason*, trans. Michael B. Smith and Claude Romano (Evanston, IL: Northwestern University Press, 2015), 87.

17. Romano goes on to argue that interpreters of Husserl often miss out on the significance of a prelinguistic consciousness. Already in *Logical Investigations*, Romano notes, "The intuitive fulfillment belongs to our prelinguistic consciousness of the world. It resides in a 'sense' that precedes *de jure* its expression, and toward which our entire corporeal existence is polarized." Romano, *At the Heart of Reason*, 87. Moreover, with respect to Heidegger, he later specifies: "Heidegger breaks away from Husserlian conceptuality by holding that all manifestation of beings in general rests on an understanding of Being, as ontological character of *Dasein*; but he specifies right away, apropos that understanding, that it is both preconceptual and prelinguistic, since meaning, that is, what can be articulated in the explanation-interpretation (*Auslegung*), particularly in the form of statement, precedes its linguistic formulation by principle." Romano, *At the Heart of Reason*, 494.

18. Schrijvers, *Introduction to Lacoste*, 159.

19. Lacoste, *Être en danger*, 199.

20. Lacoste writes: "Anthropomorphism here is significant in the extreme. The observation made by the redactor is not that of a global equivalence between the created being and the good. It is about one moment and one only. And at that moment, the (created) being and the good intersect. They intersect, on the other hand, before evil (and with its history) has entered the scene. The Sabbath that the creator grants himself, once creation has been made, will be followed, once creation has been partially defeated, by thousands of divine interventions in history, 'with a strong hand and an outstretched arm.' There was indeed a 'time,' says the text, when there was solidarity and well-being. That time has passed." Jean-Yves Lacoste, *Thèses sur le vrais* (Paris: Presses Universitaires de France, 2018), 176.

21. Lacoste, *Thèses sur le vrais*, 176.

22. Enjoyment "does not engage us *as existents*," according to Lacoste, "or if it does, the existence it supposes is minimal." Jean-Yves Lacoste, *The Appearing of God*, trans. Oliver O'Donovan (Oxford: Oxford University Press, 2018), 121.

23. Lacoste, *The Appearing of God*, 120.

24. Lacoste, *The Appearing of God*, 120.

25. Lacoste, *The Appearing of God*, 119–20.

26. Lacoste, *The Appearing of God*, 120.

27. Lacoste, *The Appearing of God*, 120–21.

28. Lacoste, *The Appearing of God*, 124.

29. Lacoste, *The Appearing of God*, 124.

30. Jean-Yves Lacoste, *Le monde et l'absence d'œuvre et autres études* (Paris: Presses Universitaire de France, 2000), 20.

31. Lacoste writes: "Certainly, I cannot be satisfied with these breaks in which I allow myself to take my time in order to the taste the happiness of the present: enjoyment is only a marginal experience, and it can only be known as such. I can certainly taste this happiness without a bad conscience, with the impression of doing things that are not really 'my own.' God 'rested' on the seventh day of creation, says the Genesis text. We do not need biblical legitimacy to accept with gratitude that a little rest is available to us, that there are interruptions in our dealings with the world and the earth." Lacoste, *Le monde et l'absence d'œuvre et autres études*, 22.

32. As Robyn Horner explains, Husserl offers a broadly defined account of intentionality that includes feelings—since feelings always have "undeniable, real relation to something objective." Horner, "Experience of Joy." Cf. Edmund Husserl, *Logical Investigations*, trans. J. N. Findlay, vol. 2 (New York: Routledge, 2001), 2, §15a, 107. However, Husserl was criticized early on for this position, since there are instances in which it is difficult to associate feelings to an object of intentionality. Horner notes that Moritz Geiger critiques Husserl's assumption that feelings can be intentional: "first, because feelings are not (theoretical) representations; second, because feelings are usually bound up with bodily sensations; and third, because feelings tend to diminish in prominence as a

focus on their theoretical correlate increases." Horner, "Experience of Joy." Cf. Michele Averchi, "Husserl and Geiger on Feelings and Intentionality," in *Feeling and Value, Willing and Action*, ed. Marta Ubiali and Maren Wehrle (Switzerland: Springer, 2015), 71, 75.

33. Horner, "Experience of Joy."
34. Horner, "Experience of Joy."
35. Jean-Louis Chrétien, "Attempting to Think beyond Subjectivity," in *Quiet Powers of the Possible: Interviews in Contemporary French Phenomenology*, ed. Tarek R. Dika and W. Chris Hackett, trans. K. Jason Wardley (New York: Fordham University Press, 2016), 232.
36. Jean-Louis Chrétien, *Spacious Joy: An Essay in Phenomenology and Literature*, trans. Anne Ashley Davenport (New York: Rowman & Littlefield, 2019), 1.
37. Chrétien, *Spacious Joy*, 184.
38. Chrétien, *Spacious Joy*, 183–84.
39. As Lacoste emphasizes, most of the time "we live in a sphere of antepredicative evidence; 'living' comes before 'judging.'" He refers to living within this sphere of antepredicative evidence as a "spontaneous reduction." Lacoste, *The Appearing of God*, 44.
40. Jean-Yves Lacoste, "Phenomenology and the Frontier," in *Quiet Powers of the Possible: Interviews in Contemporary French Phenomenology*, ed. Tarek R. Dika and W. Chris Hackett, trans. K. Jason Wardley (New York: Fordham University Press, 2016), 188.
41. Lacoste, "Phenomenology and the Frontier," 188.
42. According to Lacoste, Schleiermacher's emphasis on sensation subordinates too much of Christian doctrine to the inconsistent feelings of the believer. However, he also acknowledges that the nineteenth-century turn to the "affect" may have been an important reaction to an impersonal, overly conceptual approach to God. Jean-Yves Lacoste, *Présence et parousie*, (Genève: Ad Solem, 2006), 19.
43. Horner explains that Lacoste associates several different kinds of knowing with *connaissance* and *savoir*—affective, nonknowledge, nonexperience, conceptual knowledge—and at times it is difficult to understand how the distinction is functioning with respect to each of these terms and whether or not it is consistent. Robyn Horner, "Words That Reveal: Jean-Yves Lacoste and the Experience of God," *Continental Philosophy Review* 51 (2018): 176–79.
44. Lacoste, *The Appearing of God*, 176.
45. Lacoste, *The Appearing of God*, 179.
46. Lacoste, *The Appearing of God*, 179.
47. Lacoste, *The Appearing of God*, 182.
48. Lacoste, *The Appearing of God*, 182.
49. Horner, "Words That Reveal," 181. Cf. Jean-Yves Lacoste, *Recherches sur la parole* (Louvain: Peeters, 2015), 58.
50. Lacoste, *The Appearing of God*, 183.

51. Lacoste, *The Appearing of God*, 180.
52. Lacoste, *The Appearing of God*, 179.
53. Lacoste, *The Appearing of God*, 181.
54. All biblical quotations are taken from the New Revised Standard Version.
55. Of course, the psalm here is not concerned with "propositional" and "intuitive" knowledge. Walter Brueggemann suggests that the psalm refers to a concrete historical situation wherein "a moment of rescue is remembered. But the speaker cannot refrain from instruction that counsels others in how to consolidate and sustain the new orientation, so this psalm has strong features of wisdom instruction." Walter Brueggemann, *The Psalms: A Theological Commentary* (Minneapolis, MN: Augsberg, 1984), 133. Allen Ross notes that the moment of praise in verse 8 is "designed to be edifying" and that the two imperatives (taste and see) are "figurative" ways of encouraging people "to discover the goodness of God by acting on their faith in the Lord, i.e., seeking him and praying to him." Allen P. Ross, *A Commentary on the Psalms: Volume 1 (1–41)* (Grand Rapids, MI: Kregel, 2011), 751–52.
56. Lacoste, *The Appearing of God*, 178.
57. Lacoste, *The Appearing of God*, 85.
58. Horner, "Words That Reveal," 172. Cf. Anthony Steinbock, *Phenomenology and Mysticism: The Verticality of Religious Experience*, ed. Merold Westphal (Bloomington: Indiana University Press, 2007), 6.
59. Jean-Yves Lacoste, *Experience and the Absolute: Disputed Questions on the Humanity of Man*, trans. Mark Raftery-Skehan (New York: Fordham University Press, 2004), 102–3.
60. Romano, *At the Heart of Reason*, 498.
61. Romano, *At the Heart of Reason*, 491–92.
62. Romano, *At the Heart of Reason*, 498.
63. Romano, *At the Heart of Reason*, 498. Romano refers to Nietzsche in this context: "There are no facts [no phenomena], only interpretations. . . . But this is already an interpretation." He cites his own interpretation from Friedrich Nietzsche, "Fragments posthumes: Automne 1885–automne 1887, 7 [60]," in *Œuvres philosophiques complètes*, ed. Giorgio Colli and Mazzino Montinari, trans. Julien Hervier (Paris: Gallimard, 1979), 12:304–5. For the English, see Nietzsche, *The Will to Power*, trans. Walter Kaufmann and R. J. Hollingdale (New York: Vintage, 1967), §481, 265.
64. Lacoste, *Experience and the Absolute*, 103.
65. Lacoste's emphasis on interpretation here underscores the degree of freedom we have to interpret our surroundings. I explore the role of freedom in Chapter 5, particularly as it relates to Lacoste's account of liturgy and topology. Lacoste, *Experience and the Absolute*, 22.
66. Lacoste, *Experience and the Absolute*, 17.
67. Jean-Yves Lacoste, *Note sur le temps: Essai sur les raisons de la mémoire et de l'espérance* (Paris: Presses Universitaires de Frances, 1990), 94.

68. Lacoste, *Note sur le temps*, 86.

69. Lacoste, *Note sur le temps*, 89–90.

70. Emmanuel Falque, *The Loving Struggle: Phenomenological and Theological Debates*, trans. Lucas McCracken and Bradley Onishsi (New York: Rowman & Littlefield, 2018), 205–6.

71. Falque, *The Loving Struggle*, 206.

72. Schrijvers, *Introduction to Lacoste*, 129–31. Cf. Lacoste, *Présence et Parousie*, 163, 313.

73. Schrijvers goes on to contend that in Lacoste's account "everything that is good and meaningful must be conceived of as creation" and that "all that there is to the world can only be the negativity of death and sin." He argues that Lacoste "leaps into metaphysics" because overcoming the world is its "ultimate goal." Schrijvers then proposes that philosophy (and not just Heidegger's) "is being *misused* as a preparation for theological discourse" by Lacoste. Joeri Schrijvers, *Ontotheological Turnings? The Decentering of the Modern Subject in Recent French Phenomenology* (Albany: SUNY Press, 2012), 45–46. Schrijvers does acknowledge that this "one-sided evaluation" is less evident in Lacoste's recent work, but he maintains that it "would be a mistake" to interpret this as a "rapprochement" between world and creation. Schrijvers, *Introduction to Lacoste*, 129.

74. Lacoste, *Note sur le temps*, 90.

75. Lacoste writes: "Our facticity harbors the double possibility of atheism and of the relationship with God, and it is impossible for us rigorously to assign to one or the other the dignity of a philosophically fundamental sense of our being. The atheistic enclosure of the self, the realized ipseity as relation of self to self—as aseity—are inscribed in what we are. And their contradiction by a theological sense of experience is equally a possibility that we cannot exclude transcendentally. At the basis is therefore for us an ambiguity, the inability to decide in favor of a univocal position on being, an ontological duplicity." Lacoste, *Note sur le temps*, 83–84.

76. Lacoste, *Note sur le temps*, 83–84.

77. Lacoste, *Note sur le temps*, 88.

78. Jeffrey Bloechl, "Introduction: Eschatology, Liturgy, and the Task of Thinking," in *From Theology to Theological Thinking*, by Jean-Yves Lacoste (Charlottesville: University of Virginia Press, 2014), viii.

79. Bloechl, "Eschatology, Liturgy, Thinking," viii.

80. Lacoste, *Note sur le temps*, 89.

81. Lacoste, *Note sur le temps*, 91.

82. Lacoste writes: "On the one hand, the worldly closure of time towards death, that is to say, of the time over which death has the last word, obviously authorizes non-being as the horizon of being and that, not belonging to ourselves . . . we ultimately belong to death. On the other hand, however, the joy of being certainly is not absent from the world." Lacoste, *Note sur le temps*, 90–91. Cf. Martin Heidegger, *Being and Time*, trans. John Macquarrie and Edward Robinson (New York: Harper Perennial, 2008), 358.

83. Scholars debate whether Heidegger's frequent references to the gods and divinities in his later writing is poetry, theology, philosophy, or somewhere in between. For a recent evaluation of this problem, see Rico Gutschimdt, "The Late Heidegger and a Post-Theistic Understanding of Religion," *Religious Studies* 56 (2020): 152–68. Cf. Ben Vedder, *Heidegger's Philosophy of Religion: From God to the Gods* (Pittsburgh, PA: Duquesne University Press, 2007); Peter S. Dillard, *Heidegger and Philosophical Atheology: A Neo-scholastic Critique* (London: Continuum, 2008); Benjamin D. Crowe, *Heidegger's Phenomenology of Religion: Realism and Cultural Criticism* (Bloomington: Indiana University Press, 2008).

84. Lacoste, *Experience and the Absolute*, 14.

85. Lacoste, *Experience and the Absolute*, 21.

86. Lacoste, *Experience and the Absolute*, 14–16. The sacred becomes a more explicit theme once Heidegger includes it in the *Fourfold*: earth, sky, mortals, and the deities. Cf. Martin Heidegger, *Holderlin's Hymn "The Ister,"* trans. William McNeill and Julia Davis (Bloomington: Indiana University Press, 1996); Martin Heidegger, *Poetry Language, Thought*, trans. Albert Hofstadter (New York: Harper Perennial, 1971).

87. Lacoste, *Experience and the Absolute*, 17–18, 20.

88. Lacoste, *Experience and the Absolute*, 35.

89. Robyn Horner, "À Saint Jacques," in *The Postmodern Saints of France: Refiguring "the Holy" in Contemporary French Philosophy*, ed. Colby Dickinson (London: Bloomsbury T&T Clark, 2013), 97. Cf. Emmanuel Levinas, "Desacralization and Disenchantment," in *Nine Talmudic Readings*, trans. Annette Aronowicz (Bloomington: Indiana University Press, 1990); Jean Greisch, *Le buisson ardent et les lumières de la raison: L'invention de la philosophie de la religion*, tome III: *Vers un paradigme herméneutique* (Paris: Cerf, 2004), 717–20.

90. W. Chris Hackett explains, "The fool realizes the eschatological '*distentio animi*,' as it were, all the way even to the point of a violent fissure within itself, dwelling 'on earth' as if it were already 'in heaven.'" W. Chris Hackett, "*La Nouvelle Philosophie* . . . : On the Philosophical Significance of Sanctity in Jean-Yves Lacoste's *Experience and the Absolute*," in *The Postmodern Saints of France: Refiguring "the Holy" in Contemporary French Philosophy*, ed. Colby Dickinson (London: Bloomsbury T&T Clark, 2013), 212.

91. Lacoste, *Experience and the Absolute*, 178.

92. Lacoste, *Experience and the Absolute*, 177–80.

93. Jeffrey L. Kosky, *Arts of Wonder: Enchanting Secularity* (Chicago: University of Chicago Press, 2013), 53. Kosky quotes Hans Blumenberg, *The Legitimacy of the Modern Age*, trans. Robert Wallace (Cambridge, MA: MIT Press, 1983), 132, 137.

94. Kosky, *Arts of Wonder*, 170.

95. Kosky, *Arts of Wonder*, 176.

96. Kosky, *Arts of Wonder*, 176. Kosky proposes that religious and theological readings of art are essential and contribute to "vocabulary" that "lets me

prolong the encounter with the work of art, deepening the event of its coming intimately over me and bringing its strangeness to light." Kosky, *Arts of Wonder*, 173.

97. Kosky, *Arts of Wonder*, 133.

98. The blurred lines between religion and secularity are observed across a broad spectrum of contemporary literature on religion. Cf. Talal Asad, *Formations of the Secular: Christianity, Islam, Modernity* (Stanford, CA: Stanford University Press, 2003), 187–94; Elizabeth Shakman Hurd, *Beyond Religious Freedom: The New Global Politics of Religion* (Princeton, NJ: Princeton University Press, 2015), 19–20, 109–11; Peter Berger, *The Desecularization of the World: Resurgent Religion and World Politics* (Grand Rapids, MI: Eerdmans, 1999); Jürgen Habermas, *An Awareness of What Is Missing: Faith and Reason in a Postsecular age* (Malden, MA: Polity, 2010); William Cavanaugh, *The Myth of Religious Violence: Secular Ideology and the Roots of Modern Conflict* (New York: Oxford University Press, 2009), 57–122.

99. Charles Taylor, *A Secular Age* (Cambridge, MA: Belknap Press of Harvard University Press, 2007), 595.

100. Taylor, *A Secular Age*, 15–16.

101. Othmar Keel and Silvia Schroer, *Creation: Biblical Theologies in the Context of the Ancient Near East*, trans. Peter T. Daniels (Winona Lake, IN: Pennsylvania State University Press, 2005), 1.

102. Lacoste, *The Appearing of God*, 69.

103. Lacoste, *The Appearing of God*, 135.

104. Bradley B. Onishi, *The Sacrality of the Secular: Postmodern Philosophy of Religion* (New York: Columbia University Press, 2018), 1–3.

105. Onishi, *The Sacrality of the Secular*, 18.

106. Onishi, *The Sacrality of the Secular*, 19.

107. Onishi, *The Sacrality of the Secular*, 19.

108. For further insight into a constructive encounter with secular culture through creation theology, one might turn to Edward Schillebeeckx. See Edward Schillebeeckx, "Secularization and Christian Belief in God," in *God the Future of Man*, trans. N. D. Smith (London: Bloomsbury T&T Clark, 2014), 31–54; Daniel Minch, "Our Faith in Creation, God's Faith in Humanity: Edward Schillebeeckx and Pope Francis on Human Transcendence and an Anthropocentric Cosmos," *Theological Studies* 80, no. 4 (2019): 845–63. Also see Lieven Boeve, *God Interrupts History: Theology in a Time of Upheaval* (New York: Continuum, 2007), 82.

109. Lacoste, *The Appearing of God*, 50.

110. Romano, *At the Heart of Reason*, 88.

111. Romano, *At the Heart of Reason*, 234.

112. Romano, *At the Heart of Reason*, 234.

113. Romano, *At the Heart of Reason*, 236.

114. Romano, *At the Heart of Reason*, 236.

115. Lacoste, *The Appearing of God*, 63.

116. Lacoste, *The Appearing of God*, 63.
117. Lacoste, *The Appearing of God*, 64.
118. Romano, *At the Heart of Reason*, 500.
119. Romano, *At the Heart of Reason*, 500.
120. Jean-Luc Marion, "In Defense of Argument," in *Believing in Order to See: On the Rationality of Revelation and the Irrationality of Some Believers*, trans. Christina Gschwandtner (New York: Fordham University Press, 2017), 18.
121. Marion, "In Defense of Argument," 18.
122. Richard Kearny, "Enabling God," in *After God: Richard Kearney and the Religious Turn in Continental Philosophy* (New York: Fordham University Press, 2006), 43.

2. The Givenness of Creation's Goodness

1. Sheila Greeve Davaney, "Theology and the Turn to Cultural Analysis," in *Converging on Culture: Theologians in Dialogue with Cultural Analysis and Criticism*, ed. Delwin Brown, Sheila Greeve Davaney, and Kathryn Tanner (Oxford: Oxford University Press, 2001), 5.
2. Kathryn Tanner, *Theories of Culture: A New Agenda for Theology* (Minneapolis, MN: Fortress, 1997), 36.
3. Jean-Luc Marion, *In the Self's Place: The Approach of Saint Augustine*, trans. Jeffrey Kosky (Stanford, CA: Stanford University Press, 2012), xiii.
4. Marion, *In the Self's Place*, xiv.
5. Marion argues that metaphysics "can be defined in an almost univocal manner" and that "it appears only relatively late, but with a clear definition." It receives its canonical sense from modern philosophy and falls under this definition: "the system of philosophy from Suarez to Kant as a single science bearing at one and the same time on the universal of common being and on the being (or the beings) par excellence." Jean-Luc Marion, "Metaphysics and Phenomenology: A Relief for Theology," trans. Thomas A. Carlson, *Critical Inquiry* 20, no. 4 (1994): 573–76. As Christina Gschwandtner explains, Marion's reading of the history of metaphysics and onto-theology is much more precise than that of Heidegger. She argues that most criticisms of Marion's approach to metaphysics fail to consider that "Descartes and Pascal are at least as (if not more) significant for Marion's project of exceeding metaphysics, in terms of both definition and procedure" than Heidegger. She states: "Descartes provides both an example of Heidegger's evaluation of metaphysics and a much more refined definition of it for Marion while Pascal functions as an example of how this definition can be exceeded and put in its appropriate place." Christina M. Gschwandtner, *Reading Jean-Luc Marion: Exceeding Metaphysics* (Bloomington: Indiana University Press, 2007), 9.
6. Marion writes, "In thinking 'God' as *causa sui*, metaphysics gives itself a concept of 'God' that at once marks the indisputable experience of him and his equally incontestable limitation; by thinking "God" as an efficiency so absolutely and universally foundational into itself, metaphysics indeed constructs for

itself an apprehension of the transcendence of God, but under the figure simply of efficiency, of the cause, and of the foundation." See Jean-Luc Marion, *God without Being*, trans. Thomas A. Carlson (Chicago: University of Chicago Press, 2012), 35.

7. Jean-Luc Marion, *The Idol and Distance: Five Studies*, trans. Thomas A. Carlson (New York: Fordham University Press, 2001), 16.

8. Marion, *God without Being*, 12.

9. Marion, *In the Self's Place*, 16.

10. Marion, *In the Self's Place*, 19.

11. Marion, *In the Self's Place*, 16.

12. Jacques Derrida, "How to Avoid Speaking: Denials," in *Psyche: Inventions of the Other*, vol. 2, ed. Peggy Kamuf and Elizabeth G. Rottenberg (Stanford, CA: Stanford University Press, 2008).

13. Robyn Horner, *Rethinking God as Gift: Marion, Derrida, and the Limits of Phenomenology* (New York: Fordham University Press, 2001), 158.

14. Jean-Luc Marion, *In Excess: Studies of Saturated Phenomena*, trans. Robyn Horner and Vincent Berraud (New York: Fordham University Press, 2002), 135–36.

15. Marion, *In Excess*, 139.

16. Marion, *In Excess*, 143.

17. Marion, *In Excess*, 24.

18. Marion, *In Excess*, 24.

19. Marion, *In Excess*, 30.

20. Marion, *In Excess*, 25.

21. Marion, *In Excess*, 26.

22. Jean-Luc Marion, *Being Given: Toward a Phenomenology of Givenness*, trans. Jeffrey L. Kosky (Stanford, CA: Stanford University Press, 2002), 322. Cf. Marion, *In the Self's Place*, 45. As Jeffrey Kosky explains, the concept of *l'adonné* has multiple meanings that do not always come through in the English rendering, "the gifted." However, the term primarily refers to the sense in which *one receives oneself* from that which is *given*. Kosky also suggests that *l'adonné* "should be taken in the sense of having a talent for . . . (for converting the given into the seen) but also as a substantive made from the passive form of the verb to gift. This latter sense is meant to convey that the self, too, happens originarily in and through a givenness in which I receive myself at the same time as and along with the given." Jeffrey L. Kosky, "Translator's Note," in *In the Self's Place*, xx.

23. Jean-Luc Marion, "The Saturated Phenomenon," in *Phenomenology and the "Theological Turn": The French Debate*, trans. Thomas A. Carlson (New York: Fordham University Press, 2000), 210–11.

24. Marion, *In the Self's Place*, 100.

25. Marion, *In the Self's Place*, 232. Emmanuel Falque, "Le haut lieu du soi: Une disputatio théologique et phénoménologique," *Revue de métaphysique et de morale* 3 (2009): 363–90. Jean Greisch, "Les lieux du soi: Vers une

herméneutique du soi-même par l'Autre," *Revue de métaphysique et de morale* 3 (2009): 317–35.

26. Marion, *In the Self's Place*, 231–32.

27. Marion, *In the Self's Place*, 233.

28. While Marion acknowledges that "one can obscure the praise and posit creation as an ontic commencement," this "ontic commencement" is not the fundamental concern of a biblical theology. Marion, *In the Self's Place*, 237.

29. In *Being Given*, Marion argues that both Husserl and Heidegger used the concept of givenness; however, neither one fully conceptualized its *originary* role in the appearance of phenomena. According to Marion, "Both are familiar with givenness without officially recognizing it as such." Marion, *Being Given*, 38. Robyn Horner further explains: "Heidegger and Husserl thus effectively reach the same point. Although they make use of givenness, they do not affirm it as the key, but instead focus on other principles: objectivity and *Ereignis*. Marion's solution is to link givenness with reduction, a reduction that would not delimit any horizon. Givenness would in this way become its own horizon." Horner, *Rethinking God as Gift*, 118.

30. Jean-Luc Marion, "Hermeneutics of Givenness," in *The Enigma of the Divine: Between Phenomenology and Comparative Theology*, ed. Jean-Luc Marion and Christiaan Jacobs-Vandegeer, trans. Sarah Horton (Switzerland: Springer Nature, 2020), 18.

31. See Jocelyn Benoist, "Qu'est-ce qui est donné? La pensée et l'événement," *Archives de philosophie* 4 (1996): 629–57; François Laurelle, "L'appel et le phénomène," *Revue de Métaphysique et de Morale* 1 (1991): 27–41; and Dominique Janicaud, "The Theological Turn in French Phenomenology," in *Phenomenology and the "Theological Turn": The French Debate*, trans. Bernard G. Prusak (New York: Fordham University Press, 2000). While Marion's reading of Augustine seems to make an important concession in the sense that there may be a link between givenness and creation, he insists that it is a decisively nonmetaphysical link. However, Joeri Schrijvers suggests that *In the Self's Place* reveals that the question of whether "the phenomenology of givenness was or was not a covert theology—has now, it seems, been answered by Marion himself. And Marion is to be applauded, of course, for not shrinking back from some of the equations that this book bluntly makes: yes, givenness can be linked to creation." Joeri Schrijvers, "In (the) Place of the Self: A Critical Study of Jean-Luc Marion's 'Au lieu de soi. L'approche de Saint Augustin,'" *Modern Theology* 25, no. 4 (October 2009): 679.

32. Marion, *In the Self's Place*, 243–44.

33. Marion, *In the Self's Place*, 248.

34. Marion, *In the Self's Place*, 249.

35. Marion, *In the Self's Place*, 235–36.

36. Marion, *In the Self's Place*, 194.

37. Marion, *In the Self's Place*, 237.

38. Marion, *In the Self's Place*, 234.

39. Marion, *In the Self's Place*, 234.

40. Jean-Yves Lacoste, *Experience and the Absolute: Disputed Questions on the Humanity of Man*, trans. Mark Raftery-Skehan (New York: Fordham University Press, 2004), 103.

41. Jean-Luc Marion and Dan Arbib, *The Rigor of Things: Conversations with Dan Arbib*, trans. Christina M. Gschwandtner (New York: Fordham University Press, 2017), 28–29.

42. Bradley B. Onishi, "Introduction to English Translation: Is the Theological Turn Still Relevant? Finitude, Affect, and Embodiment," in *The Loving Struggle: Phenomenological and Theological Debates*, by Emmanuel Falque, trans. Bradley B. Onishi and Lucas McCracken (New York: Rowman & Littlefield, 2018), xvii.

43. Onishi, "Introduction to English Translation."

44. Charles Taylor, *A Secular Age* (Boston: Belknap Press of Harvard University Press, 2007), 488.

45. In *The Rigor of Things*, Marion suggests that any "denunciation of the 'thought of '68' will remain superficial because, when it comes down to it, there was no single or coherent 'thought of '68.'" For more on his impression of the period, see Marion, *The Rigor of Things*, 9–11.

46. Marion, *God without Being*, xxi.

47. Marion, *God without Being*, 30. It is helpful to recall that Marion's first explicit engagement with the death of god is offered in *The Idol and Distance*. Marion notes that this first text was "was an occasional book, but it tackled a haunting or even stubborn problem, one that occupied me and many others for years—the question of the 'death of God.'" Marion explains that he wrote *God without Being* following discussions about *The Idol and Distance* at a conference held in June 1979. Marion, *The Rigor of Things*, 106–8.

48. Marion, *God without Being*, 31.

49. Marion, *The Rigor of Things*, 11.

50. Jean-Luc Marion, "In Defense of Argument," in *Believing in Order to See: On the Rationality of Revelation and the Irrationality of Some Believers*, trans. Christina Gschwandtner (New York: Fordham University Press, 2017), 14. This article was first published as "Apologie de l'argument," *Revue Catholique Internationale Communio* 27, no. 100 (1992): 12–33.

51. Marion, "In Defense of Argument," 15.

52. Marion, "In Defense of Argument," 28. For more context regarding what Marion means by another kind of reason, see Chapter 1.

53. Marion, *Being Given*, 35–36.

54. Marion, *In Excess*, 11, 13, 15. It is also worth noting that in *In the Self's Place* his sole reference to nihilism remains precisely in the context of an alternative reading of the self that cannot attain access to the self by the self—finding precisely the limit of the will to power. Marion, *In the Self's Place*, 168–69.

55. Jean-Luc Marion, "Faith and Reason," in *Believing in Order to See*, 8–9.

56. Jean-Luc Marion, "Faith and Reason," in *The Visible and the Revealed*, trans. Christina M. Gschwandtner (New York: Fordham University Press, 2008), 151. He also uses nihilism as a short-hand description for the current age in Jean-Luc Marion, *The Reason of the Gift*, trans. Stephan Lewis (Charlottesville: University of Virginia Press, 2011), 69.

57. Jean-Luc Marion, *Negative Certainties*, trans. Stephan E. Lewis (Chicago: University of Chicago Press, 2015), 1, 33, 29, 51, 112, 115, 207. As Christina M. Gschwandtner confirms, Marion's concern with nihilism "emerges much more fully" in his later work. Christina M. Gschwandtner, *Degrees of Givenness: On Saturation in Jean-Luc Marion* (Bloomington: Indiana University Press, 2014), 132.

58. Marion, *Negative Certainties*, 1, 37.

59. Marion, *Negative Certainties*, 33.

60. Marion, *Negative Certainties*, 33.

61. Jean-Luc Marion, *A Brief Apology for a Catholic Moment*, trans. Stephen E. Lewis (Chicago: University of Chicago Press, 2021), 58.

62. Marion, *A Brief Apology for a Catholic Moment*, 58.

63. Marion, *A Brief Apology for a Catholic Moment*, 65–66.

64. Marion, *A Brief Apology for a Catholic Moment*, 30.

65. Marion, *A Brief Apology for a Catholic Moment*, 57–58.

66. Marion, *A Brief Apology for a Catholic Moment*, 58.

67. Marion, *A Brief Apology for a Catholic Moment*, 58.

68. Marion, *A Brief Apology for a Catholic Moment*, 59.

69. Marion, *A Brief Apology for a Catholic Moment*, 60.

70. Marion, *A Brief Apology for a Catholic Moment*, 61.

71. Marion, *A Brief Apology for a Catholic Moment*, 60.

72. Marion, *A Brief Apology for a Catholic Moment*, 64.

73. Marion, *God without Being*, 180.

74. Marion, *God without Being*, 172.

75. Marion, *God without Being*, 172.

76. Marion, *A Brief Apology for a Catholic Moment*, 63.

77. Marion, *A Brief Apology for a Catholic Moment*, 63–64.

78. Marion, *The Rigor of Things*, 172.

79. Marion, *The Rigor of Things*, 164.

80. Marion, *The Rigor of Things*, 171–72.

81. Marion, *The Rigor of Things*, 28–29.

82. Quoted in the previous section. Marion, "In Defense of Argument," 28.

83. Tom Conley, introduction to *The Certeau Reader*, ed. Graham Ward (New York: Blackwell, 2000), 58. Cf. Michel de Certeau, "A Symbolic Revolution," in *The Certeau Reader*, 64.

84. Michel de Certeau, "The Weakness of Believing," in *The Certeau Reader*, 214–43.

85. Gschwandtner notes that Marion's strategy for combating nihilism in *Negative Certainties* is to affirm that the gift is "able to function as a response to contemporary nihilism." Gschwandtner, *Degrees of Givenness*, 132.

86. Jens Zimmermann, *Reimagining the Sacred: Richard Kearney Debates God*, ed. Richard Kearney and Jens Zimmermann (New York: Columbia University Press, 2016), 192.

87. Marion makes a similar point in *Negative Certainties*: "Indeed, the gift extends beyond the space not yet rendered economic, to that which can in no way become economic: the events of death and birth, which, at least for the flesh that I find myself to be, remain unforeseeable, unavailable, non-negotiable, unappreciable, unsubstitutable. Just like pain and pleasure, love and hate, confidence and despair, desire and fear—in short, all that without which I would not experience myself. This is given and happens, but is not exchanged, or shared, and even less so is it fungible." Marion, *Negative Certainties*, 30. For more on the potential of Marion's gift to escape the logic of economic exchange in relation to creation theology (and eco-theology), see the second chapter in Mark Manolopoulos, *If Creation Is a Gift* (Albany: SUNY Press, 2009).

88. Gschwandtner, *Degrees of Givenness*, 137.

89. Gschwandtner, *Degrees of Givenness*, 137.

90. Gschwandtner, *Degrees of Givenness*, 141.

91. Marion, *Negative Certainties*, 110.

92. Horner, *Rethinking God*, 246–47.

93. Marion, *In Excess*, 34.

94. Marion, *In Excess*, 30.

95. Marion, *In Excess*, 31.

96. Marion, *In Excess*, 32.

97. Marion, *In Excess*, 32.

98. Marion, *In Excess*, 33.

99. Marion, *In Excess*, 34.

100. Claude Romano, *At the Heart of Reason*, trans. Michael B. Smith and Claude Romano (Evanston, IL: Northwestern University Press, 2015), 498.

101. Marion, "Hermeneutics of Givenness," 39–45. Marion notes, "Thus I am in accord with C. Romano's thesis: '[. . .] genuine hermeneutics is phenomenology and phenomenology is only achieved as hermeneutics.'" Marion, "Hermeneutics of Givenness," 44. Cf. Romano, *At the Heart of Reason*, 485.

102. Marion, "Hermeneutics of Givenness," 39.

103. Marion, "Hermeneutics of Givenness," 39. Marion's emphasis on our limits to receive and integrate phenomena can be seen across his oeuvre. It coincides with his analysis of idolatry noted earlier but also with a much broader critique of the modern philosophical subject. For instance, he develops the concept of the *saturated phenomenon*, which challenges the formal conditions of transcendental philosophy. He asks what would happen if phenomena could appear "in spite of and in disagreement with the conditions of possibility of experience—by imposing an impossible experience." Specifically challenging Kant's categories, he asks, "What would occur phenomenologically if a phenomenon did not 'agree' with or 'correspond' to the I's power of knowing?" According to Marion, the Kantian answer is that the phenomenon would either

not appear or that "there would not be any phenomenon at all, but an object-less aberration." However, Marion imagines a situation where the eye "sees nothing distinctly, but clearly experiences its impotence before the unmeasuredness of the visible, and thus above all experiences a perturbation of the visible, the noise of a poorly received message, the obfuscation of finitude." The phenomenon suspends its "subjection to the I," inverting its relation so that the I now becomes constituted by the phenomenon, becoming a "me," a witness of the excess of donation. Marion aims to reverse the order of things, emphasizing our own modification, rather than the capacity of the subject to make appear or anticipate the meaning of that which manifests. Marion, "Saturated Phenomenon," 209–11.

104. Marion, "Hermeneutics of Givenness," 32.

105. One of the most persistent criticisms of Marion's work has been a perceived lack of hermeneutics in his phenomenology of givenness. Jean Greisch and Jean Grondin were the first to raise this issue and more recently, Shane Mackinlay, Tamsin Jones, Christina Gschwandtner, and Richard Kearney have pressed the issue. Mackinlay, for instance, argues that Marion's *l'adonné* does not leave enough room for "an active reception." Gschwandtner argues that Marion has not emphasized the degrees of givenness within his broader project and proposes that more emphasis on the "hermeneutic dimension" of phenomenology would address this issue. Jones argues Marion does not give enough attention to preparatory practices and the lack of criteria one might use to judge phenomena. Meanwhile, James Alvis has questioned aspects of these critiques by arguing that Marion's concept of the *adonné* maintains a degree of volition, specifically with an emphasis on the role of desire and love. While these are important issues with respect to the status of hermeneutics in Marion's phenomenology, my intention here is not to adjudicate the various critiques of Marion's work but to focus on how Marion's own phenomenology of givenness undermines his interpretation of culture and the differences he perceives along confessional lines. At the same time, I also aim to show that his phenomenology of givenness further refines the description of a prelinguistic goodness. Jean Greisch, "L'herméneutique dans la 'phénoménologie comme telle': Trois questions à propos de 'Réduction et donation,'" *Revue de Métaphysique et de Morale* 96, no. 1 (1991): 43–63; Jean Grondin, "La phénoménologie sans herméneutique," *Internationale Zeitschrift für Philosophie* 1 (1992): 146–53; Shane Mackinlay, *Interpreting Excess: Jean-Luc Marion, Saturated Phenomena, and Hermeneutics* (New York: Fordham University Press, 2010); Tamsin Jones, *A Genealogy of Marion's Philosophy of Religion: Apparent Darkness* (Bloomington: Indiana University Press, 2011); Gschwandtner, *Degrees of Givenness*; Richard Kearney, *Debates in Continental Philosophy: Conversations with Contemporary Thinkers* (New York: Fordham University Press, 2004), 15–32; James Alvis, *Marion and Derrida on the Gift and Desire: Debating the Generosity of Things* (Switzerland: Springer International, 2016), 45.

106. Marion, "Hermeneutics of Givenness," 32.

107. Romano explains: "For how could hermeneutic phenomenology bring phenomena, that is, 'what gives itself of itself' to light, by means of the most accurate interpretation, if phenomena, the things or the subject matter of the phenomenologist, are *only* given by means of interpretation? If we reject this distinction, if we maintain that the phenomenon depends, in order to appear (assuming that it appears), on a hermeneutic stage, we inevitably fall into a circle—a *vicious* circle, and not a hermeneutic one: the phenomenon in order to appear needs interpretation, but interpretation must draw its source not in inherited (or 'popular') concepts and theories, but in phenomena themselves." Romano, *At the Heart of Reason*, 498.

108. Marion, "Hermeneutics of Givenness," 33.

109. Norman Wirzba, *Food and Faith: A Theology of Eating* (Cambridge: Cambridge University Press, 2011), 2.

110. As Paul Helm explains, according to Calvin, "common grace is an aspect of God's providence by which, despite the Fall, he maintains human society and culture and restrains evil. Such grace, 'common' in the sense that it is universally distributed, is the source of human goodness and giftedness in people who do not necessarily experience the special or regenerating grace of God." Paul Helm, *Calvin at the Centre* (New York: Oxford University Press, 2010), 308.

111. Rudi A. te Velde submits that for Aquinas, "the word 'creation' does not immediately come into play when the natural world is considered in itself, as object of physical knowledge. It pertains to an invisible dimension of meaning and orientation which the natural world receives from elsewhere, from God who has brought the world of nature into existence for the sake of a goal which itself is beyond nature." Rudi A. te Velde, "Creation, Fall, and Providence," in *The Oxford Handbook of the Reception of Aquinas*, ed. Matthew Levering and Marcus Plested (New York: Oxford University Press, 2021), 644.

3. Transfigured Goodness

1. Brian Treanor, *Melancholic Joy: On Life Worth Living* (New York: Bloomsbury, 2021), 15.

2. Regarding his own work, Falque writes, "In reality, everything depends on the relationship maintained with contemporary culture, or at least with modern man as a 'figure of finitude.'" Emmanuel Falque, *Parcours d'embûchés: S'expliquer* (Paris: Éditions Franciscaines, 2016), 95.

3. Emmanuel Falque, "The Collision of Phenomenology and Theology," in *Quiet Powers of the Possible: Interviews in Contemporary French Phenomenology*, ed. Tarek R. Dika and W. Chris Hackett, trans. K. Jason Wardley (New York: Fordham University Press, 2016), 211–12. See Chapter 2 for more on how the cultural moment of 1960s Paris influenced Marion's work.

4. Falque, "The Collision of Phenomenology and Theology," 212. There is an important conceptual background to the cultural analysis here. Falque develops a particular reading of the "death of God," arguing that Marion's own

engagement with the theme fails to hear "the *double* echo of the mad cry of Nietzsche." Not only is God dead, but God *remains* dead, and such a statement is a direct challenge to the reality of the resurrection. Emmanuel Falque, *The Metamorphosis of Finitude: An Essay on Birth and Resurrection*, trans. Georges Hughes (New York: Fordham University Press, 2012), 32.

5. Bradley B. Onishi, "Introduction to the English Translation: Is the Theological Turn Still Relevant? Finitude, Affect, and Embodiment," in *The Loving Struggle: Phenomenological and Theological Debates*, by Emmanuel Falque, trans. Bradley B. Onishi and Lucas McCracken (New York: Rowman & Littlefield, 2018), xxii.

6. Seeking to take advantage of this newfound openness, Falque also founded Lien Inter Philosophé et Théologie (1996–2006), a group dedicated to breaking up the isolation between the various Christian institutions—spiritual, intellectual, and ecclesial that grew up in response to post-1970 French culture. Instead of simply being content with a role in the university, Falque suggests that this group openly pursued engagement across the culture in order to be informed and even "transformed" by their contemporaries. They sought "tolerance and differentiation" and aimed to not flee their own transformation by others. Falque, *Parcours d'embûchés*, 54–56. Working in this context eventually leads to Falque's controversial thesis: "The more we theologize, the better we philosophize." Emmanuel Falque, *Crossing the Rubicon: The Borderlands of Philosophy and Theology*, trans. Reuben Shank (New York: Fordham University Press, 2016), 25.

7. Falque, *The Metamorphosis of Finitude*, 34. Jocelyn Benoist, "Le tournant théologique," in *L'idée de la phénoménologie* (Paris: Beauchesne, 2001), 81, 84, 85.

8. Falque, *The Metamorphosis of Finitude*, 34.

9. Falque, *The Metamorphosis of Finitude*, 34.

10. Joseph O'Leary, "Phenomenology and Theology: Respecting the Boundaries," *Philosophy Today* 62, no. 1 (2018): 105.

11. O'Leary, "Phenomenology and Theology," 105.

12. O'Leary, "Phenomenology and Theology," 105.

13. Lucas McCracken, translator's preface to *The Loving Struggle*, ix.

14. Falque, *The Loving Struggle*, 3.

15. Onishi, "Introduction to the English Translation," xxiii.

16. Falque, *The Metamorphosis of Finitude*, 164.

17. Falque, *The Metamorphosis of Finitude*, 13. Falque is developing a specifically Heideggerian account of finitude here. He writes, "See §65 for the determining of finitude as a positive limit starting from 'Temporality as the Ontological Meaning of Care' (in particular S. 330), and §72 for the definition of *Dasein* as 'between' the two, caught between birth and death (in particular S. 374)." Falque, *The Metamorphosis of Finitude*, 158.

18. Falque, *Parcours d'embûchés*, 88. Emmanuel Falque, *The Guide to Gethsemane: Anxiety, Suffering, Death*, trans. George Hughes (New York:

Fordham University Press, 2019), 7–9. Emmanuel Falque, "Pascal and the Anxiety of Faith," *Louvain Studies* 42 (2019): 151–74.

19. Falque, *The Guide to Gethsemane*, 17.

20. With respect to the influence of Lacoste on his work, Falque proposes that "it is necessary to read Lacoste, probably above anyone else, in order to see and to understand the degree to which theology itself actually insists upon and does not contradict finitude as such (understood as the limiting horizon of our existence). '[T]he ordinary comes before,' Lacoste emphasizes in a critical methodological remark in *Presence et parousia* [Presence and Parousia], 'and only when we are capable of speaking of [the ordinary] in a sufficiently precise and subtle manner . . . will we also be capable of speaking of the extraordinary.'" Falque, *The Loving Struggle*, 196.

21. Jeffrey Bloechl, "Introduction: Eschatology, Liturgy, and the Task of Thinking," in *From Theology to Theological Thinking*, by Jean-Yves Lacoste (Charlottesville: University of Virginia Press, 2014), viii.

22. Falque does not question the Christian affirmation that God "is 'already there' in the world" but rather the idea that one might have immediate access to this knowledge. Falque, *The Metamorphosis of Finitude*, 13–14. While I do not question Falque's heuristic approach to finitude as a "pure nature" in this chapter, it would interesting to contrast Falque's account with the kind of analysis that suggests that God's presence is somehow available within the first givens of life. For instance, see Hans Urs von Balthasar, *Unless You Become Like This Child*, trans. Erasmo Leiva Merikakis (San Francisco: Ignatius, 1991).

23. Falque, *The Metamorphosis of Finitude*, 13. Falque then reinforces this position in *Parcours d'embûchés*, submitting that "a phenomenology of the resurrection should first of all be rooted in what is most 'phenomenal' in man and therefore most apparent. Finitude and the horizon of the death 'stamp' what appears to us 'at first sight, and the most often'—to use the terms of Martin Heidegger." Falque, *Parcours d'embûchés*, 87–88.

24. Falque, *The Metamorphosis of Finitude*, 16.

25. Falque, *The Metamorphosis of Finitude*, 16.

26. Falque, *Parcours d'embûchés*, 96. Emmanuel Gabellieri, "Entre 'vérité du monde' et 'vérité de Dieu', l''homme tout court'?," in *Une analytique du passage*, ed. Claude Brunier-Coulin (Paris: Éditions Franciscaines, 2016), 191–218.

27. Karl Rahner SJ, "Concerning the Relation between Nature and Grace," in *Theological Investigations*, vol. 1: *God, Christ, Mary, and Grace*, 2nd ed., trans. Cornelius Ernst (Baltimore, MD: Helicon, 1963), 298.

28. Rahner, "Concerning the Relation between Nature and Grace," 298.

29. Karen Kilby, *Karl Rahner: Theology and Philosophy* (New York: Routledge, 2004), 54.

30. Hans Boersma, *Nouvelle Théologie and Sacramental Ontology: A Return to Mystery* (New York: Oxford University Press, 2009), 98.

31. Falque, *The Metamorphosis of Finitude*, 16–17.

32. Matthew Farley, introduction to *Crossing the Rubicon*, 1.

33. Falque, *The Metamorphosis of Finitude*, 34. Cf. John XXIII, "Discours d'ouverture du concile Vatican II," in *Vatican II: Les seize documents conciliaires* (Paris: Fides, 1967), 587.

34. Falque, *The Metamorphosis of Finitude*, 3. Cf. Claude Romano, *Event and World*, trans. Shane Mackinlay (New York: Fordham University Press, 2009), 16–21.

35. Falque himself acknowledges that Romano's work provided him with "if not the impulse, then at least the idea of using birth to connect the *existentiale* of death and the significance of the Resurrection within a philosophically interrogated Christian framework." Falque, *The Loving Struggle*, 238. However, Falque also raises questions about whether the "weight of finitude as such" is "sufficiently accounted for" in Romano's work. Falque, *The Loving Struggle*, 239.

36. Falque, *The Metamorphosis of Finitude*, 129. Romano, *Event and World*, 1–23.

37. Falque, *The Metamorphosis of Finitude*, 131.

38. Romano, *Event and World*, 47.

39. Falque, *The Metamorphosis of Finitude*, 127. Romano argues that birth is a paradigmatic *large-scale* event that configures one's various possibilities in the world and reverberates over the course of life. One might look back on their birth and relate to it in a variety of ways over the course of their life. Romano, *Event and World*, 47.

40. Sarah LaChance Adams and Caroline Lundquist argue that "since women have largely been excluded from the practice of academic philosophy, their experiences have rarely found just representation in the canon. As a result, philosophy has a long history of ignoring, misunderstanding, reappropriating, and denigrating pregnancy, childbirth, and mothering." Sarah LaChance Adams and Caroline R. Lundquist, "Introduction: The Philosophical Significance of Pregnancy, Childbirth, and Mothering," in *Coming to Life: Philosophies of Pregnancy, Childbirth, and Mothering*, ed. Sarah LaChance Adams and Caroline R. Lundquist (New York: Fordham University Press, 2013), 1. I am focusing on the "mother" in this context, since "historically and culturally, women, mothers, and gestation have been profoundly linked," but I am not seeking to exclude transgender pregnancies or the rise in surrogate mothers—there are clearly important exceptions to the historically understood role of the mother. Alison Stone, *Being Born: Birth and Philosophy* (New York: Oxford University Press, 2019), 2, 9.

41. Florinteien Verhage, "The Vision of the Artist/Mother: The Strange Creativity of Painting and Pregnancy," in *Coming to Life: Philosophies of Pregnancy, Childbirth, and Mothering*, ed. Sarah LaChance Adams and Caroline R. Lundquist (New York: Fordham University Press, 2013), 302. Cf. Imogen Tyler, "Reframing Pregnant Embodiment," in *Transformations: Thinking through Feminism*, ed. Sarah Ahmed et al. (London: Routledge, 2000), 291. Christine Battersby, *The Phenomenal Woman: Feminist Metaphysics and the Patterns of Identity* (New York: Routledge, 1998), 18.

42. Falque writes, "Only a mother in the pains of her womb will be able to confirm that it was from her that I was taken . . . nobody knows better than she does that *I was born*, because it was *through her* that I was placed in the world, or phenomenologically 'thrown' into the world." Falque, *The Metamorphosis of Finitude*, 131.

43. Louise Levesque-Lopman, "Decision and Experience: A Phenomenological Analysis of Pregnancy and Childbirth," *Human Studies* 6, no. 1 (1983): 267.

44. Iris Marion Young, *On Female Body Experience: "Throwing Like a Girl" and Other Essays* (New York: Oxford University Press, 2005), 50.

45. Young, *On Female Body Experience*, 50.

46. Romano, *Event and World*, 144.

47. Stone, *Being Born*, 87.

48. Stone, *Being Born*, 85.

49. Stone, *Being Born*, 88.

50. Richard Kearney, "The Wager of Carnal Hermeneutics," in *Carnal Hermeneutics*, ed. Richard Kearney and Brian Treanor (New York: Fordham University Press, 2015), 28.

51. Adams, "The Philosophical Significance of Pregnancy," 11–15.

52. For a more detailed analysis of this "saturation," one might consider Marion's critique of the Kantian category of *quality*, wherein "the intensity of the real intuition exceeds all the anticipations of perception." Finitude, in this context, is defined not by the "given before our gaze" but by a gaze that cannot measure "the amplitude of the *donation*." Jean-Luc Marion, "The Saturated Phenomenon," in *Phenomenology and the "Theological Turn": The French Debate*, trans. Thomas A. Carlson (New York: Fordham University Press, 2000), 200–2.

53. Marion, *Being Given*, 289.

54. The affirmation of "goodness" most likely follows when a caregiver (usually the mother) meets the needs of a newborn following the event. However, if it is important to focus on that which is *most* initial to experience it might be helpful to recall that the relationship between mother and child even predates the event of birth. To this end, in *Event and World* Romano makes an important distinction between the *originary* and the *original*. The originary implies Heidegger's existential analysis of death as that which is "the origin of all self-authenticity and selfhood." Death, in the context of *Being and Time*, implies "a mode of *Being* of *Dasein*, in which it is related, through the ordeal of anxiety, to the uttermost possibility of the impossibility of the possibilities in which it is thrown from the outset of its existence." Stated more simply, death is inextricable from *Dasein*'s existence, and as such it is not like an event that "happens" from the outside. However, Romano's account of birth represents *"the original nonoriginarity of existence and mineness with respect to the impersonal event that is their condition."* Prior to *Dasein* realizing anything like its originary existence is an *original* existence that is by definition not originary. Romano argues that this introduces *"the original disparity between the originary and the original* that on its own introduces a rupture in the origin, a hiatus, an opening,

a fissure that will never be filled." Romano, *Event and World*, 19–21. However, I would interject into this issue by pointing out that there is something still *more original* to the event of birth at play between the mother and child. During gestation, there is already a substantial amount that is "happening" to both the mother and the embryo or fetus that is worth exploring further.

55. Falque, *The Metamorphosis of Finitude*, 104. Cf. Jean-Paul Sartre, *Existentialism Is a Humanism*, trans. Carol Macomber (New Haven, CT: Yale University Press, 2007). Maurice Merleau-Ponty, *Nature: Course Notes from the Collège de France (1956–1957)*, ed. Dominique Segland (Evanston, IL: Northwestern University Press, 2003). Hannah Arendt, *Condition de l'homme moderne* (Paris: Pocket, 1998).

56. Falque, *The Loving Struggle*, 195–219.

57. For instance, in *The Loving Struggle* Falque acknowledges that "anyone can identify" with enjoyment. He cites the popularity of Phillipe Delerm's *La première gorge de bière* as a good example of an experience that is "common" to humanity: "The first sip of beer is the only one that counts. . . . You drink it right away . . . and in that moment you already know, you've had the best part. You put your glass back down, sliding it away from you on the drink napkin. . . . By an entire ritual of wisdom and patience one wishes to master the miracle that both produces and escapes itself." Falque, *The Loving Struggle*, 219. Phillipe Delerm, *La première gorge de bière* (Paris: Gallimard, 1997), 31–32.

58. See Chapter 1 for an explanation of "propositional knowledge" in the context of Lacoste's work.

59. Falque, *The Metamorphosis of Finitude*, 7. Falque often uses the terms *transformation* and *metamorphosis* interchangeably. I describe Falque's theology of "transformation" rather than "metamorphosis" in order to emphasize its theological content. Falque touches on the distinction between the two terms himself in *Parcours d'embûchés*: "I propose that the 'metamorphoses of Ovid' and of the 'metamorphosis of the finitude' cannot be used 'in the same way,' since the first determines only progressive changes in the man and the second designates the definitive transformation of the man in the figure of the Man-God. One can easily go from the pagan to the Christian, but the homology of the term 'metamorphosis' does not imply an equivalence with transformation. The gap between the 'human metamorphoses' and the 'resurrection of the Lord' remains in reality unbridgeable, except by God himself. For it is not a question of 'transforming' or 'metamorphosing' oneself, in Christianity of course, but of 'being resurrected' or raised by another." Falque, *Parcours d'embûchés*, 89.

60. Falque, *Crossing the Rubicon*, 132. Cf. Emmanuel Falque, *Saint Bonaventure and the Entrance of God into Theology: The* Breviloquium *as a* Summa Theologica, trans. Brian Lapsa and Sarah Horton, rev. William C. Hackett (New York: Franciscan Institute Publications, 2018), 242–48. Falque does not go to great historical lengths to explain why Bonaventure's Trinitarian theology is a "monadology." A footnote in the Bonaventure text explains that

the Bonaventurian monadology is formulated by Alain de Libera in *La philosophie médiévale*. Falque writes that Bonaventure fuses Avicenna and Dionysius; however, the idea of monadology "enters theology more than it does philosophy for Bonaventure, since, to tell the truth, it makes absolutely no sense outside of the reality of the Trinity that carries it and sustains it." Falque, *Saint Bonaventure*, 120. Cf. Alain de Libera, *La philosophie médiévale* (Paris: Presses Universitaires de France, 1993), 405.

61. Falque, *The Metamorphosis of Finitude*, 83.
62. Falque, *Crossing the Rubicon*, 114.
63. Falque, *Crossing the Rubicon*, 114.
64. Anthony Godzieba, *A Theology of the Presence and Absence of God* (Collegeville, MN: Liturgical Academic Press, 2018), 280.
65. Rowan Williams, *Christ the Heart of Creation* (New York: Bloomsbury Continuum, 2018), xii.
66. Falque, *The Metamorphosis of Finitude*, 7–8.
67. Falque, *Crossing the Rubicon*, 115.
68. Falque, *The Metamorphosis of Finitude*, 88.
69. Falque, *Crossing the Rubicon*, 115. Cf. Falque, *The Metamorphosis of Finitude*, 115.
70. Jean-Louis Chrétien, *Spacious Joy: An Essay in Phenomenology and Literature*, trans. Anne Ashley Davenport (New York: Rowman and Littlefield International, 2019), 58.
71. Chrétien, *Spacious Joy*, 56.
72. Chrétien, *Spacious Joy*, 56.
73. Chrétien, *Spacious Joy*, 58.
74. Falque, *The Metamorphosis of Finitude*, 108.
75. Chrétien notices that the love of neighbor, for instance, is not disconnected from the practice of *contemplation* for Gregory. Chrétien, *Spacious Joy*, 56–58.
76. Falque proposes that transformation is "seen through its effects rather than an actual moment of transformation." Falque, *The Metamorphosis of Finitude*, 44.
77. Falque develops an analogy between the *event of rebirth* and the *event of birth* by appropriating several of Romano's central concepts. He writes: "What is true of birth, in the obscurity of the *act of being* born for the one who is born, is true also of the mystery of the *act of being reborn* for the one who is reborn. I experience only the effects of my rebirth, or my resurrection, and never the reason for it, nor the goal. It is not that my rebirth or my birth is without reason or goal, but that neither reasons nor goals (that is, my parents, my love for my neighbor, the search for blessedness or for God, etc.) are fully sufficient to justify it. Whether it was wished for or not, my birth (and rebirth) seems to me always *something for which I cannot take responsibility*, in the sense that 'it happens to me impersonally, even before I could begin to take responsibility for it in the first person.'" Falque, *The Metamorphosis of Finitude*, 129–30. Cf. Romano, *Event and World*, 73.

78. In the context of this quote Chrétien references Augustine in particular, noting: "Augustine's theological and mystical model long predates contemporary philosophies 'of the event' that develop similar approaches." Chrétien, *Spacious Joy*, 26. Chrétien has argued for this point at length elsewhere; see Jean-Louis Chrétien, *The Unforgettable and the Unhoped For*, trans. Jeffrey Bloechl (New York: Fordham University Press, 2002).

79. Chrétien, *Spacious Joy*, 26.

80. Rahner, "Concerning the Relation between Nature and Grace," 300.

81. Jean-Yves Lacoste, *The Appearing of God*, trans. Oliver O'Donovan (Oxford: Oxford University Press, 2018), 179–81.

82. Lacoste, *The Appearing of God*, 183.

83. Lacoste, *The Appearing of God*, ix.

84. Lacoste, *The Appearing of God*, 72–73.

85. Lacoste, *The Appearing of God*, 73.

86. Lacoste, *The Appearing of God*, 75. Lacoste makes a similar point by identifying another theological tension: "God gives himself to be known by giving himself to be loved, whether in the 'natural' or 'supernatural' order so-called, and love's response to love is never necessitated. To be able to agree that God exists, we must decide freely, and must make up our minds." Lacoste, *The Appearing of God*, 88.

87. Lacoste, *The Appearing of God*, 87.

88. The relationship between ambiguity and feelings relates to Lacoste's critique of philosophies of religion that use a concept of religious experience as feeling or sentiment in order to confirm the *presence* of God. Jean-Yves Lacoste, "Phenomenology and the Frontier," in *Quiet Powers of the Possible: Interviews in Contemporary French Phenomenology*, trans. K. Jason Wardley, ed. Tarek R. Dika and W. Chris Hackett (New York: Fordham University Press, 2016), 188.

89. Lacoste, *The Appearing of God*, 181.

90. The reference to "affective tonalities" refers to Lacoste's extended examination of Heidegger's *Befindlichkeit*. See Chapter 1 for more on Lacoste's account of affection. Lacoste, *The Appearing of God*, 30.

91. Lacoste, *The Appearing of God*, 180.

92. See Chapter 1, where I explain Lacoste's skepticism of philosophies of religion that rely on a concept of religious experience as sentiment or feeling (he associates this philosophical approach with Friedrich Schleiermacher and William James).

93. Lacoste suggests that as a "safe rule" one should "let propositional knowledge be the judge of intuitive knowledge to the extent that it is capable of it." Previously quoted in Chapter 1; see Lacoste, *The Appearing of God*, 181.

94. As Lacoste notes, "In the Bible (no less!) we frequently find love commanded ('You shall love . . .'), and commands are hardly calculated to arouse feeling." Lacoste, *The Appearing of God*, 95.

95. Love of one's enemies follows the experiential contours of the event here. Romano notes, "The beginning of a love, the start of a friendship, are always

already 'lost': once an event 'is brought about,' it is already too late; we are never contemporaries of its actualization and can only experience it when it has already taken place, and this is why an event, in its eventness, happens only according to the secret of its latency." Romano, *Event and World*, 47.

96. Merold Westphal, "The Importance of Overcoming Metaphysics for the Life of Faith," *Modern Theology* 23, no. 2 (April, 2007): 264.

97. Williams, *Christ the Heart of Creation*, 247.

98. Williams, *Christ the Heart of Creation*, 247. Cf. Erich Przyawara, *Analogia Entis: Metaphysics: Original Structure and Universal Rhythm*, trans. John R. Betz and David Bentley Hart (Grand Rapids, MI: Eerdmans, 2014), 314.

99. Williams, *Christ the Heart of Creation*, 243.

100. There are two different influences in the background of my claim here. First, there are Falque's comments on the importance of the credibility of Christianity. He explains: "I tried to find the credibility of Christianity, and I think the aim of Christianity today is not to convert others. Credibility is not only belief but is also the philosophical act of showing that Christianity always has a meaning for today. . . . It is first necessary that religion be credible, and afterward the question of believing in God is raised." Emmanuel Falque, "Embrace and Differentiation: A Phenomenology of Eros," in *Somatic Desire: Recovering Corporeality in Contemporary Thought*, ed. Sarah Horton et al., trans. Christina Gschwandtner (New York: Lexington, 2019), 88. Second, I am also influenced from the position Williams outlines in the preface to *Christ the Heart of Creation*, when he suggests that he aims to "give more depth and substance to imagining what it is like to believe and what new connections and possibilities are opened up" by reflecting on the language of doctrine. Williams, *Christ the Heart of Creation*, xi.

101. Bloechl, "From Theology to Theological Thinking," xvi.

102. Williams goes on to explain, "God and the world are not two things to be added together. Neither are they two things that are 'really' one thing. They exist in an asymmetrical relation in which one depends wholly on the other, yet is fully itself, made to be and to act according to its own logic and structure." Williams, *Christ the Heart of Creation*, xii–xiii.

103. Williams, *Christ the Heart of Creation*, 222.

104. Williams, *Christ the Heart of Creation*, 244–45.

105. Previously quoted in the Introduction. Francis, *Laudato si' of the Holy Father Francis: On Care for Our Common Home*, encyclical letter, May 24, 2015, https://www.vatican.va/content/francesco/en/ency clicals/documents/papa -francesco_20150524_enciclica-laudato-si.html.

106. Elizabeth A. Johnson, *Ask the Beasts: Darwin and the God of Love* (New York: Bloomsbury, 2014), 3.

107. Johnson, *Ask the Beasts*, 3. Francis adds, "Clearly, the Bible has no place for a tyrannical anthropocentrism unconcerned for other creatures. . . . By virtue of our unique dignity and our gift of intelligence, we are called to respect creation and its inherent laws, for 'the Lord by wisdom founded the

earth' (Prov 3:19). In our time, the Church does not simply state that other creatures are completely subordinated to the good of human beings, as if they have no worth in themselves and can be treated as we wish." Francis, *Laudato si'*.

4. Obscured Goodness

1. Brian Treanor, *Melancholic Joy: On Life Worth Living* (New York: Bloomsbury, 2021), 3.

2. Ian A. McFarland, *In Adam's Fall: A Meditation on the Christian Doctrine of Original Sin* (West Sussex: Wiley-Blackwell, 2010), 45–46.

3. Eleonore Stump, *Wandering in Darkness: Narrative and the Problem of Suffering* (New York: Oxford University Press, 2010), 3. Alvin Plantinga's examination of the problem of evil only goes so far as to claim that the "existence of God is neither precluded nor rendered improbable by the existence of evil." Alvin Plantinga, *God, Freedom, Evil* (Grand Rapids, MI: Eerdmans, 1974), 63.

4. Lucas McCracken, translator's preface to *The Loving Struggle: Phenomenological and Theological Debates*, by Emmanuel Falque, trans. Bradley B. Onishi and Lucas McCracken (New York: Rowman & Littlefield, 2018), ix.

5. Emmanuel Falque, *The Wedding Feast of the Lamb: Eros, the Body, and the Eucharist*, trans. George Hughes (New York: Fordham University Press, 2016), 119–20.

6. Falque, *The Wedding Feast of the Lamb*, 1, 21.

7. Falque, *The Wedding Feast of the Lamb*, 104–5.

8. Falque, *The Wedding Feast of the Lamb*, 24.

9. Falque, *The Wedding Feast of the Lamb*, 105.

10. Falque, *The Wedding Feast of the Lamb*, 25.

11. Falque, *The Wedding Feast of the Lamb*, 41. Falque's comparison with animals here alludes to a much broader theme in *The Wedding Feast of the Lamb*. He understands animality as an "ontological zone" of the body that operates beneath consciousness or language. Falque does not attempt to "spiritualize" evolutionary biology but instead uses animality to "clarify"—to the extent that it is possible—"how our well-being (or our ill-being) is rooted in life at the level of our most basic corporality." In other words, animality is *capable* of being life giving (or not), and as such it marks an ontological "zone" of the body embedded in a struggle for life. Falque, *The Wedding Feast of the Lamb*, 26–28.

12. Falque, *The Wedding Feast of the Lamb*, 40–41.

13. Falque argues that "the principle of entropy" does not allow us to forget that we are moving toward death—as such the material body causes us to be concerned with death. Falque, *The Wedding Feast of the Lamb*, 66.

14. Falque, *The Wedding Feast of the Lamb*, 18.

15. Falque, *The Wedding Feast of the Lamb*, 16. Falque capitalizes, shortens, and does not use italics with respect to the biblical reference to *tohu wabohu* throughout *Wedding Feast of the Lamb*. In a translator's note, George Hughes explains that "'Tohu-Bohu' is a Hebrew term found in Genesis 1:2, usually translated as 'formless and void' (or empty), or 'without form and void.' In modern

English, or French, it can also be used informally to mean a state of chaos or utter confusion." George Hughes, in Falque, *The Wedding Feast of the Lamb*, 3.

16. Falque, *The Wedding Feast of the Lamb*, 18.

17. Othmar Keel and Silvia Schroer, *Creation: Biblical Theologies in the Context of the Ancient Near East*, trans. Peter T. Daniels (Winona Lake, IN: Pennsylvania State University Press, 2015), 117–18.

18. Falque relates the meaning of the Tohu-Bohu to the following myths: "Sumerian (the primeval sea [*apsu*]), Chinese (the primordial chaos), or Egyptian (the primeval ocean)." Falque, *The Wedding Feast of the Lamb*, 16, 18.

19. Keel and Schroer explain that in "Psalm 74 (the Temple, a cosmos-constructing place, is threatened) and Psalm 89 (the Davidic dynasty, a cosmos-constructing historical power, is threatened)." The psalmists remind YHWH that "he did indeed act in creation in primeval times in order to defeat chaos in a mighty battle (Ps 74:12–17, 89:10–15). Why does he now give chaos free rein? Why does he not show the 'dragon' and his 'kingdom of evil' to the door once again?" Keel and Schroer, *Creation*, 148–49.

20. Keel and Schroer propose that the chaos of creation accords "a certain degree of freedom" by God and decenters Job's anthropocentric concerns. Keel and Schroer, *Creation*, 169–70.

21. Jon Levenson, *Creation and the Persistence of Evil: The Jewish Drama of Divine Omnipotence* (Princeton, NJ: Princeton University Press, 1988), 14.

22. R. W. L. Moberly, *The Theology of the Book of Genesis* (Cambridge: Cambridge University Press, 2009), 43.

23. Only after God separates the land from the water and organizes time through the creation of day and night does God affirm that "it is good." Keel and Schroer, *Creation*, 133–34. Cf. Claus Westermann, *Genesis 1–11: A Commentary* (Minneapolis, MN: Augsburg, 1984), 125.

24. Janet Soskice provides a good example of this position when she argues that the concept of *creatio ex nihilo* arose to preserve God's absolute freedom and implies that the "world is graced in its createdness, which is happening all the time." Janet Soskice, "Creation and the Glory of Creatures," in *Being-in-Creation: Human Responsibility in an Endangered World*, ed. Bruce Ellis Benson, Norman Wirzba, and Brian Treanor (New York: Fordham University Press, 2015), 155–58.

25. Levenson, *Creation and the Persistence of Evil*, 14–26. Levenson, however, also emphasizes the importance of "order" for the Genesis narrative. He writes, "Two and a half millennia of Western theology have made it easy to forget that throughout the ancient Near Eastern world, including Israel, the point of creation is not the production of matter out of nothing, but rather the emergence of a stable community in a benevolent and life-sustaining order. The defeat by YHWH of the forces that have interrupted that order is intrinsically an act of creation. The fact that order is being restored rather than instituted was not a difference of great consequence in ancient Hebrew culture." Levenson, *Creation and the Persistence of Evil*, 12.

26. Catherine Keller, *Face of the Deep: A Theology of Becoming* (New York: Routledge, 2003), 50.

27. Falque alludes to a middle ground where the "ambiguity of the *de nihilo*" in Augustine's Latin can mean both "God created starting from (*ex*) nothing" as well as "God created with (*de*) the nothingness." Falque, *The Wedding Feast of the Lamb*, 16–17. Cf. Jean-Luc Marion, *In the Self's Place: The Approach of Saint Augustine*, trans. Jeffrey Kosky (Stanford, CA: Stanford University Press, 2012), 246.

28. Ian A. McFarland argues that one of the primary "theological trajectories" shaping Western doctrines of the Fall stretches "back to the earliest periods of Christian theological reflection"—namely, why do human beings suffer? McFarland, *In Adam's Fall*, 45–46.

29. James K. A. Smith, "What Stands in the Fall? A Philosophical Exploration," in *Evolution and the Fall*, ed. William T. Cavanaugh and James K. A. Smith (Grand Rapids, MI: Eerdmans, 2017), 49–50. More precisely, the doctrine of original sin is "an attempt to come to terms with an origin that is double: totally good, because it comes from God, but somehow corrupted, and thereby drawing on another origin that cannot, nevertheless, exceed the first." Robyn Horner, "Problème du mal et péché des origines," *Recherches de Science Religieuse* 90, no. 1 (2002): 63 (the unpublished English version of the text was provided by the author).

30. Scholars like Richard Cross and David Albert Jones make the connection between biological death and the loss of an additional gift of immortality through original sin in the work of Aquinas. Richard Cross, "Aquinas on Physical Impairment: Human Nature and Original Sin," *Harvard Theological Review* 110, no. 3 (July 2017): 329. David Albert Jones, *Approaching the End: A Theological Exploration of Death and Dying* (Oxford: Oxford University Press, 2007), 114–15. However, the relationship between biological death and original sin in Aquinas is less clear according to Angus Brook. He argues that Aquinas does not claim that "death is unnatural, but rather, that original justice perfected human nature in such a way that death was not necessary for humans. With the loss of original justice and the weakening of the will, there is a corresponding disordering of the powers of human nature. It is this disordering of the soul more than anything else which subjects humans to death inasmuch as a disordered soul tends more to a lack of self-rule and ordering, self-destructive actions, and equally, in a community of disordered souls, to death by external violence." Angus Brook, "Thomas Aquinas on Effects of Original Sin: A Philosophical Analysis," *Heythrop Journal* 59, no. 4 (2018): 727. Aquinas himself writes in the *Summa Theologiae*: "When God first made the human being he conferred on him the favour of being exempt from the necessity resulting from such matter. However, this favour was withdrawn due to the sin of the first parents. Accordingly death is both natural on account of a condition attaching to matter, and a punishment on account of the loss of the Divine gift preserving the human being from death." Thomas Aquinas, *Summa Theologiae*, trans. Fathers of the English Dominican Province (New York:

Benziger Bros., 1947), II–II, q 164. 1 A.D. 1, https://www.ccel.org/a/aquinas/summa/home.html.

31. Celia Deane-Drummond, "In Adam All Die? Questions at the Boundary of Niche Construction, Community Evolution, and Original Sin," in *Evolution and the Fall*, ed. William T. Cavanaugh and James K. A. Smith (Grand Rapids, MI: Eerdmans, 2017), 26.

32. J. R. Middleton, "Reading Genesis 3 Attentive to Human Evolution: Beyond Concordism and Non-Overlapping Magisteria," in *Evolution and the Fall*, ed. William T. Cavanaugh and James K. A. Smith (Grand Rapids, MI: Eerdmans, 2017), 67–69.

33. For example, David Bentley Hart writes: "The very notion of an 'inherited guilt' is a logical absurdity, rather on the order of a 'square circle.' All that the doctrine can truly be taken to assert, speaking logically, is that God willfully imputes to innocent creatures a guilt they can never have really contracted, out of what from any sane perspective can only be called malice." David Bentley Hart, *That All Shall Be Saved: Heaven, Hell, and Universal Salvation* (New Haven, CT: Yale University Pres, 2019), 75.

34. Emmanuel Falque, *The Guide to Gethsemane: Anxiety, Suffering, Death*, trans. George Hughes (New York: Fordham University Press, 2019), 23.

35. Falque, *The Guide to Gethsemane*, 23–24. Falque acknowledges that his more existential position runs counter to the *Catechism of the Catholic Church*'s statements on original sin. But he submits that there is room for differing interpretations based on the *French Bishops' Catechism for Adults* if one is able to "read the lines." Falque, *The Guide to Gethsemane*, 11, 120.

36. Middleton, "Reading Genesis 3," 79.

37. Middleton, "Reading Genesis 3," 79.

38. Danielle Shroyer offers a compelling case against associating creation's goodness with a concept of *perfection*. She contends, "God designed the world to develop and function in a certain way, while allowing for creation to live freely into its potential." Danielle Shroyer, *Original Blessing: Putting Sin in Its Rightful Place* (Minneapolis, MN: Fortress, 2016), 67.

39. As Brian Treanor explains, death often appears as an "offense, in part, because every death is the loss of an entire world—constellations of love and intimacy, imagination and meaning, hopes and dreams." Treanor, *Melancholic Joy*, 2.

40. As noted in the Introduction to this study, David Fergusson argues that Genesis 1 clearly intends to describe the ongoing goodness of creation—not something that is to be associated with a prelapsarian world. I clearly adopt a similar position. David Fergusson, "Creation," in *The Oxford Handbook of Systematic Theology*, ed. Kathryn Tanner, John Webster, and Iain Torrance (New York: Oxford University Press, 2007), 78.

41. Falque only mentions this in passing and promises to develop it in a future text: *Le mystère de l'iniquité*. See Emmanuel Falque, *Parcours d'embûches: S'expliquer* (Paris: Éditions Franciscaines, 2016), 49.

42. Falque, *Parcours d'embûchés*, 49. Falque also relates the "struggle" more positively to love. See Falque, *The Loving Struggle*, 6; Falque, *The Wedding Feast of the Lamb*, 158.

43. Alison Stone also argues that the "negative aspect" of birth is integral to the "positive aspect," since "to be born is to come into the world and thereby become susceptible to various harms, but concomitantly to become able to enter into enriching, empowering, and rewarding relationships and endeavours of many kinds." Alison Stone, *Being Born: Birth and Philosophy* (New York: Oxford University Press, 2019), 70.

44. Recalling his struggle with cancer, Christian Wiman submits that all the beauty and goodness in the world does not mean much "when some pain is tearing your heart in two. . . . One considers the meaning of suffering only when one is not actually suffering." Christian Wiman, "The Cancer Chair," *Harper's Magazine*, February 2020, https://harpers.org/archive/2020/02/the-cancer-chair/.

45. Emmanuel Falque, "Toward an Ethics of the Spread Body," in *Somatic Desire: Recovering Corporeality in Contemporary Thought*, ed. Sarah Horton et al., trans. Christina Gschwandtner (New York: Lexington, 2019). Gschwandtner offers a translator's note on the language of a "splayed" or "spread body." She writes, "The French term 'épandu' can mean 'stretched out,' 'spread out,' 'splayed out' (as on a bed), 'expanded' (over an entire area), or even 'extended' (as in water covering a flooded plain)." Gschwandtner, in Falque, "Toward an Ethics of the Spread Body," 112.

46. Falque, "Toward an Ethics of the Spread Body," 91–92. Falque's emphasis on silence here repeats an earlier intuition in which he proposes: "Let all discourse cease and let pain speak: that should probably be the first, and the most compelling, commandment of a 'phenomenology of suffering.'" Falque, *The Guide to Gethsemane*, 88.

47. Falque, "Toward an Ethics of the Spread Body," 99. Elsewhere, Falque also acknowledges that some approaches to suffering may be more helpful than others depending on the circumstances—for instance, one person might find suffering to be cathartic, but this particular experience cannot be used to normalize suffering and will not be helpful in every instance. Falque, *The Guide to Gethsemane*, 105.

48. Falque proposes that Merleau-Ponty laid out a "vision for philosophy" in his later work that he never had the opportunity to explore fully because of his untimely death. As a result, it now "falls upon us to take up his project and to strive to achieve it." Falque, *The Loving Struggle*, 45. Cf. Maurice Merleau-Ponty, "La nature ou le monde de silence," in *Maurice Merleau-Ponty*, ed. Emmanuel de Saint-Aubert (Paris: Herman, 2008), 53.

49. Falque, *The Loving Struggle*, 54.

50. Falque, "Toward an Ethics of the Spread Body," 112.

51. Falque, "Toward an Ethics of the Spread Body," 96.

52. Falque, "Toward an Ethics of the Spread Body," 104.

53. Emmanuel Falque, "Evil and Finitude," in *Evil, Fallenness, and Finitude*, ed. Bruce Ellis Benson and B. Keith Putt (Cham: Palgrave Macmillan, 2017), 89. Cf. Emmanuel Levinas, *Existence and Existents*, trans. Alphonso Lingis (Pittsburgh, PA: Duquesne University Press, 2001).

54. Falque, *Evil and Finitude*, 90; emphasis added. Levinas writes: "My being doubles with a *having*; I am *encumbered by myself*. And this is *material existence*. . . . To understand the body starting with its materiality . . . is to reduce it to an ontological event." Emmanuel Levinas, *Time and the Other*, trans. Richard A. Cohen (Pittsburgh, PA: Duquesne University Press, 1987), 56; emphasis added by Falque.

55. Wiman, "The Cancer Chair."

56. Drew Leder, *The Absent Body* (Chicago: University of Chicago Press, 1990), 83.

57. Leder, *The Absent Body*, 83. See also Martin Heidegger, *Being and Time*, trans. John Macquarrie and Edward Robinson (New York: Harper Perennial, 2008), 95–107.

58. Leder, *The Absent Body*, 103, 76.

59. Leder, *The Absent Body*, 76.

60. Leder, *The Absent Body*, 82.

61. I explain the distinction between joy and enjoyment in Chapter 1. Lacoste argues that *joy* is an existentially significant experience associated with Heidegger's account of *Befindlichkeit*, whereas *enjoyment* is related to particular things like reading a good book or discovering an old friend. I argued joy and enjoyment are closer than Lacoste seems to acknowledge, but my central point was that they are both experiences that introduce one to a prelinguistic quality of "goodness" associated with the first chapter of Genesis.

62. Claude Romano, *At the Heart of Reason*, trans. Michael B. Smith and Claude Romano (Evanston, IL: Northwestern University Press, 2015), 87.

63. Claude Romano, *Event and World*, trans. Shane Mackinlay (New York: Fordham University Press, 2009), 40.

64. Romano, *Event and World*, 40.

65. Romano, *Event and World*, 41.

66. Romano, *Event and World*, 41–42.

67. Romano, *Event and World*, 178.

68. Romano, *Event and World*, 178.

69. Iris Marion Young, *On Female Body Experience: "Throwing Like a Girl" and Other Essays* (New York: Oxford University Press, 2005), 156–61.

70. Young, *On Female Body Experience*, 162.

71. Young explains: "He had no space in which he could array and store some of the meaningful things of his life. Even if he had more space, he would not have wanted his things, because he had no privacy in which to enjoy them. He did not want some of his paintings hanging on the wall across from his bed and chair, because the ever changing roommates would gaze upon them as much as he. The staff would likely come in and cheerfully start conversation

about them that he would have to answer. He rejected the idea of having a locked box under his bed with some important mementos of his life, because he would not have the opportunity to look through them undisturbed. He would not have been able to share the stories they carried for his life with a few privileged visitors without allowing the strangers in his room to partake of them as well. The things that had meaning in his cottage as the materialization of his achievements and relationships would have lost their meaning in such a public and anonymous space. So he preferred not to have them." Young, *On Female Body Experience*, 162.

72. Thomas Sheehan, *Making Sense of Heidegger: A Paradigm Shift* (New York: Roman & Littlefield, 2015), 161.

73. Jack Gilbert, "A Brief for the Defense," in *Refusing Heaven* (New York: Knopf, 2005), 3. Cf. Christian Wiman, "Still Wilderness," *American Scholar*, Autumn 2017, 45. Chrétien observes a similar point when he suggests that people who work in medicine can attest to the excessive beauty of a smile that transfigures "the face of people suffering grave illness, or whose illness has devastated their features." Jean-Louis Chrétien, *The Unforgettable and the Unhoped For*, trans. Jeffrey Bloechl (New York: Fordham University Press, 2002), 122.

74. Andrew Prevot, *Thinking Prayer: Theology and Spirituality amidst the Crisis of Modernity* (Notre Dame, IN: University of Notre Dame Press, 2015), 298–304. Cf. James Cone, *The Spirituals and the Blues: An Interpretation* (Maryknoll, NY: Orbis, 2008), 44.

75. Francis, *Laudato si' of the Holy Father Francis: On Care for Our Common Home*, encyclical letter, May 24, 2015, https://www.vatican.va/content/francesco/en/encyclicals/documents/papa-francesco_20150524_enciclica-laudato-si.html.

76. Falque writes, "But what lay behind my reading of the Gospels here was something that was all the more crucial in that it happened so suddenly: the unbearable coincidence of the accidental death of one friend, and the suicide of another." Falque, *The Guide to Gethsemane*, xxxi.

77. Johnson argues that "over the centuries for a variety of reasons . . . theology narrowed its interests to focus on human beings almost exclusively. Our special identity, capacities, roles, sinfulness, and need for salvation became the all-consuming interest. The result was a powerful anthropocentric paradigm in theology that shaped every aspect of endeavor." Elizabeth A. Johnson, *Ask the Beasts: Darwin and the God of Love* (New York: Bloomsbury, 2014), 2.

78. Falque, *The Guide to Gethsemane*, 98.

79. Falque, *The Guide to Gethsemane*, 98.

80. Falque, *The Guide to Gethsemane*, 98.

81. Falque, *The Guide to Gethsemane*, 106. Cf. Hans Urs von Balthasar, *Unless You Become Like This Child*, trans. Erasmo Leiva-Merikakis (San Francisco: Ignatius, 1991), 7. The association between tears and children alludes to a description of extreme suffering by Levinas in *Time and the Other*: "This is

not just in the instant of suffering where, backed against being, I still grasp it and am still the subject of suffering, but in the crying and sobbing toward which suffering is inverted. Where suffering attains its purity, where there is no longer anything between us and it, the supreme responsibility of this extreme assumption turns into supreme irresponsibility, into infancy." Levinas, *Time and the Other*, 72.

82. Falque, *The Guide to Gethsemane*, 99.

83. Falque, *The Guide to Gethsemane*, 101. Christian Wiman helps explain that the Christian sense of becoming like a child does not imply that "you must shuck all knowledge and revert to an innocence—or, worse, a state of helpless dependence—that you have lost or outgrown. The operative word in the injunction is *become*. (The Greek word is *strepho*, which is probably more accurately translated as 'convert,' a word that suggests an element of will and maturation)." Christian Wiman, "I Will Love You in Summertime," *American Scholar*, February 2016, https://theamericanscholar.org /i-will-love-you-in-the-summertime/#.XAw9NxNKjBI.

84. Falque, *The Guide to Gethsemane*, 99.

85. Falque, *The Guide to Gethsemane*, 99.

86. Falque, *The Guide to Gethsemane*, 70.

87. Falque, *The Guide to Gethsemane*, 70.

88. Falque, *The Guide to Gethsemane*, 53–56.

89. Falque, *The Guide to Gethsemane*, 100.

90. Falque, *The Guide to Gethsemane*, 10, 17, 37, 63, 154.

91. Falque, *The Guide to Gethsemane*, 102.

92. Falque, *The Guide to Gethsemane*, 102.

93. Falque, *The Guide to Gethsemane*, 77.

94. Falque, *The Guide to Gethsemane*, 101.

95. Falque gives his account of the impassibility of God in *God, the Flesh, and the Other*—arguing God is not without compassion but remains impassible. He argues that Bernard of Clairvaux takes Origen's understanding of the *passion* of God and turns it into the *compassion* of God, protecting (or even correcting) Origen's arguments regarding the passion of God from the threat of anthropomorphism. He suggests that "charity" is the very being of God, and as such, the "passion" of God is always translated into "com-passion" (*com-passio*), at least in the sense that God is not indifferent to anything human. However, God is not affected by humanity's affection (God does not suffer what humanity suffers). For the details of this analysis, see Emmanuel Falque, *God, the Flesh, and the Other: From Irenaeus to Duns Scotus*, trans. W. C. Hackett (Evanston, IL: Northwestern University Press, 2015), 207–30.

96. Falque, *The Guide to Gethsemane*, 103. According to Moltmann, the Father and Son are "most deeply separated in forsakenness and at the same time are most inwardly one in their surrender." Jürgen Moltmann, *The Crucified God: The Cross of Christ as the Foundation and Criticism of Christian Theology*, trans. R. A. Wilson and John Bowden (Minneapolis, MN: Fortress, 1991),

243–44. Falque's approach is heavily influenced by Balthasar's focus on the "horror which isolates." Falque, *The Guide to Gethsemane*, 54. Cf. Hans Urs von Balthasar, *Mysterium Paschale*, trans. Aidan Nichols (San Francisco: Ignatius, 01990), 100. Falque goes on to argue that the cry of dereliction ("My God, my God, why have you forsaken me?") indicates Christ's intense feelings of separation from the Father but proposes it is also a moment of profound intimacy in which the Son fully relinquishes himself to the Father. He writes, "We do not have to interpret the cry of dereliction made by Jesus on the cross as a sign of distress of the man in a death where God no longer replies to him and would be eliminated because of his absence. On the contrary, as Gustave Martelet says, this cry can be understood as 'a lament made to be heard by God and answered in the Resurrection.'" Falque, *The Guide to Gethsemane*, 55. Cf. Gustave Martelet, "Dieu n'a pas créé la mort," *Christus* 168 (1995): 461.

97. Johnson, *Ask the Beasts*, 183–84, 187.
98. Johnson, *Ask the Beasts*, 185.
99. Johnson, *Ask the Beasts*, 185.
100. Johnson, *Ask the Beasts*, 186.
101. Johnson, *Ask the Beasts*, 183.
102. Johnson, *Ask the Beasts*, 195.
103. Johnson, *Ask the Beasts*, 195.

104. In his more recent work, Falque suggests *sarx* "sends us back, first of all in scriptural terms, to the biological aspect of human existence, even if it does not reduce things to this aspect." Falque, *Wedding Feast of the Lamb*, 101. In this sense, *sarx* is related to "*Fleisch* in German, *flesh* in English, and *chair* in French. In every case the flesh as commonly understood is 'linked to blood, to meat, to that soft substance of the body which is opposed to the bones. It is unstable, fluid and soft in character and reduces the structural stature of the body.'" Falque, *Wedding Feast of the Lamb*, 14. Cf. Natalie Depraz, "Leib," in *Vocabulaire européen des philosophies*, ed. Barbara Cassin (Paris: Éditions du Seuil, 2004), 707.

105. In the context of the citation provided here, Chrétien does not directly refer to Christ's tears; however, it is consistent with the overall argument of Chrétien's essay to suggest that the Word remains in intimate relation with a suffering creation: "Tears of men or tears of the ocean, it is always within the Word that they will have been spilled." Jean-Louis Chrétien, *Hand to Hand: Listening to the Work of Art*, trans. Stephen E. Lewis (New York: Fordham University Press, 2003), 152, 162.

106. Wiman, "The Cancer Chair." Jean-Louis Chrétien also brought my attention to the connection between joy and suffering (also with a focus on human suffering) in *Under the Gaze of the Bible* when he writes: "The joyous night of Easter does not forget Good Friday, nor the agony of Christ continued ceaselessly in the prisons and the camps, on the rude paths of exodus, among the humans who are its effectual and possible members. It is not a matter of sporting on our faces a perpetual smile of a surfeited idol, stewing in his

circular nothingness. 'Rejoice,' says the Epistle to the Romans, 'with those who are joyful, weep with those who weep, full of the same kindness for all alike . . .' (12:15–16). In the image of Christ, we are to strive to be everything to all, and to partake of the sufferings as well as the joys of our human brothers and sisters." Jean-Louis Chrétien, *Under the Gaze of the Bible*, trans. John Marson Dunaway (New York: Fordham University Press, 2015), 58.

107. Jan Zwicky, "A Ship from Delos," in *Learning to Die: Wisdom in the Age of the Climate Crisis* (Regina: University of Regina Press, 2018), 63.

108. Zwicky, "A Ship from Delos," 63.

109. By using the language of *resistance* here I am thinking of Edward Schillebeeckx's concept of "negative contrast experience," which suggests that human resistance *to* suffering "reveals that there is something positive beneath the negativity that is immediately at hand." Dan Minch, *Eschatological Hermeneutics: The Theological Core of Experience and the Hope of Our Salvation* (London: Bloomsbury, 2018), 107. Cf. Edward Schillebeeckx, "Correlation between Human Question and Christian Answer," in *The Understanding of Faith: Interpretation and Criticism* (London: Bloomsbury T&T Clark, 2014), 80. Minch goes on to explain that for Schillebeeckx, "the human subject experiences suffering, and an overwhelming feeling of impending negation, and recoils from it because the experience is identified *as suffering* and as being *negative*. The subject as self-transcending goes beyond itself in experience, but recoils from this particular experience, exercising a veto on the suffering it undergoes in the form of the recognition that the affliction should be replaced with something else." Minch, *Eschatological Hermeneutics*, 109.

110. Treanor, *Melancholic Joy*, 120–22, 140.

111. Treanor, *Melancholic Joy*, 140.

112. Rowan Williams, *Christ the Heart of Creation* (New York: Bloomsbury Continuum, 2018), 244–45.

113. Annie Dillard, *Pilgrim at Tinker Creek* (New York: Harper Perennial, 1985), 119, 220, 269.

5. Not Good Enough

1. Jean-Yves Lacoste, *Experience and the Absolute: Disputed Questions on the Humanity of Man*, trans. Mark Raftery-Skehan (New York: Fordham University Press, 2004), 137–40.

2. Brian Treanor, "Joy and the Myopia of Finitude," *Comparative and Continental Philosophy* 8, no. 1 (March 2016): 17.

3. Jeffrey Bloechl, "The Life and Things of Faith: A Partial Reading of Jean-Yves Lacoste," *Revista Portuguesa de Filosofia* 76, no. 2–3 (2020): 693.

4. Judith Wolfe, *Heidegger's Eschatology: Theological Horizons in Martin Heidegger's Early Work* (Oxford: Oxford University Press, 2013), 1.

5. Wolfe, *Heidegger's Eschatology*, 2.

6. Wolfe, *Heidegger's Eschatology*, 2.

7. Wolfe, *Heidegger's Eschatology*, 114–15. Cf. Martin Heidegger, "Phenomenology and Theology," in *Pathmarks*, ed. William McNeil, trans. James G. Hart and John C. Maraldo (Cambridge: Cambridge University Press, 1998).

8. Wolfe, *Heidegger's Eschatology*, 2.

9. As I noted in the first chapter, Lacoste does not "reject" Heidegger's philosophy but instead identifies it with an authentically secular way of being in the world. See Jeffrey Bloechl, "Introduction: Eschatology, Liturgy, and the Task of Thinking," in *From Theology to Theological Thinking*, by Jean-Yves Lacoste (Charlottesville: University of Virginia Press, 2014), xi.

10. See Chapter 1 for details of Lacoste's engagement with *Befindlichkeit*.

11. Heidegger writes, "As one of Dasein's possibilities of Being, anxiety—together with Dasein itself as disclosed in it—provides the phenomenal basis for explicitly grasping Dasein's primordial totality of Being." Martin Heidegger, *Being and Time*, trans. John Macquarrie and Edward Robinson (New York: Harper Perennial, 2008), 227.

12. Claude Romano, *At the Heart of Reason*, trans. Michael B. Smith and Claude Romano (Evanston, IL: Northwestern University Press, 2015), 239.

13. Heidegger, *Being and Time*, 232. Judith Wolfe states, "Because Dasein is ineluctably temporal (and thus also finite), this future includes the ineluctable possibility of his non-being, his death. Consequently, *Angst* (anxiety, affliction) and not hope is the dominant mood of eschatological expectation and the mood most revelatory of Dasein's own being." Wolfe, *Heidegger's Eschatology*, 83, see also 118–20.

14. Bloechl clarifies further, explaining: "One may wish to debate Heidegger on any number of points, but one also has to admit that the force of his analysis does bring before us an inescapable complication for the attempt to understand the things that belong properly to faith. Believers no less than non-believers must come to terms with their mortality, and this surely means coming to terms with the claims made on us all by this world and its exigencies. Unless we wish to deny all of that, the first order of business must be to challenge the topos of the latter as it presents itself—a topos which, as traced for us by Heidegger, suggests that we are first and last our anxiety at death." Bloechl, "Life and Things of Faith," 692–93.

15. Jean-Yves Lacoste, *Être en danger* (Paris: Les Éditions du Cerf, 2011), 182.

16. Lacoste, *Être en danger*, 182. Heidegger describes the "vulgar" concept of time as a uniform set of "nows" that appear in the present: "This time is that which is *counted* and which shows itself when one follows the travelling pointer, counting and making present in such a way that this making-present temporalizes itself in an ecstatic unity with the retaining and awaiting which are horizonally open according to the 'earlier' and 'later.'" Heidegger, *Being and Time*, 472. Cf. Simon Critchley, "Heidegger's Being and Time: Part 8," *Guardian*, July 27, 2009, https://www.theguardian.com/commentisfree/belief/2009/jul/27/heidegger-being-time-philosophy.

17. Lacoste, *Être en danger*, 182–83.

18. Lacoste, *Être en danger*, 186.

19. The language Lacoste uses here is nuanced. He is not arguing that being-at-peace is a fundamental mood or affection (*Grundbefindlichkeit*)—at least not in the Heideggerian sense, since Heidegger exclusively associates that concept with the prospect of nonbeing. Instead, Lacoste attributes "to peace the status of *Grundstimmung*, of fundamental tonality—not the sole mood [*affect*] that unveils what is played out at the heart of us, but a mood [*affect*] amongst those that unveil this stake. We evidently would be right to say: the phenomenon of being-at-peace unveils an aptitude for experience that goes to the depth of us." Lacoste, *Être en danger*, 185.

20. Lacoste, *Être en danger*, 184.

21. Lacoste, *Être en danger*, 190.

22. In Kearney's account, microeschatologies represent a return to "the everyday: that is, back to the natural world of simple embodied life where we may confront again the other 'face-to-face.'" These microeschatologies are part of a broader sense that Kearney describes as *return* to religion—he describes this as "religion *beyond* religion, *before* religion, and *after* religion." His use of the concept leads to a more wide-ranging set of issues than Lacoste. Richard Kearney, "Epiphanies of the Everyday: Toward a Micro-Eschatology," in *After God: Richard Kearney and the Religious Turn in Continental Philosophy*, ed. John Panteleimon Manoussakis (New York: Fordham University Press, 2006), 5–8.

23. Lacoste, *Être en danger*, 287.

24. Lacoste, *Être en danger*.

25. Lacoste, *Être en danger*, 300.

26. Lacoste, *Être en danger*, 284.

27. Lacoste Jean-Yves Lacoste, *Le monde et l'absence d'œuvre et autre études* (Paris: Presses Universitaires de France, 2000), 20–22.

28. Lacoste writes: "We spoke of liturgy to indicate a possible break with the world and earth, a new term of theological origin that can be used to indicate schematically what is comfortable: we will say that it is a *sabbatical* experience. . . . The liturgy anticipates the Kingdom, so it should be said that ease returns us to creation. What I enjoy during the minutes taken away from the worries of work can be received with gratitude, as part of what, in the beginning, was declared 'good' and 'very good.'" Lacoste, *Le monde et l'absence d'œuvre*, 21–22.

29. Lacoste writes: "If we respectfully secularize the biblical text, the double aprioristic possibility of doing and resting nevertheless manifests an entire abundance of meaning. The man of whom the biblical account speaks is at the same time a laboring animal and an animal capable of finding himself at ease in the world." Jean-Yves Lacoste, *Thèses sur le vrais* (Paris: Presses Universitaires de France, 2018), 178.

30. Lacoste, *Être en danger*, 283, 289.

31. Lacoste, *Être en danger*, 289. Lacoste's qualified account of the eschatological anticipation suggests that it remains defined by an apophatic sense of

hope. While the significance of *hope* for eschatological anticipation remains undeveloped in this chapter, one would do well to turn to David Newheiser's *Hope in a Secular Age* for further insight. He articulates a concept of hope that remains subject to ongoing revision and uncertainty while still leaving room for certain affirmations. In Newheiser's account, hope is an experience that crosses religious and secular divisions, and his analysis corresponds with (and helped inspire) my own interest in common experiences in this book. See David Newheiser, *Hope in a Secular Age: Deconstruction, Negative Theology, and the Future of Faith* (New York: Cambridge University Press, 2019).

32. Jeffrey Bloechl explains: "What Lacoste here calls 'peace' and sometimes 'ease' does not manifest only our existing, but existing as inscribed in an eventual limit, or else—if we cede the word 'existing' to Heidegger's sense of what Dasein cares for—it does not manifest existing at all; peace would instead manifest an 'elsewhere' (*une ailleurs*) and an 'otherwise than existing' (*une autrement qu'exister*) toward death, and thus a form of living that is no longer circumscribed in dying." Bloechl, "Life and Things of Faith," 694.

33. Lacoste broadly defines liturgy as "everything that embodies the relation of man to God." While this definition of liturgy may include specific rituals and practices, he is more interested in how "being-before-God" discloses something particular about human beings and the world than concrete liturgical practices. Jean-Yves Lacoste, *Experience and the Absolute: Disputed Questions on the Humanity of Man*, trans. Mark Raftery-Skehan (New York: Fordham University Press, 2004), 22. Cf. Trevor Maine, "Knowing through Worship: The Epistemological Underpinnings of Liturgical Theology," PhD diss., Katholieke Universiteit Leuven, 2018, 89–90; Jean Greisch, *Le buisson ardent et les lumières de la raison. L'invention de la philosophie de la religion*, Tome II: *Les approches phénoménologiques et analytiques* (Paris: Cerf, 2002), 269.

34. Lacoste, *Experience and the Absolute*, 11.

35. Lacoste, *Experience and the Absolute*, 12.

36. Lacoste, *Experience and the Absolute*, 39.

37. Lacoste, *Experience and the Absolute*, 22.

38. Lacoste, *Experience and the Absolute*, 25.

39. Lacoste, *Experience and the Absolute*, 25.

40. Bloechl, "Life and Things of Faith," 695.

41. Lacoste, *Être en danger*, 305.

42. Lacoste, *Être en danger*, 306. Lacoste suggests that the Latin expresses the idea better: "*in hoc corpore constituti non solun pietatis tuae cotidianos experimur effectus, sed aeternitatis etiam pignora jam tenemus.*" See *Missale Romanum*, 1969.

43. Lacoste, *Être en danger*, 306.

44. Lacoste, *Être en danger*, 306–7.

45. Lacoste, *Être en danger*, 307.

46. Bloechl, "Eschatology, Liturgy, Thinking," xiii.

47. Bloechl, "Eschatology, Liturgy, Thinking," x.

48. In a defining question posed at the beginning of *Experience and the Absolute*, Lacoste asks: "If phenomenology, and phenomenology alone, furnishes us the coordinates with which to coherently question who we are, and with which to rigorously debate what we are, will it not also provide us with the means to understand how Dasein, how mortals, who concern themselves solely with an atheistic world and a familiar earth, with the sky and the deities, can also be concerned with a God with whom they maintain a relation steeped in ambiguity?" Lacoste, *Experience and the Absolute*, 2.

49. Christina M. Gschwandtner, *Welcoming Finitude: Towards a Phenomenology of Orthodox Liturgy* (New York: Fordham University Press, 2019), 69. This is part of a broader argument, in which Gschwandtner argues that philosophy tends to be far too focused on "doctrine or abstract faith statements"; however, if "one wants to understand how a faith or a tradition functions, one must look at its habits, practices, and experiences." Gschwandtner, *Welcoming Finitude*, xii.

50. Gschwandtner goes on to argue: "Although Lacoste affirms that the tension between our earthly corporeality and spatiality in the world and the eschatological suspension of this in a non-place and non-experience always remains, it is clear that he expects them to be severed in the parousia, in which our 'liturgical being' will be lived fully and not only temporarily." Gschwandtner, *Welcoming Finitude*, 96.

51. Gschwandtner, *Welcoming Finitude*, 76.

52. Lacoste summarizes his project as an attempt to "develop a non-'religious' (i.e., anti-Schleiermacherian and anti-Jamesian) logic of 'liturgy' (not worship!)—that is, of what man does *coram Deo* (before the face of/in the presence of God) as subverting the Heideggerian logic of being-in-the-world." Jean-Yves Lacoste, "Continental Philosophy," in *The Routledge Companion to Philosophy of Religion* (New York: Routledge, 2013), 729. Cf. Joeri Schrijvers, *An Introduction to Jean-Yves Lacoste* (New York: Ashgate, 2012), 181.

53. Lacoste, *Experience and the Absolute*, 103.

54. Abraham Olivier, "Understanding Place," in *Place, Space, and Hermeneutics*, ed. Bruce B. Janz (Cham: Springer International, 2017), 9–10. Cf. Dan Zahavi, *Subjectivity and Selfhood* (Cambridge, MA: MIT Press, 2005), 4, 5.

55. Hans Dieter Betz, *The Sermon on the Mount* (Minneapolis, MN: Augsburg Fortress, 1995), 423. In the Sermon on the Mount, Jesus is portrayed as "a new Moses who, like his predecessor, goes up a mountain (Matt. 5:1; cf. Exod. 19:3) to expound God's law (Matt. 5:17; cf. Exod. 19:7)." Ian A. McFarland, "Sermon on the Mount," in *Cambridge Dictionary of Christian Theology*, ed. Ian A. McFarland et al. (New York: Cambridge University Press, 2011).

56. Ulrich Luz, *Matthew 1–7: A Commentary*, trans. James E. Crouch (Minneapolis, MN: Fortress, 2007), 339.

57. Kierkegaard influence on Lacoste's work is particularly evident in *The Appearing of God*, wherein he examines Kierkegaard's *Fragments* and *Edifying*

Discourses in order to explore the interactions between philosophy, theology, and worship. Jean-Yves Lacoste, *The Appearing of God*, trans. Oliver O'Donovan (Oxford: Oxford University Press, 2018), 11–17, 72, 76, 176–98. Jason Kenneth Wardley explores the connections between the two authors at length in *Praying to a French God* (Burlington, VT: Ashgate, 2014), 49–72. See also Maine, *Knowing through Worship*, 105.

58. Paul Ricoeur, *The Rule of Metaphor: The Creation of Meaning in Language*, trans. Robert Czerny with Kathleen McLaughlin and John Costello (Toronto: Toronto University Press, 1977; repr. New York: Routledge, 2003), 361–62. Citations refer to the Routledge edition.

59. Ricoeur, *The Rule of Metaphor*, 74–245.

60. Kevin Hart, *Poetry and Revelation: For a Phenomenology of Religious Poetry* (London: Bloomsbury Academic, 2017), xii.

61. Mary Oliver, *The Truro Bear and Other Adventures: Poems and Essays* (Boston: Beacon, 2008), 25.

62. Margaret Renkl, *Late Migrations: A Natural History of Love and Loss* (Minneapolis, MN: Milkweed Editions, 2019), 218.

63. Walter Brueggemann, *Genesis: A Bible Commentary for Teaching and Preaching* (Atlanta: John Knox, 1984), 89. Claus Westermann, *Genesis*, trans. David E. Green (London: T&T Clark, 1987), 12.

64. Previously quoted in the Introduction. See Ellen Davis, *Scripture, Culture, Agriculture: An Agrarian Reading of the Bible* (New York: Cambridge University Press, 2009), 43.

65. Luz, *Matthew 1–7*, 341. Cf. Johannes Weiss, *Die Predigt Jesu vom Reiche Gottes*, 3rd ed. (Göttingen, Germany: Vandenhoeck & Ruprecht, 1964), 293. Some commentators argue that the passage "is a good symbol of the economic naïveté" or even "laziness." Cf. Ernst Bloch, *Atheism in Christianity: The Religion of the Exodus and the Kingdom*, trans. J. T. Swann (New York: Herder & Herder, 1972), 138; and Karl Kautsky, *Foundations of Christianity: A Study in Christian Origins* (New York: International Publishers, 1925), 346. But Dennis Edwards notes: "The saying about every sparrow that falls to the ground reflects the ancient biblical understanding of the Creator's care for all creatures (Ps. 84.3; 104.27–28). It is consistent with other passages where Jesus speaks about God's care for birds and flowers as well as human beings (Mt. 6.25–34; Lk. 12.22–33)." Denis Edwards, "Every Sparrow That Falls to the Ground: The Cost of Evolution and the Christ Event," *Ecotheology* 11, no. 1 (2006): 103.

66. Hans Dieter Betz, for instance, argues that Jesus's teaching is "set into the larger context of creation of the world by God and divine providence." Betz, *Sermon on the Mount*, 460. And Ulrich Luz proposes that Kierkegaard's reading of the text is helpful for thinking about its relevance today. Luz, *Matthew 1–7*, 348.

67. Lacoste, *The Appearing of God*, 186.

68. In reference to Kierkegaard's *Edifying Discourses* Lacoste explains: "The discourse will speak *of* God, usually through Scriptural exposition, but not

before it has spoken *to* God. The terms are thus set at the beginning, so that we can never accuse the author of ignoring the horizon within which he speaks of God. We shall never be able to forget that well-formed theological language speaks *to* God before speaking *of* him, and speaks *of* him only as it is presumed capable of speaking *to* him." Lacoste, *The Appearing of God*, 186. Lacoste also submits that Kierkegaard uses the resources of propositional or didactic theology in the discourses while also maintaining a stance of eschatological anticipation (definitive of liturgy) by continually emphasizing that God "exceeds all propositions." Lacoste, *The Appearing of God*, 184–85.

69. Søren Kierkegaard, *The Lily of the Field and the Bird of the Air: Three Godly Discourses*, trans. Bruce H. Kirmmse (Princeton, NJ: Princeton University Press, 2016), 30.

70. George Pattison, *Kierkegaard's Upbuilding Discourses: Philosophy, Theology, and Literature* (New York: Routledge, 2002), 95–96.

71. Pattison, *Kierkegaard's Upbuilding Discourses*, 96.

72. Lacoste, *Experience and the Absolute*, 151–52.

73. Lacoste, *Experience and the Absolute*, 150.

74. Kierkegaard, *The Lily of the Field and the Bird of the Air*, 29.

75. Kierkegaard, *The Lily of the Field and the Bird of the Air*, 30–31.

76. Kierkegaard, *The Lily of the Field and the Bird of the Air*, 30.

77. Kierkegaard, *The Lily of the Field and the Bird of the Air*, 31–32.

78. Kierkegaard, *The Lily of the Field and the Bird of the Air*, 32.

79. Bruce H. Kirmmse, "Introduction: Letting Nature Point beyond Nature," in Kierkegaard, *The Lily of the Field and the Bird of the Air*, xxi.

80. Given my earlier argument that Lacoste is too quick to dismiss the category of the "sacred" (Chapter 1), it is important to point out that I seek to develop a more complex understanding of the relationship between Christian concepts of creation and other religious or spiritual traditions than either Lacoste or Kierkegaard display. The idea that a human being is "fragmentary" or "incompletely realized" without a sense of divine transcendence understood in relation to the Christian God is highly contestable (to say the least). For instance, in my Canadian context, one would have to first explore the rich and complex Inuit concept of *Sila* in detail before making such an expansive claim. This would be the bare minimum given the fact that so many Christian concepts have been used to justify atrocious acts against the Indigenous peoples of Canada. Cf. Zoe Todd, "An Indigenous Feminist's Take on the Ontological Turn: 'Ontology' Is Just Another Word for Colonialism," *Journal of Historical Sociology* 29, no. 1 (March, 2016): 4–22. For more on the Inuit concept of *Sila*, see Keavy Martin, *Stories in a New Skin: Approaches to Inuit Literature* (Winnipeg: University of Winnipeg Press, 2012), 4–5.

81. Lacoste submits that the God of the *Wholly-other* "is bound to appear as numinous and yet not-numinous, fascinating and yet not-fascinating, sacred and yet not-sacred, etc., etc. He is even bound to appear as 'other and yet not-other,' *valde aluid* and *non aluid*. He is bound to put in question all the

experience that lays claim to him, which is what happens, in fact, in Barth." However, according to Lacoste, Kierkegaard's "infinite qualitative difference" is a more appropriate approach to divine transcendence. Lacoste, *The Appearing of God*, 32–33.

82. Lacoste, *The Appearing of God*, 22. Lacoste then goes on to propose that this ordinary transcendence is relevant for understanding Janicaud's "elementary phenomenological error in championing a phenomenology which has only to do with the visible, audible, etc., a phenomenology for which the play of sensory 'matter' and intentional 'form' gives access to more than what is visible, etc." Lacoste, *The Appearing of God*, 23. Cf. Dominque Janicaud, "The Theological Turn in French Phenomenology," in *Phenomenology and the "Theological Turn": The French Debate*, trans. Bernard G. Prusak (New York: Fordham University Press, 2000), 16–103.

83. Lacoste, *The Appearing of God*, 24.

84. Joris Geldhof argues that the concept of "salvation" is central to understanding what distinguishes Christianity from concepts of the sacred—at least as the concept is presented in twentieth-century European thought. He writes: "Both Heidegger and Eliade have forgotten about salvation, so that one does not know actually whether it shows itself *through* being or not. It surely shows itself *in* being, that is, within the milieu of beings, and *in* the existence of human persons, relations between them, and surroundings around them. But it may be possible that the origin of salvation is not being qua being itself in a way similar to being's situation at the origin of the discovery of the sacred. Perhaps one has to incorporate that origin beyond being as well if one wants to arrive at liturgy." Joris Geldhof, *Liturgy and Secularism: Beyond the Divide* (Collegeville, MN: Liturgical Press, 2018), chap. 3.

85. Lacoste, *Experience and the Absolute*, 97.

86. David Bentley Hart, *The Hidden and the Manifest: Essays in Theology and Metaphysics* (Grand Rapids, MI: Eerdmans, 2017), 100.

87. Hart, *The Hidden and the Manifest*, 100.

88. Rowan Williams, *Christ the Heart of Creation* (New York: Bloomsbury, 2018), 4. Rowan Williams suggests that there has to be a sense in which "the Word: the divine suppost, is the agency whereby the created order is sustained in coherence: it is thus related to every form of finite agency as that which draws it towards harmony, internal and external." Williams, *Christ the Heart of Creation*, 38.

89. Further engagement on this issue would benefit from examining how a phenomenological concept of transcendence (described by Lacoste) interacts with the current debates over natural theology and the validity of *analogia entis*. For contemporary scholarship on this issue, see Keith L. Johnson, *Karl Barth and the* Analogia Entis (New York: T&T Clark, 2010); John R. Betz, "Beyond the Sublime: The Aesthetics of the Analogy of Being (Part Two)," *Modern Theology* 22, no. 1 (2006): 1–50; David Bentley Hart, "The Offering of Names:

Metaphysics, Nihilism, and Analogy," in *Reason and the Reasons of Faith*, ed. Paul J. Griffiths and Reinhard Hütter (New York: T&T Clark, 2005).

90. Ken Koltun-Fromm, *Imagining Jewish Authenticity* (Bloomington: Indiana University Press, 2015), 142.

91. Koltun-Fromm, *Imagining Jewish Authenticity*, 142.

92. Abraham Joshua Heschel, *The Sabbath: Its Meaning for Modern Man* (New York: Noonday, 2005), 4.

93. Heschel, *The Sabbath*, 10.

94. Heschel, *The Sabbath*, 8.

95. Heschel, *The Sabbath*, 7–8.

96. Susannah Heschel, introduction to Heschel, *The Sabbath*, xiii.

97. Abraham Joshua Heschel, *God in Search of Man: A Philosophy of Judaism* (New York: Harper & Row, 1966), 210–11. Emphasis added.

98. Heschel, *God in Search of Man*, 208, 143.

99. Heschel, *The Sabbath*, 60.

100. Heschel, *The Sabbath*, 59.

101. Heschel, *The Sabbath*, 60.

102. Edward Kaplin, *Spiritual Radical: Abraham Joshua Heschel in America, 1940–1972* (New Haven, CT: Yale University Press, 2005), 85–86.

103. Heschel, *The Sabbath*, 79.

104. Emmanuel Levinas, "Desacralization and Disenchantment," in *Nine Talmudic Readings*, trans. Annette Aronowicz (Bloomington: Indiana University Press, 1990), 141. Cf. Robyn Horner, "À Saint Jacques," in *The Postmodern Saints of France: Refiguring 'the Holy' in Contemporary French Philosophy*, ed. Colby Dickinson (London: Bloomsbury T&T Clark, 2013), 97.

105. Heschel, *The Sabbath*, 9.

106. Heschel, *The Sabbath*, 9. Susannah Heschel further explains: "My father defines Judaism as a religion centrally concerned with holiness in time. Some religions build great cathedrals or temples, but Judaism constructs the Sabbath as an architecture of time. Creating holiness in time requires a different sensibility than building a cathedral in space: 'We must conquer space in order to sanctify time.' My father did not mean to imply, as some have suggested, a denigration of space or a denial of the significance of the land of Israel. His commitment to Israel and its sanctity is attested to in his book *Israel: An Echo of Eternity*. In the cases of both the Sabbath and Israel, he emphasizes that sanctification is dependent upon human behavior and attitude. Sanctifying the Sabbath is part of our imitation of God, but it also becomes a way to find God's presence." Susannah Heschel, introduction to Heschel, *The Sabbath*, xiii.

107. Heschel, *The Sabbath*, 30.

108. Heschel, *The Sabbath*, 13.

109. Joris Geldhof describes this function of liturgy in some detail. He argues that liturgy has the potential to play "a proactive and leading role" in "the de-ideologization of the many modern(ist) and secular(ist) discourses."

Geldhof is speaking of Christian liturgical contexts, but there remains a similar consequence that can be drawn from Heschel's analysis of the Sabbath. Geldhof, *Liturgy and Secularism*, introduction.

110. Heschel, *The Sabbath*, 6.
111. Heschel, *The Sabbath*, 31–32.
112. Heschel, *The Sabbath*, 23.
113. Heschel, *The Sabbath*, 74.
114. Heschel, *The Sabbath*, 23. Later in the text Heschel explains, "According to the Talmud, the Sabbath is *me'en'olam ha-ba*, which means: somewhat like eternity or the world to come." Heschel, *The Sabbath*, 74.
115. Heschel, *The Sabbath*, 76.
116. Lacoste, *Experience and the Absolute*, 103.
117. Lacoste, *Experience and the Absolute*, 103.
118. Lacoste, *The Appearing of God*, 149. A helpful example of how "being-before-God" might permeate one's horizon of place is provided by Erazim Kohák in *The Embers and the Stars*. He submits that an "incredibly blue sky" on a July summer day "is not a function of the gray dawn which preceded it nor of the greenish-yellow which will follow it at dusk. It simply is, blue with a perennial validity unaffected by the passing of time." This "perennial validity," according to Kohák, is a matter of "seeing the present not in its relation to what preceded and what will follow it, but in its absolute being—in its relation to what, clumsily, we describe as eternity." Of course, various manifestations of goodness will appear and disappear over the course of time, but the *value* of creation (its goodness) is of the "order" of eternity. "Eternity, so understood, is not an extension of time, not even an infinite time. It is, rather, a vertical dimension cutting through time at each of its moments." In other words, the incredibly blue sky in July participates in the same eternity that one is exposed to on the Sabbath. Erazim Kohák, *The Embers and the Stars: A Philosophical Inquiry into the Moral Sense of Nature* (Chicago: University of Chicago Press, 1984), 82–83.
119. Lacoste, *Experience and the Absolute*, 22.

Conclusion: The Credibility of Creation's Goodness

1. First quoted in the Introduction. Richard Kearney, "The Wager of Carnal Hermeneutics," in *Carnal Hermeneutics*, ed. Richard Kearney and Brian Treanor (New York: Fordham University Press, 2015), 48. Cf. Paul Ricoeur, *Freedom and Nature: The Voluntary and Involuntary*, trans. Erizam V. Kohák (Evanston, IL: Northwestern University Press, 1996), 94.

2. Francis, *Laudato si' of the Holy Father Francis: On Care for Our Common Home*, encyclical letter, May 24, 2015, 69, https://www.vatican.va/content/francesco/en/encyclicals/documents/papa-francesco_20150524_enciclica-laudato-si.html.

3. Brian Treanor, "Joy and the Myopia of Finitude," *Comparative and Continental Philosophy* 8, no. 1 (March, 2016): 8.

4. Brian Treanor, *Melancholic Joy: On Life Worth Living* (New York: Bloomsbury, 2021), 140.

5. Emmanuel Falque, *The Metamorphosis of Finitude: An Essay on Birth and Resurrection*, trans. Georges Hughes (New York: Fordham University Press, 2012), 104.

6. Rowan Williams, *Christ the Heart of Creation* (New York: Bloomsbury Continuum, 2018), xi.

7. For more on the relationship between credibility and politics in Christianity, see Stephan van Erp, "The World and Sacrament: Foundations of the Political Theology of the Church," *Louvain Studies* 39 (2015–2016): 102–20. This essay has influenced my thinking on political theology and philosophy substantially.

8. Francis goes a long way toward addressing these misinterpretations in *Laudato si'*: "We are not God. The earth was here before us and it has been given to us. This allows us to respond to the charge that Judaeo-Christian thinking, on the basis of the Genesis account which grants man 'dominion' over the earth (cf. Gen 1:28), has encouraged the unbridled exploitation of nature by painting him as domineering and destructive by nature. This is not a correct interpretation of the Bible as understood by the Church. Although it is true that we Christians have at times incorrectly interpreted the Scriptures, nowadays we must forcefully reject the notion that our being created in God's image and given dominion over the earth justifies absolute domination over other creatures." Francis, *Laudato si'*, 67.

9. The Catholic Church has recently apologized for the doctrine of discovery. Of course, the consequence of its framework continues to impact Indigenous land claims. Mark Charles and Soong-Chan Rah, *Unsettling Truths: The Ongoing Dehumanizing Legacy of the Doctrine of Discovery* (Downers Grove, IL: Intervarsity, 2019), 15.

10. Some good examples are Celia Deane-Drummond, *Theological Ethics through a Multispecies Lens: The Evolution of Wisdom*, vol. (Oxford: University of Oxford Press, 2019). Elizabeth Johnson, *Creation and the Cross: The Mercy of God for a Planet in Peril* (Maryknoll, NY: Orbis, 2019). Norman Wirzba, *This Sacred Life: Humanity's Place in a Wounded World* (Cambridge: Cambridge University Press, 2021).

11. Jan Zwicky, "A Ship from Delos," in *Learning to Die: Wisdom in the Age of the Climate Crisis* (Regina: University of Regina Press, 2018), 64–65.

12. Zwicky, "A Ship from Delos," 65.

13. Zwicky, "A Ship from Delos," 66, 44.

14. William Cavanaugh, "Return of the Golden Calf: Economy, Idolatry, and Secularization since *Gaudium et spes*," *Theological Studies* 76, no. 4 (2015): 716.

Bibliography

Aertsen, Jan A. "The Goodness of Being." *Recherches de théologie et philosophie médiévales* 78, no. 2 (2011): 281–95.
Alvis, James. *Marion and Derrida on the Gift and Desire: Debating the Generosity of Things*. Switzerland: Springer International, 2016.
Aquinas, Thomas. *Summa Theologiae*. Trans. Fathers of the English Dominican Province. New York: Benziger Bros., 1947. http://ccel.org/a/aquinas/summa/home.html.
Arendt, Hannah. *Condition de l'homme moderne*. Paris: Pocket, 1998.
Asad, Talal. *Formations of the Secular: Christianity, Islam, Modernity*. Stanford, CA: Stanford University Press, 2003.
Augustine. *City of God*. Trans. Marcus Dods. In *The Nicene and Post-Nicene Fathers*, series 1, vol. 2. Edinburgh: T&T Clark, 1887. http://www.ccel.org/ccel/schaff/npnf102.toc.html.
Averchi, Michele. "Husserl and Geiger on Feelings and Intentionality." In *Feeling and Value, Willing and Action*, ed. Marta Ubiali and Maren Wehrle, 71–91. Switzerland: Springer, 2015.
Balthasar, Hans Urs von. *Mysterium Paschale*. Trans. Aidan Nichols. San Francisco: Ignatius, 1990.
———. *Unless You Become Like This Child*. Trans. Erasmo Leiva-Merikakis. San Francisco: Ignatius, 1991.
Battersby, Christine. *The Phenomenal Woman: Feminist Metaphysics and the Patterns of Identity*. New York: Routledge, 1998.
Benoist, Jocelyn. "Le tournant théologique." In *L'idée de la phénoménologie*, 81–104. Paris: Beauchesne, 2001.

———. "Qu'est-ce qui est donné? La pensée et l'événement." *Archives de philosophie* 4 (1996): 629–57.
Berger, Peter. *The Desecularization of the World: Resurgent Religion and World Politics*. Grand Rapids, MI: Eerdmans, 1999.
Betz, Hans Dieter. *The Sermon on the Mount*. Minneapolis, MN: Augsburg Fortress, 1995.
Betz, John R. "Beyond the Sublime: The Aesthetics of the Analogy of Being (Part Two)." *Modern Theology* 22, no. 1 (2006): 1–50.
Bloch, Ernst. *Atheism in Christianity: The Religion of the Exodus and the Kingdom*. Trans. J. T. Swann. New York: Herder & Herder, 1972.
Bloechl, Jeffrey. "Introduction: Eschatology, Liturgy, and the Task of Thinking." In *From Theology to Theological Thinking*, by Jean-Yves Lacoste, vii–xxi. Charlottesville: University of Virginia Press, 2014.
———. "The Life and Things of Faith: A Partial Reading of Jean-Yves Lacoste." *Revista Portuguesa de Filosofia* 76, no. 2–3 (2020): 689–704.
Blumenberg, Hans. *The Legitimacy of the Modern Age*. Trans. Robert Wallace. Cambridge, MA: MIT Press, 1983.
Boersma, Hans. *Nouvelle Theologie and Sacramental Ontology: A Return to Mystery*. New York: Oxford University Press, 2009.
Boeve, Lieven. *God Interrupts History: Theology in a Time of Upheaval*. New York: Continuum, 2007.
Brook, Angus. "Thomas Aquinas on Effects of Original Sin: A Philosophical Analysis." *Heythrop Journal* 59, no. 4 (2018): 721–32.
Brown, Peter. *The Body and Society: Men, Women, and Sexual Renunciation in Early Christianity*. New York: Columbia University Press, 1988.
Brueggemann, Walter. *Genesis: A Bible Commentary for Teaching and Preaching*. Atlanta: John Knox, 1984.
———. *The Psalms: A Theological Commentary*. Minneapolis, MN: Augsberg, 1984.
Calvin, John. *Complete Old Testament Commentaries*. Trans. John King, James Anderson, C. W. Bingham, and William Pringle. Grand Rapids, MI: Eerdmans, 1948.
Caputo, John D. *The Weakness of God: A Theology of the Event*. Bloomington: Indiana University Press, 2006.
Cavanaugh, William. *The Myth of Religious Violence: Secular Ideology and the Roots of Modern Conflict*. New York: Oxford University Press, 2009.
———. "Return of the Golden Calf: Economy, Idolatry, and Secularization since *Gaudium et spes*." *Theological Studies* 76, no. 4 (2015): 698–717.
Charles, Mark, and Soong-Chan Rah. *Unsettling Truths: The Ongoing Dehumanizing Legacy of the Doctrine of Discovery*. Downers Grove, IL: Intervarsity, 2019.
Chrétien, Jean-Louis. "Attempting to Think beyond Subjectivity." In *Quiet Powers of the Possible: Interviews in Contemporary French Phenomenology*, ed. Tarek R. Dika and W. Chris Hackett, trans. K. Jason Wardley, 228–38. New York: Fordham University Press, 2016.

———. *Hand to Hand: Listening to the Work of Art.* Trans. Stephen E. Lewis. New York: Fordham University Press, 2003.
———. *Spacious Joy: An Essay in Phenomenology and Literature.* Trans. Anne Ashley Davenport. New York: Rowman & Littlefield, 2019.
———. *Under the Gaze of the Bible.* Trans. John Marson Dunaway. New York: Fordham University Press, 2015.
———. *The Unforgettable and the Unhoped For.* Trans. Jeffrey Bloechl. New York: Fordham University Press, 2002.
Cone, James. *The Spirituals and the Blues: An Interpretation.* Maryknoll, NY: Orbis, 2008.
Conley, Tom. Introduction to *The Certeau Reader*, ed. Graham Ward, 55–60. New York: Blackwell, 2000.
Critchley, Simon. "Heidegger's Being and Time: Part 8." *Guardian*, July 27, 2009, https://www.theguardian.com/commentisfree/belief/2009/jul/27/heidegger-being-time-philosophy.
Cross, Richard. "Aquinas on Physical Impairment: Human Nature and Original Sin." *Harvard Theological Review* 110, no. 3 (July, 2017): 317–38.
Crowe, Benjamin D. *Heidegger's Phenomenology of Religion: Realism and Cultural Criticism.* Bloomington: Indiana University Press, 2008.
Davaney, Sheila Greeve. "Theology and the Turn to Cultural Analysis." In *Converging on Culture: Theologians in Dialogue with Cultural Analysis and Criticism*, ed. Delwin Brown, Sheila Greeve Davaney, and Kathryn Tanner, 3–16. Oxford: Oxford University Press, 2001.
Davis, Ellen. *Scripture, Culture, Agriculture: An Agrarian Reading of the Bible.* New York: Cambridge University Press, 2009.
de Certeau, Michel. "A Symbolic Revolution." In *The Certeau Reader*, ed. Graham Ward, 61–68. New York: Blackwell, 2000.
———. "The Weakness of Believing." In *The Certeau Reader*, ed. Graham Ward, 214–43. New York: Blackwell, 2000.
de Libera, Alain. *La philosophie médiévale.* Paris: Presses Universitaires de France, 1993.
De Maeseneer, Yves. "Truth as Performance? History, Transcendence, and 'As If.'" In *Orthodoxy, Process, and Product*, ed. Lieven Boeve, Mathijs Lamberigts, and Terrence Merrigan. Leuven: Peeters, 2009.
Deane-Drummond, Celia. "In Adam All Die? Questions at the Boundary of Niche Construction, Community Evolution, and Original Sin." In *Evolution and the Fall*, ed. William T. Cavanaugh and James K. A. Smith, 23–47. Grand Rapids, MI: Eerdmans, 2017.
———. *Theological Ethics through a Multispecies Lens: The Evolution of Wisdom.* Vol. 1. Oxford: University of Oxford Press, 2019.
Delerm, Phillipe. *La première gorge de bière.* Paris: Gallimard, 1997.
Depraz, Natalie. "Leib." In *Vocabulaire européen des philosophies*, ed. Barbara Cassin. Paris: Éditions du Seuil, 2004.

Derrida, Jacques. "How to Avoid Speaking: Denials." In *Psyche: Inventions of the Other*, ed. Peggy Kamuf and Elizabeth G. Rottenberg, 2:143–95. Stanford, CA: Stanford University Press, 2008.

Dillard, Annie. *Pilgrim at Tinker Creek*. New York: Harper Perennial, 1985.

Dillard, Peter S. *Heidegger and Philosophical Atheology: A Neo-scholastic Critique*. London: Continuum, 2008.

Dyrness, William A. *Reformed Theology and Visual Culture: The Protestant Imagination from Calvin to Edwards*. Cambridge: Cambridge University Press, 2004.

Edwards, Denis. *Christian Understandings of Creation: A Historical Trajectory*. Minneapolis, MN: Fortress, 2017.

———. "Every Sparrow That Falls to the Ground: The Cost of Evolution and the Christ-Event." *Ecotheology* 11, no. 1 (2006): 103–23.

Falque, Emmanuel. "The Collision of Phenomenology and Theology." In *Quiet Powers of the Possible: Interviews in Contemporary French Phenomenology*, ed. Tarek R. Dika and W. Chris Hackett, trans. K. Jason Wardley, 211–27. New York: Fordham University Press, 2016.

———. *Crossing the Rubicon: The Borderlands of Philosophy and Theology*. Trans. Reuben Shank. New York: Fordham University Press, 2016.

———. "Embrace and Differentiation: A Phenomenology of Eros." In *Somatic Desire: Recovering Corporeality in Contemporary Thought*, ed. Sarah Horton, Stephen Mendelsohn, Christine Rojcewicz, and Richard Kearney, 71–90. New York: Lexington, 2019.

———. "Evil and Finitude." In *Evil, Fallenness, and Finitude*, ed. Bruce Ellis Benson and B. Keith Putt, 77–96. Cham: Palgrave Macmillan, 2017.

———. *God, the Flesh, and the Other: From Irenaeus to Duns Scotus*. Trans. W. C. Hackett. Evanston, IL: Northwestern University Press, 2015.

———. *The Guide to Gethsemane: Anxiety, Suffering, Death*. Trans. George Hughes. New York: Fordham University Press, 2019.

———. "Le haut lieu du soi: Une disputatio théologique et phénoménologique." *Revue de métaphysique et de morale* 3 (2009): 363–90.

———. *The Loving Struggle: Phenomenological and Theological Debates*. Trans. Lucas McCracken and Bradley Onihsi. New York: Rowman & Littlefield, 2018.

———. *The Metamorphosis of Finitude: An Essay on Birth and Resurrection*. Trans. Georges Hughes. New York: Fordham University Press, 2012.

———. *Parcours d'embûchés: S'expliquer*. Paris: Éditions Franciscaines, 2016.

———. "Pascal and the Anxiety of Faith." *Louvain Studies* 42 (2019): 151–74.

———. *Saint Bonaventure and the Entrance of God into Theology: The* Breviloquium *as a* Summa Theologica. Trans. Brian Lapsa and Sarah Horton, rev. William C. Hackett. New York: Franciscan Institute Publications, 2018.

———. "Toward an Ethics of the Spread Body." *In Somatic Desire: Recovering Corporeality in Contemporary Thought*, trans. Christina Gschwandtner, ed.

Sarah H. Horton, Stephen Mendelsohn, Christine Rojcewicz, and Richard Kearney, 91–116. New York: Lexington, 2019.

———. *The Wedding Feast of the Lamb: Eros, the Body, and the Eucharist*. Trans. George Hughes. New York: Fordham University Press, 2016.

Farley, Matthew. Introduction to *Crossing the Rubicon: The Borderlands of Philosophy and Theology*, by Emmanuel Falque, trans. Reuben Shank, 1–13. New York: Fordham University Press, 2016.

Fergusson, David. "Creation." In *The Oxford Handbook of Systematic Theology*, ed. Kathryn Tanner, John Webster, and Iain Torrance, 72–90. New York: Oxford University Press, 2007.

Francis. *Laudato si' of the Holy Father Francis: On Care for Our Common Home*. Encyclical Letter. May 24, 2015. https://www.vatican.va/content/francesco/en/encyclicals/ documents/papa-francesco_20150524_ enciclica-laudato-si.html.

Gabellieri, Emmanuel. "Entre 'vérité du monde' et 'vérité de Dieu', l'homme tout court'?". In *Une analytique du passage*, ed. Claude Brunier-Coulin, 191–218. Paris: Éditions Franciscaines, 2016.

Geldhof, Joris. *Liturgy and Secularism: Beyond the Divide*. Collegeville, MN: Liturgical Press, 2018.

Gilbert, Jack. "A Brief for the Defense." In *Refusing Heaven*, 3. New York: Knopf, 2005.

Godzieba, Anthony. "Adventures in Chiasmus and Sacramentality: Merleau-Ponty Saves the World." *Louvain Studies* 44, no. 3 (2021): 277–97.

———. *A Theology of the Presence and Absence of God*. Collegeville, MN: Liturgical Academic Press, 2018.

Greisch, Jean. "L'herméneutique dans la 'phénoménologie comme telle': Trois questions à propos de 'Réduction et donation.'" *Revue de Métaphysique et de Morale* 96, no. 1 (1991): 43–63.

———. *Le buisson ardent et les lumières de la raison: L'invention de la philosophie de la religion*. Tome II: *Les approches phénoménologiques et analytiques*. Paris: Cerf, 2002.

———. *Le buisson ardent et les lumières de la raison: L'invention de la philosophie de la religion*, Tome III: *Vers un paradigme herméneutique*. Paris: Cerf, 2004.

———. "Les lieux du soi: Vers une herméneutique du soi-même par l'Autre." *Revue de métaphysique et de morale* 3 (2009): 317–35.

Grondin, Jean. "La phénoménologie sans herméneutique." *Internationale Zeitschrift für Philosophie* 1 (1992): 146–53.

Gschwandtner, Christina M. *Degrees of Givenness: On Saturation in Jean-Luc Marion*. Bloomington: Indiana University Press, 2014.

———. *Postmodern Apologetics? Arguments for God in Contemporary Philosophy*. New York: Fordham University Press, 2012.

———. *Reading Jean-Luc Marion: Exceeding Metaphysics*. Bloomington: Indiana University Press, 2007.

———. "The Truth of Christianity: Michel Henry's Words of Christ." *Journal of Scriptural Reasoning* 13, no. 1 (June 2014): https://jsr.lib.virginia.edu/vol-13-no-1-june-2014-phenomenology-and-scripture/the-truth-of-christianity-michel-henrys-words-of-christ/.

———. *Welcoming Finitude: Towards a Phenomenology of Orthodox Liturgy*. New York: Fordham University Press, 2019.

Gunton, Colin. *The Triune Creator: A Historical and Systematic Study*. Edinburgh: Edinburgh University Press, 1998.

Gutschimdt, Rico. "The Late Heidegger and a Post-Theistic Understanding of Religion." *Religious Studies* 56 (2020): 152–68.

Habermas, Jürgen. *An Awareness of What Is Missing: Faith and Reason in a Postsecular Age*. Malden, MA: Polity, 2010.

Hackett, W. Chris. "*La Nouvelle Philosophie* . . . : On the Philosophical Significance of Sanctity in Jean-Yves Lacoste's *Experience and the Absolute*." In *The Postmodern Saints of France: Refiguring "the Holy" in Contemporary French Philosophy*, ed. Colby Dickinson, 201–216. London: Bloomsbury T&T Clark, 2013.

———. "Translator's Foreword." In *God, the Flesh, and the Other: From Irenaeus to Duns Scotus*, by Emmanuel Falque, ix–xviii. Evanston, IL: Northwestern University Press, 2015.

Hart, David Bentley. *The Hidden and the Manifest: Essays in Theology and Metaphysics*. Grand Rapids, MI: Eerdmans, 2017.

———. "The Offering of Names: Metaphysics, Nihilism, and Analogy." In *Reason and the Reasons of Faith*, ed. Paul J. Griffiths and Reinhard Hütter. New York: T&T Clark, 2005.

———. *That All Shall Be Saved: Heaven, Hell, and Universal Salvation*. New Haven, CT: Yale University Press, 2019.

Hart, Kevin. *Poetry and Revelation: For a Phenomenology of Religious Poetry*. London: Bloomsbury Academic, 2017.

Heidegger, Martin. *Being and Time*. Trans. John Macquarrie and Edward Robinson. New York: Harper Perennial, 2008.

———. "Die Idee der Philosophie und das Weltanschauungsproblem (Auszug aus der Nachschrift Brecht)." *Heidegger Studies* 12 (1996): 9–14.

———. *Hölderlin's Hymn "The Ister."* Trans. William McNeill and Julia Davis. Bloomington: Indiana University Press, 1996.

———. *Identity and Difference*. Trans. Joan Stambaugh. New York: Harper & Row Publishers, 2002.

———. "Phenomenology and Theology." In *Pathmarks*, ed. William McNeil, trans. James G. Hart and John C. Maraldo, 39–62. Cambridge: Cambridge University Press, 1998.

———. *Poetry Language, Thought*. Trans. Albert Hofstadter. New York: Harper Perennial, 1971.

———. *The Question Concerning Technology and Other Essays*. Trans. William Lovitt. New York: Harper & Row, 1977.

Helm, Paul. *Calvin at the Centre*. New York: Oxford University Press, 2010.
Henry, Michel. *Words of Christ*. Trans. Christina M. Gschwandtner. Grand Rapids, MI:. Eerdmans, 2012.
Heschel, Abraham Joshua. *God in Search of Man: A Philosophy of Judaism*. New York: Harper & Row, 1966.
———. *The Sabbath: Its Meaning for Modern Man*. New York: Noonday; Farrar, Straus, and Giroux, 2005.
Heschel, Susannah. Introduction to *The Sabbath: Its Meaning for Modern Man*, by Abraham Joshua Heschel, vii–xvi. New York: Noonday; Farrar, Straus, and Giroux, 2005.
Hildegard. *Book of Divine Works, with Letters and Songs*. Ed. Matthew Fox. Trans. Robert Cunningham. Santa Fe, NM: Bear & Company, 1987.
Horner, Robyn. "À Saint Jacques." In *The Postmodern Saints of France: Refiguring "the Holy" in Contemporary French Philosophy*, ed. Colby Dickinson, 95–108. London: Bloomsbury T&T Clark, 2013.
———. "The Experience of Joy: Saturation and Non-Experience." In *Routledge Handbook on Phenomenology and Theology*, ed. Joseph Rivera and Joseph O'Leary. London: Routledge, forthcoming.
———. "Is Anxiety Fundamental? Lacoste's Reading of Heidegger." In *Heidegger and Contemporary French Philosophy. New Yearbook for Phenomenology and Phenomenological Philosophy*. London: Routledge, 2022.
———. "Problème du mal et péché des origines." *Recherches de Science Religieuse* 90, no. 1 (2002): 63–86. The unpublished English version of the text was provided by the author.
———. *Rethinking God as Gift: Marion, Derrida, and the Limits of Phenomenology*. New York: Fordham University Press, 2001.
———. "Words That Reveal: Jean-Yves Lacoste and the Experience of God." *Continental Philosophy Review* 51 (2018): 169–92.
Hurd, Elizabeth Shakman. *Beyond Religious Freedom: The New Global Politics of Religion*. Princeton, NJ: Princeton University Press, 2015.
Husserl, Edmund. *Logical Investigations*. Vol. 2. Trans. J. N. Findlay. New York: Routledge, 2001.
Janicaud, Dominique. "The Theological Turn in French Phenomenology." In *Phenomenology and the "Theological Turn": The French Debate*, trans. Bernard G. Prusak, 16–103. New York: Fordham University Press, 2000.
John XXIII. "Discours d'ouverture du concile Vatican II." In *Vatican II: Les seize documents conciliaires*, 587. Paris: Fides, 1967.
Johnson, Elizabeth. *Ask the Beasts: Darwin and the God of Love*. New York: Bloomsbury, 2014.
———. *Creation and the Cross: The Mercy of God for a Planet in Peril*. Maryknoll, NY: Orbis, 2019.
Johnson, Keith L. *Karl Barth and the* Analogia Entis. New York: T&T Clark, 2010.
Jones, David Albert. *Approaching the End: A Theological Exploration of Death and Dying*. Oxford: Oxford University Press, 2007.

Jones, Tamsin. *A Genealogy of Marion's Philosophy of Religion: Apparent Darkness*. Bloomington: Indiana University Press, 2011.

Kaplin, Edward. *Spiritual Radical: Abraham Joshua Heschel in America, 1940–1972*. New Haven, CT: Yale University Press, 2005.

Kasper, Walter. *An Introduction to Christian Faith*. Trans. V. Green. New York: Paulist, 1980.

Kautsky, Karl. *Foundations of Christianity: A Study in Christian Origins*. New York: International Publishers, 1925.

Kearney, Richard. *Anatheism: Returning to God after God*. New York: Columbia University Press, 2010.

———. *Debates in Continental Philosophy: Conversations with Contemporary Thinkers*. New York: Fordham University Press, 2004.

———. "Enabling God," in *After God: Richard Kearney and the Religious Turn in Continental Philosophy*. New York: Fordham University Press, 2006.

———. "Epiphanies of the Everyday: Toward a Micro-Eschatology." In *After God: Richard Kearney and the Religious Turn in Continental Philosophy*, ed. John Panteleimon Manoussakis, 3–20. New York: Fordham University Press, 2006.

———. "The Wager of Carnal Hermeneutics." In *Carnal Hermeneutics*, ed. Richard Kearney and Brian Treanor. New York: Fordham University Press, 2015.

Keel, Othmar, and Silvia Schroer. *Creation: Biblical Theologies in the Context of the Ancient Near East*. Trans. Peter T. Daniels. Winona Lake, IN: Pennsylvania State University Press, 2015.

Keller, Catherine. *Face of the Deep: A Theology of Becoming*. New York: Routledge, 2003.

Kierkegaard, Søren. *The Lily of the Field and the Bird of the Air: Three Godly Discourses*. Trans. Bruce H. Kirmmse. Princeton, NJ: Princeton University Press, 2016.

Kilby, Karen. *Karl Rahner: Theology and Philosophy*. New York: Routledge, 2004.

Kirmmse, Bruce H. "Introduction: Letting Nature Point beyond Nature." In *The Lily of the Field and the Bird of the Air: Three Godly Discourses*, by Søren Kierkegaard, vii–xxxv. Princeton, NJ: Princeton University Press, 2016.

Kohák, Erazim. *The Embers and the Stars: A Philosophical Inquiry into the Moral Sense of Nature*. Chicago: University of Chicago Press, 1984.

Koltun-Fromm, Ken. *Imagining Jewish Authenticity*. Bloomington: Indiana University Press, 2015.

Kosky, Jeffrey L. *Arts of Wonder: Enchanting Secularity*. Chicago: University of Chicago Press, 2013.

———. "Translator's Note." In *In the Self's Place: The Approach of Saint Augustine*, by Jean-Luc Marion, xix–xxii. Stanford, CA: Stanford University Press, 2012.

LaChance Adams, Sarah, and Caroline R. Lundquist. "Introduction: The Philosophical Significance of Pregnancy, Childbirth, and Mothering." In

Coming to Life: Philosophies of Pregnancy, Childbirth, and Mothering, ed. Sarah LaChance Adams and Caroline R. Lundquist, 1–30. New York: Fordham University Press, 2013.

Lacoste, Jean-Yves. *The Appearing of God*. Trans. Oliver O'Donovan. Oxford: Oxford University Press, 2018.

———. *Être en danger*. Paris: Les Éditions du Cerf, 2011.

———. *Experience and the Absolute: Disputed Questions on the Humanity of Man*. Trans. Mark Raftery-Skehan. New York: Fordham University Press, 2004.

———. *Le monde et l'absence d'œuvre et autre études*. Paris: Presses Universitaires de France, 2000.

———. *Note sur le temps: Essai sur les raison de la mémoire et de l'espérance*. Paris: Presses Universitaires de Frances, 1990.

———. "Phenomenology and the Frontier." In *Quiet Powers of the Possible: Interviews in Contemporary French Phenomenology*, ed. Tarek R. Dika and W. Chris Hackett, trans. K. Jason Wardley, 188–210. New York: Fordham University Press, 2016.

———. *Présence et parousie*. Geneva, Switzerland: Ad Solem, 2006.

———. *Recherches sur la parole*. Louvain: Peeters, 2015.

———. *Thèses sur le vrai*. Paris: Presses Universitaires de France, 2018.

———. "The Work and Compliment of Appearing." In *Religious Experience and the End of Metaphysics*, ed. Jeffrey Bloechl, 68–93. Bloomington: Indiana University Press, 2003.

Lamberigts, Mathijs. "Was Augustine a Manichaean? The Assessment of Julian of Aeclanum." In *Augustine and Manichaeism in the Latin West: Proceedings of the Fribourg-Utrecht International Symposium of the International Association of Manichaean Studies (IAMS)*, ed. Johannes van Oort, Otto Wermelinger, and Gregor Wurst, 113–36. Boston: Brill, 2001.

Laurelle, François. "L'appel et le phénomène." *Revue de Métaphysique et de Morale* 1 (1991): 27–41.

Leder, Drew. *The Absent Body*. Chicago: University of Chicago Press, 1990.

Levenson, Jon. *Creation and the Persistence of Evil: The Jewish Drama of Divine Omnipotence*. Princeton, NJ: Princeton University Press, 1988.

Levesque-Lopman, Louise. "Decision and Experience: A Phenomenological Analysis of Pregnancy and Childbirth." *Human Studies* 6, no. 1 (1983): 247–77.

Levinas, Emmanuel. "Desacralization and Disenchantment." In *Nine Talmudic Readings*, trans. Annette Aronowicz, 136–60. Bloomington: Indiana University Press, 1990.

———. *Existence and Existents*. Trans. Alphonso Lingis. Pittsburgh, PA: Duquesne University Press, 2001.

———. *Time and the Other*. Trans. Richard A. Cohen. Pittsburgh, PA: Duquesne University Press, 1987.

Luz, Ulrich. *Matthew 1–7: A Commentary*. Trans. James E. Crouch. Minneapolis, MN: Fortress, 2007.

Mackinlay, Shane. *Interpreting Excess: Jean-Luc Marion, Saturated Phenomena, and Hermeneutics*. New York: Fordham University Press, 2010.
Maine, Trevor. "Knowing through Worship: The Epistemological Underpinnings of Liturgical Theology." PhD diss., Katholieke Universiteit Leuven, 2018.
Malpas, Jeff. *Heidegger's Topology: Being, Place, World*. Cambridge, MA: MIT Press, 2006.
Manolopoulos, Mark. *If Creation Is a Gift*. Albany: SUNY Press, 2009.
Marion, Jean-Luc. "Apologie de l'argument." *Revue Catholique Internationale Communio* 27, no. 100 (1992): 12–33.
———. *Being Given: Toward a Phenomenology of Givenness*. Trans. Jeffrey L. Kosky. Stanford, CA: Stanford University Press, 2002.
———. *A Brief Apology for a Catholic Moment*. Trans. Stephen E. Lewis. Chicago: University of Chicago Press, 2021.
———. "Faith and Reason." In *Believing in Order to See: On the Rationality of Revelation and the Irrationality of Some Believers*, trans. Christina Gschwandtner, 3–13. New York: Fordham University Press, 2017.
———. "Faith and Reason." In *The Visible and the Revealed*, trans. Christina M. Gschwandtner, 145–54. New York: Fordham University Press, 2008.
———. *God without Being*. Trans. Thomas A. Carlson. Chicago: University of Chicago Press, 2012.
———. "Hermeneutics of Givenness." In *The Enigma of the Divine: Between Phenomenology and Comparative Theology*, ed. Jean-Luc Marion and Christiaan Jacobs- Vandegeer, trans. Sarah Horton, 17–47. Switzerland: Springer Nature, 2020.
———. *The Idol and Distance: Five Studies*. Trans. Thomas A. Carlson. New York: Fordham University Press, 2001.
———. "In Defense of Argument." In *Believing in Order to See: On the Rationality of Revelation and the Irrationality of Some Believers*, trans. Christina Gschwandtner, 14–29. New York: Fordham University Press, 2017.
———. *In Excess: Studies of Saturated Phenomena*. Trans. Robyn Horner and Vincent Berraud. New York: Fordham University Press, 2002.
———. *In the Self's Place: The Approach of Saint Augustine*. Trans. Jeffrey Kosky. Stanford, CA: Stanford University Press, 2012.
———. "Metaphysics and Phenomenology: A Relief for Theology." Trans. Thomas A. Carlson. *Critical Inquiry* 20, no. 4 (1994): 572–91.
———. *Negative Certainties*. Trans. Stephan E. Lewis. Chicago: University of Chicago Press, 2015.
———. *The Reason of the Gift*. Trans. Stephan Lewis. Charlottesville: University of Virginia Press, 2011.
———. *The Rigor of Things: Conversations with Dan Arbib*. Trans. Christina M. Gschwandtner. New York: Fordham University Press, 2017.
———. "The Saturated Phenomenon." In *Phenomenology and the "Theological Turn": The French Debate*, trans. Thomas A. Carlson, 176–216. New York: Fordham University Press, 2000.

Martelet, Gustave. "Dieu n'a pas créé la mort." *Christus* 168 (1995): 456–67.
Martin, Keavy. *Stories in a New Skin: Approaches to Inuit Literature*. Winnipeg: University of Winnipeg Press, 2012.
Matthews, Charles. "A Worldly Augustinianism: Augustine's Sacramental Vision of Creation." *Augustinian Studies* 41 (2010): 333–48.
McCracken, Lucas. Translator's preface to *The Loving Struggle: Phenomenological and Theological Debates*, by Emmanuel Falque, trans. Bradley B. Onishi and Lucas McCracken, ix–x. New York: Rowman & Littlefield, 2018.
McFarland, Ian A. *In Adam's Fall: A Meditation on the Christian Doctrine of Original Sin*. West Sussex: Wiley-Blackwell, 2010.
———. "Sermon on the Mount." In *Cambridge Dictionary of Christian Theology*, ed. Ian A. McFarland, David A. S. Fergusson, Karen Kilby, and Iain R. Torrance, 468. New York: Cambridge University Press, 2011.
McGinn, Bernard. *Thomas Aquinas's Summa Theologiae: A Biography*. Princeton, NJ: Princeton University Press, 2014.
Merleau-Ponty, Maurice. *Nature: Course Notes from the Collège de France (1956–1957)*. Ed. Dominique Segland. Evanston, IL: Northwestern University Press, 2003.
———. "La nature ou le monde de silence." In *Maurice Merleau-Ponty*, ed. Emmanuel de Saint-Aubert, 44–53. Paris: Herman, 2008.
———. *Phenomenology of Perception*. Trans. Donald A. Landes. London: Routledge, 2012.
Middleton, J. R. "Reading Genesis 3 Attentive to Human Evolution: Beyond Concordism and Non-Overlapping Magisteria." In *Evolution and the Fall*, ed. William T. Cavanaugh and James K. A. Smith, 67–97. Grand Rapids, MI: Eerdmans, 2017.
Minch, Daniel. *Eschatological Hermeneutics: The Theological Core of Experience and the Hope of Our Salvation*. London: Bloomsbury, 2018.
———. "Our Faith in Creation, God's Faith in Humanity: Edward Schillebeeckx and Pope Francis on Human Transcendence and an Anthropocentric Cosmos." *Theological Studies* 80, no. 4 (2019): 845–63.
Moberly, R. W. L. *The Theology of the Book of Genesis*. Cambridge: Cambridge University Press, 2009.
Moltmann, Jürgen. *The Crucified God: The Cross of Christ as the Foundation and Criticism of Christian Theology*. Trans. R. A. Wilson and John Bowden. Minneapolis, MN: Fortress, 1991.
Newheiser, David. *Hope in a Secular Age: Deconstruction, Negative Theology, and the Future of Faith*. New York: Cambridge University Press, 2019.
Newman, Barbara. "St. Hildegard, Doctor of the Church, and the Fate of Feminist Theology." *Spiritus* 13 (2013): 36–55.
Nietzsche, Friedrich. "Fragments posthumes: Automne 1885–automne 1887." In *Œuvres philosophiques complètes*, vol. 12, ed. Giorgio Colli, trans. Julien Hervier and Mazzino Montinari. Paris: Gallimard, 1979.

---. *The Will to Power*. Trans. Walter Kaufmann and R. J. Hollingdale. New York: Vintage, 1967.

O'Leary, Joseph. "Phenomenology and Theology: Respecting the Boundaries." *Philosophy Today* 62, no. 1 (2018): 99–117.

Oliver, Mary. *The Truro Bear and Other Adventures: Poems and Essays*. Boston: Beacon, 2008.

Olivier, Abraham. "Understanding Place." In *Place, Space, and Hermeneutics*, ed. Bruce B. Janz, 9–22. Cham: Springer International Publishing, 2017.

Onishi, Bradley B. "Introduction to English Translation: Is the Theological Turn Still Relevant? Finitude, Affect, and Embodiment." In *The Loving Struggle: Phenomenological and Theological Debates*, by Emmanuel Falque, trans. Bradley B. Onishi and Lucas McCracken, xi–xxix. New York: Rowman & Littlefield, 2018.

---. "Philosophy and Theology: Emmanuel Falque and the Theological Turn." In *Evil, Fallenness, and Finitude*, ed. Bruce Ellis Benson and B. Keith Putt, 77–96. Cham: Palgrave Macmillan, 2017.

---. *The Sacrality of the Secular: Postmodern Philosophy of Religion*. New York: Columbia University Press, 2018.

Pattison, George. *Kierkegaard's Upbuilding Discourses: Philosophy, Theology, and Literature*. New York: Routledge, 2002.

Plantinga, Alvin. *God, Freedom, Evil*. Grand Rapids, MI: Eerdmans, 1974.

Prevot, Andrew. *Thinking Prayer: Theology and Spirituality amidst the Crisis of Modernity*. Notre Dame, IN: University of Notre Dame Press, 2015.

Przywara, Erich. *Analogia Entis: Metaphysics: Original Structure and Universal Rhythm*. Trans. John R. Betz and David Bentley Hart. Grand Rapids, MI: Eerdmans, 2014.

Rad, Gerhard von. *Genesis: A Commentary*. Philadelphia: Westminster, 1973.

Rahner, Karl. "Concerning the Relation between Nature and Grace." In *Theological Investigations*, vol. 1: *God, Christ, Mary, and Grace*, 2nd ed., trans. Cornelius Ernst, 297–318. Baltimore, MD: Helicon, 1963.

Renkl, Margaret. *Late Migrations: A Natural History of Love and Loss*. Minneapolis, MN: Milkweed Editions, 2019.

Ricoeur, Paul. "Experience and Language in Religious Discourse." In *Phenomenology and the "Theological Turn": The French Debate*, trans. Thomas A. Carlson, 127–46. New York: Fordham University Press, 2000.

---. *Freedom and Nature: The Voluntary and Involuntary*. Trans. Erizam V. Kohák. Evanston, IL: Northwestern University Press, 1996.

---. *Interpretation Theory: Discourse and the Surplus of Meaning*. Fort Worth: Texas Christian University Press, 1976.

---. *The Rule of Metaphor: The Creation of Meaning in Language*. Trans. Robert Czerny with Kathleen McLaughlin and John Costello. Toronto: Toronto University Press, 1977. Reprint, New York: Routledge, 2003.

Romano, Claude. *At the Heart of Reason*. Trans. Michael B. Smith and Claude Romano. Evanston, IL: Northwestern University Press, 2015.

———. *Event and World*. Trans. Shane Mackinlay. New York: Fordham University Press, 2009.

Ross, Allen P. *A Commentary on the Psalms: Volume 1 (1–41)*. Grand Rapids, MI: Kregel, 2011.

Sartre, Jean-Paul. *Existentialism Is a Humanism*. Trans. Carol Macomber. New Haven, CT: Yale University Press, 2007.

Schillebeeckx, Edward. "Correlation between Human Question and Christian Answer." In *The Understanding of Faith: Interpretation and Criticism*, vol. 5. Trans. N. D. Smith. London: Bloomsbury T&T Clark, 2014.

———. "Secularization and Christian Belief in God." In *God the Future of Man*, trans. N. D. Smith, 31–54. London: Bloomsbury T&T Clark, 2014.

Schrijvers, Joeri. "In (the) Place of the Self: A Critical Study of Jean-Luc Marion's 'Au lieu de soi. L'approche de Saint Augustin.'" *Modern Theology* 25, no. 4 (October 2009): 661–86.

———. *An Introduction to Jean-Yves Lacoste*. New York: Ashgate, 2012.

———. *Ontotheological Turnings? The Decentering of the Modern Subject in Recent French Phenomenology*. Albany: SUNY Press, 2012.

Sheehan, Thomas. *Making Sense of Heidegger: A Paradigm Shift*. New York: Roman & Littlefield, 2015.

Shroyer, Danielle. *Original Blessing: Putting Sin in Its Rightful Place*. Minneapolis, MN: Fortress, 2016.

Smith, James K. A. "What Stands in the Fall? A Philosophical Exploration." In *Evolution and the Fall*, ed. William T. Cavanaugh and James K. A. Smith, 48–64. Grand Rapids, MI: Eerdmans, 2017.

Soskice, Janet. "Creation and the Glory of Creatures." In *Being-in-Creation: Human Responsibility in an Endangered World*, ed. Bruce Ellis Benson, Norman Wirzba, and Brian Treanor, 143–58. New York: Fordham University Press, 2015.

Steenberg, M. C. *Irenaeus on Creation: The Cosmic Christ and the Saga of Redemption*. Boston: Brill, 2008.

Steinbock, Anthony. *Phenomenology and Mysticism: The Verticality of Religious Experience*. Ed. Merold Westphal. Bloomington: Indiana University Press, 2007.

Stone, Alison. *Being Born: Birth and Philosophy*. New York: Oxford University Press, 2019.

Stump, Eleonore. *Wandering in Darkness: Narrative and the Problem of Suffering*. New York: Oxford University Press, 2010.

Tanner, Kathryn. *Theories of Culture: A New Agenda for Theology*. Minneapolis, MN: Fortress, 1997.

Taylor, Charles. *A Secular Age*. Cambridge, MA: Belknap Press of Harvard University Press, 2007.

te Velde, Rudi A. "Creation, Fall, and Providence." In *The Oxford Handbook of the Reception of Aquinas*, ed. Matthew Levering and Marcus Plested, 643–57. New York: Oxford University Press, 2021.

Todd, Zoe. "An Indigenous Feminist's Take on the Ontological Turn: 'Ontology' Is Just Another Word for Colonialism." *Journal of Historical Sociology* 29, no. 1 (March 2016): 4–22.

Treanor, Brian. "Joy and the Myopia of Finitude." *Comparative and Continental Philosophy* 8, no.1 (March 2016): 6–25.

———. *Melancholic Joy: On Life Worth Living*. New York: Bloomsbury Academic, 2021.

Turner, Denys. *Thomas Aquinas: A Portrait*. New Haven, CT: Yale University Press, 2013.

Tyler, Imogen. "Reframing Pregnant Embodiment." In *Transformations: Thinking Through Feminism*, ed. Sarah Ahmed, Jane Kilby, Celia Lury, Maureen McNeil, and Beverley Skeggs, 288–302. London: Routledge, 2000.

van Erp, Stephan. "The World and Sacrament: Foundations of the Political Theology of the Church." *Louvain Studies* 39 (2015–2016): 102–20.

van Erp, Stephan, and Daniel Minch. "Introduction: Reading Edward Schillebeeckx from His Texts and Context." In *T&T Clark Reader in Edward Schillebeeckx*. London: Bloomsbury, 2023.

Vedder, Ben. *Heidegger's Philosophy of Religion: From God to the Gods*. Pittsburgh, PA: Duquesne University Press, 2007.

Verhage, Florinteien. "The Vision of the Artist/Mother: The Strange Creativity of Painting and Pregnancy." In *Coming to Life: Philosophies of Pregnancy, Childbirth, and Mothering*, ed. Sarah LaChance Adams and Caroline R. Lundquist, 300–20. New York: Fordham University Press, 2013.

Walton, John C. *The Lost World of Genesis One: Ancient Cosmology and the Origins Debate*. Westmont, IL: Intervarsity, 2009.

Wardley, Jason Kenneth. *Praying to a French God*. Burlington, VT: Ashgate, 2014.

Webster, John. "Love Is Also a Lover of Life: *Creatio Ex Nihilo* and Creaturely Goodness." *Modern Theology* 29, no. 2 (2013): 156–71.

Weiss, Johannes. *Die Predigt Jesu vom Reiche Gottes*. 3rd ed. Göttingen: Vandenhoeck & Ruprecht, 1964.

Westermann, Claus. *Genesis*. Trans. David E. Green. London: T&T Clark, 1987.

———. *Genesis 1–11: A Commentary*. Minneapolis, MN: Augsburg, 1984.

Westhelle, Vitor. "Creation Motifs in the Search for a Vital Space: A Latin American Perspective." In *Lift Every Voice: Constructing Christian Theologies from the Underside*, ed. Susan B. Thistlethwaite and Mary Potter Engel. San Francisco: Harper, 1990.

Westphal, Merold. "The Importance of Overcoming Metaphysics for the Life of Faith." *Modern Theology* 23, no. 2 (April 2007): 253–78.

Williams, Rowan. *Christ the Heart of Creation*. New York: Bloomsbury, 2018.

———. "'Good for Nothing'? Augustine on Creation." *Augustinian Studies* 25 (1994): 9–24.

Wiman, Christian. "The Cancer Chair." *Harper's*, February, 2020. https://harpers.org/archive/ 2020/02/the-cancer-chair/.

———. "I Will Love You in Summertime." *American Scholar*, February 2016. https://theamericanscholar.org /i-will-love-you-in-the-summertime/#.XAw9 NxNKjBI.

———. "Still Wilderness." *American Scholar*, Autumn 2017.

Wingren, Gustaf. *Man and the Incarnation: A Study in the Biblical Theology of Irenaeus*. Trans. Ross Mackenzie. Edinburgh: Oliver & Boyd, 1959.

Wirzba, Norman. *Food and Faith: A Theology of Eating*. Cambridge: Cambridge University Press, 2011.

———. *This Sacred Life: Humanity's Place in a Wounded World*. Cambridge: Cambridge University Press, 2021.

Wolfe, Judith. *Heidegger's Eschatology: Theological Horizons in Martin Heidegger's Early Work*. Oxford: Oxford University Press, 2013.

Young, Iris Marion. *On Female Body Experience: "Throwing Like a Girl" and Other Essays*. New York: Oxford University Press, 2005.

Zahavi, Dan. *Subjectivity and Selfhood*. Cambridge, MA: MIT Press, 2005.

Zimmermann, Jens. *Reimagining the Sacred: Richard Kearney Debates God*. Edited by Richard Kearney and Jens Zimmermann. New York: Columbia University Press, 2016.

Zwicky, Jan. "A Ship from Delos." In *Learning to Die: Wisdom in the Age of the Climate Crisis*, 41–73. Regina: University of Regina Press, 2018.

Index

Aertsen, Jan A., 153n58
agnosticism, 14, 17, 22, 24, 41–42, 141
Alvis, James, 168n105
anthropocentrism, 93, 96, 108, 110, 179n20, 184n7
anxiety, 19, 128, 141; Falque on, 84, 98, 108, 110, 142; Heidegger on, 23, 39, 66, 120–21, 173n54, 188n11, 188n13–14
Aquinas, Thomas, 99, 169n111, 180n30
Arendt, Hannah, 174n55
atheism, 14, 17, 22, 37, 42, 75–79, 141, 142
Augustine, 7, 49–54, 152n33, 164n31, 176n78

Balthasar, Hans Urs von, 186n96
Benoist, Jocelyn, 75
Betz, Hans Dieter, 192n66
birth, 64, 173n54; childbirth and, 80–84, 171n40; Falque on, 73, 74, 77, 79–81, 142, 172n39
Bloechl, Jeffrey, 37, 120, 125, 188n14, 190n32
bodies: childbirth and, 81–82; Chrétien on, 28; Falque on, 94, 96–98, 100, 101–2, 178n11, 178n13, 182n45–48; Kearney on, 12; Lacoste on, 25; Romano on, 104–5; suffering and, 103–4, 106–7
Brown, Peter, 7
Brueggemann, Walter, 5, 158n55

Calvin, John, 5–6, 35, 169n110
Caputo, John D., 9
chaos, 6, 95, 97–99, 179n19; Falque on, 95–97, 102, 178–79n15, 179n18
Chrétien, Jean-Louis, 28, 75, 77, 87–88, 90, 175n75, 176n78, 184n73, 185n106, 186n105
Christology, 11, 36, 107–15
climate crisis, 17, 62, 94, 144
commonality: entangled topologies and, 41, 45–46; experience and, 79, 143; prelinguistic experience and, 21–22
Cone, James, 106
confession of faith, 1, 15, 16, 19, 21, 45, 47, 70, 71, 72, 79–80, 114, 126, 140, 143, 145; Falque on, 74, 84; Lacoste on, 29, 38, 122, 142; Marion on, 48–50, 52–55, 62, 63, 64, 66, 70, 71, 141, 168n105
creatio ex nihilo, 95, 98, 101; Catherine Keller on, 98; Falque on, 100

215

creation's goodness, 1–8, 10–11, 13–19, 20–21, 47–49, 72–74, 94–96, 113–16, 117–19, 126–27, 138–39, 140–45; affectivity and, 29–32; entangled topologies and, 35, 38–39, 41–42, 45–46; eschatology and, 127–30, 133–34; death and, 98–101; givenness and, 66–71; hermeneutics, 33–35; Marion on, 54–55; prelinguistic experience and, 22, 24–28, 42–44, 79–81, 83–84; suffering and, 101, 103–4, 106–7; transfigured goodness and, 84–86, 92–93, 110, 112, 137–38
creation's groaning, 95–96; Falque on, 107–10; Johnson on, 110–12
culture, 14, 47–49, 62–65, 70–71, 73, 142–45; Falque on, 74–75, 79; Marion on, 55–61, 66; Taylor on, 40; theology and, 17, 19–20

Davis, Ellen, 5, 130, 115n16
de Certeau, Michel, 63
death, 6–7, 18, 94–96, 107, 113, 128, 133; Christ and, 107–10, 112; death of God and, 56–57, 75, 165n47; Falque on, 77, 80, 96–100, 169n4, 178n13; Heidegger on, 37–38, 118, 120, 138–39, 173n54, 188n13, 188n24; Lacoste on, 125, 159n82; original sin and, 180n30; Treanor on, 181n39
Derrida, Jacques, 50, 77
diversity, experience and, 1–2, 15, 21–22, 29, 35, 38, 42, 45–46, 47, 77, 83, 92, 101, 115, 123, 140–41, 143, 145

earth, Heidegger on, 38–42
Edwards, Denis, 7, 192n65
enjoyment, 43, 45, 67, 103; Falque on, 84; Lacoste on, 17, 22–23, 25–30, 33, 38, 41, 66, 68, 143, 189n31
entangled topologies, 17, 22, 35–42, 46, 48, 55, 126, 141, 143
eschatology, 18, 117, 118, 127, 138–39, 160n90; Heidegger on, 119–20, 188n13; Heschel on, 137–38; Kierkegaard on, 128, 130, 133; Lacoste on, 119–25
event, childbirth and, 82–84; Chrétien on, 87–88; Falque on, 73, 80–81, 87–88; Marion on, 57, 64, 65, 67–68, 83; phenomenology of, 3, 25; Romano on, 80–81, 104–5
evil, 10, 18, 95, 99, 141, 178n3
experience: ambiguity and, 1–2, 17, 22, 27, 29, 37, 38, 41, 74, 85, 88–91, 107, 115, 138, 141, 143, 159n75, 176n88, 191n48; prelinguistic and, 13–16, 17, 21–22, 25, 28, 34, 45, 66, 68, 70, 74, 82, 93, 94, 103–4, 114–15

Falque, Emmanuel, 3, 9, 13, 17, 19, 36, 52, 72–74, 95, 123, 141–42; Christ's suffering and, 107–10, 112; event of birth and, 79–81, 84; finitude and, 74–81; struggle for life and, 96–100; suffering and, 101–3; transformation and, 85–87
Fall, the, 150n15, 169n110, 180n28
feminism, phenomenology and, 81–83, 172n40
Fergusson, David, 6–7
finitude, 19, 36, 73–74, 118, 127, 138, 141; Falque on, 74–81, 169n2, 170n17, 171n20, 171n22, 172n35; Lacoste on, 120, 125; Marion on, 173n52, transformation and, 84–86, 174n59
flesh, 2, 12, 25, 80; Christ and, 109, 111–12; Falque on, 96, 105, 186n104; Kearney on, 2, 82
Francis, Pope, 11, 93, 107, 112, 177n107, 197n8

Gabellieri, Emmanuel, 74
gift: creation and, 5, 17, 41, 86; Marion and, 44, 48, 58, 61, 62, 64–66, 163n22, 167n87
Gilbert, Jack, 106
givenness: Marion and, 17, 48, 51, 53, 58, 66–67, 69, 70, 83, 163n22, 164n29, 164n31, 168n105; phenomenology and, 120
Gnosticism, 95, 100
Godzieba, Anthony, 9, 86
grace, 70, 111, 138, 179n24; common grace and, 71, 169n110; nature and, 16–17, 71, 73–74, 78–79, 85–86, 88, 92, 107, 139, 141

Greisch, Jean, 52
Gschwandtner, Christina M., 3, 64–65, 123, 125, 149n6, 154n68, 162n5, 168n105, 182n45, 191n49, 191n50

Hackett, W. Chris, 160n90
Hart, David Bentley, 181n33
Hart, Kevin, 129
Heidegger, Martin: anxiety and, 81, 119–21, 173n54, 188n11, 188n13, 188n14; finitude and, 73, 78, 170n17; fundamental moods and, 23–25, 66, 189n19; earth and, 38–41; givenness and, 164n29; gods and, 160n83, 160n86; hermeneutics and, 12; metaphysics and, 8–10, 49, 52, 153n51, 162n5, 188n16; nihilism and, 61, 71; prelinguistic experience and, 155n17; ready-to-hand and, 103; topology and, 126, 154n79; world and, 35–38, 78, 123–24, 126, 138
Henry, Michel, 12, 153n63, 154n68
Heschel, Abraham Joshua, 18, 119, 195n106; the Sabbath and, 134–38
Hildegard of Bingen, 5, 35
holiness, 39, 136
Horner, Robyn, 27, 65, 156n32, 157n43, 164n29, 180n9
Husserl, Edmund: *Erlebnis* and, 23; essences, 42–43; flesh, 82; givenness and, 164n29 hermeneutics and, 12, 153n63; intentionality and, 156n32; prelinguistic experience and, 155n17

icon, 49
idol, 49–50, 56–57, 145
immanence, 36, 39–41, 71, 78, 80, 132

Janicaud, Dominique, 194n82
Johnson, Elizabeth, 7, 93, 108, 110–12, 184n77
Jones, Tamsin, 158n105
joy, 5, 6, 17, 22–24, 38, 43, 45; 66–8, 92, 96, 123, 138, 141, 150n18, 159n82; affectivity and, 29–32; enjoyment and, 24–28, 103, 105–6, 143, 183n61; peace and, 122; suffering and, 112, 186n106

Kasper, Walter, 149n6
Kearney, Richard, 9, 12, 64, 82, 121, 189n22
Keel, Othmar, 4, 179n19, 179n20, 179n23
Keller, Catherine, 6, 98
Kierkegaard, Søren, 18, 118, 128, 130–33, 191n57, 192n68, 193n80, 194n81
Kirmmse, Bruce H., 132
knowledge: intuitive and, 29–32, 89–90, 158n55, 176n93; propositional and, 29–33, 85, 89–90, 158n55, 176n93, 193n68
Kohák, Erazim, 196n118
Kosky, Jeffrey, 39–41, 160n96, 163n22

LaChance Adams, Sarah, 172n40
Lacoste, Jean-Yves, 3, 17, 18–19, 21–22, 44, 75, 80, 134, 136–38, 141–42, 156n20, 156n22, 176n86, 183n61, 189n29, 193n80, 193n81, 193–94n82; affectivity and, 29–33, 157n42–43; ambiguity and, 88–90, 159n75, 176n88, 191n48; enjoyment and, 25–27, 66; entangled topologies, 35–41; Falque on, 77–78, 171n20; joy and, 22–25, 66, 156n31, 159n82; Kierkegaard and, 128, 130–33, 192n68; liturgy and, 55, 123–27, 139, 189n28, 191n52; peace and, 119, 189n19, 190n32, 190n33; prelinguistic experience and, 157n39; secondary evidence and, 33–35, 68, 115; topology and, 16, 158n55
Leder, Drew, 103
Levenson, Jon, 98, 179n25
Levesque-Lopman, Louise, 81
Levinas, Emmanuel, 25, 27, 102, 136, 183n54, 184–85n81
liturgy, 3, 139, 191n49, 194n84, 195n109; Heschel and, 119, 134; Lacoste and, 16, 21, 33–34, 123–27, 128, 131–33, 137–38, 158n65, 189n28, 190n33, 191n52
Lundquist, Caroline R., 172n40

Mackinlay, Shane, 168n105
Malpas, Jeff, 154n79
Manolopoulos, Mark, 167n87

Marion, Jean-Luc, 3, 9–10, 16, 17, 19, 47–48; *l'adonné*, 163n22; *confessio* and, 52–55, 164n28; culture, 59–62, 70–71, 141–42, 145; event and, 83; Falque and, 75–77, 169n4; gift and, 62–66; givenness and, 66–70, 115, 164n29, 167n100, 168n105, 173n52; metaphysics and, 49–52, 162n5, 162n6, 164n31, 165n47; nihilism and, 55–59, 165n54, 166n56, 166n57, 166n85; revelation and, 44; 167n87; saturated phenomena, 167n103
Martelet, Gustave, 185–85n96
Matthew 6, 118, 127–33
McCracken, Lucas, 76
McFarland, Ian A., 180n28
menuha, 137
Merleau-Ponty, Maurice: childbirth 81; descriptive psychology and, 11–12; Falque and, 182n48, flesh and, 25; prelinguistic, 102
metaphysics, 8–11; Lacoste and, 32, 159n73; Marion and, 47, 49–52, 60–61, 64, 75, 162n5, 162–3n6, 164n31
micro-eschatologies, 121, 125, 128, 130, 137, 189n22
Middleton, J. R., 99–100
Moberly, R. W. L., 6–7, 150n15
Moltmann, Jürgen, 109, 185n96

nature. *See* grace
Nietzsche, Friedrich, 8–9; Falque and, 169–70n4; nihilism and, 56–59, 61, 63, 71; Romano and, 158n63; will to power and, 62
nihilism, 17, 19, 48–49, 55–65, 70, 80, 142, 144, 156n54, 166n56–57, 166n85
nonplace, 118, 123–28, 132, 133, 136–39

O'Leary, Joseph, 74, 76
Oliver, Mary, 129–30
Olivier, Abraham, 15
Onishi, Bradley B., 41–42, 75
onto-theology, 7–10, 32, 49, 52, 162n5
order, 6–7, 95, 97–99, 101, 179n19
original sin, 11, 95, 99–101, 180n29, 180n30, 181n35

Pattison, George, 131
peace: being-at-peace and, 18, 27, 119–23, 125, 130, 137, 189n19, 190n32
phenomenology, 4, 7, 10–11, 15–20, 22–28; affectivity and, 28–25, 89–91; birth and, 79–84; eschatology and, 119–27; event, 79, 87–88, 104–5; flesh, 96; the gift and, 65; givenness and, 58, 66–70; hermeneutics and, 11–14, 16; intentionality and, 27; materiality and, 96, 102–3; realism and, 42–46; reduction and, 13–14, 22, 129, 140, 157n39, 164n29; suffering and, 95, 101–7; topology and, 15–16, 35–41
prelinguistic experience: commonality and diversity and, 45–46, 70–71, 74, 79; entangled topologies and, 38, 41–42; givenness and, 66–70; goodness and, 13–15, 17, 21–29, 80–85, 103–5, 114–15, 126, 140–43, 168n105, 183n61; phenomenology and, 12, 155n17; secondary evidence and, 33–35; transfigured goodness and, 92–93, 106

Rahner, Karl, 88
realism: phenomenology and, 1, 42–45, 129, 143
relativism, 1–2, 17, 22, 36, 42–45, 75, 140, 143
Renkl, Margaret, 129–30
Ricoeur, Paul, 2, 12–14, 128
Romano, Claude, 3, 16, 24, 28, 153n63, 155n17; event and, 80–81, 83, 95, 104–5, 135, 172n35, 172n39, 173n54, 175n77, 176–77n95; hermeneutics and, 12–14, 34, 44, 68, 115, 158n63, 167n100, 169n100; realism and, 43–44

Sabbath, 18, 119, 133–38, 156n20, 195n106
sacrality, 22, 36, 38–42, 80, 132, 136, 141, 160n86, 193n80, 193n81, 194n84
sacrament, 125, 134
Sartre, Jean-Paul, 81
Schillebeeckx, Edward, 161n108, 187n109

Schrijvers, Joeri, 36–37, 123, 159n73, 164n31
secondary evidence, 16, 33–35, 43, 52, 67, 115, 121, 138
secularity, 37, 39–42, 55, 115, 122, 145, 161n98, 161n108, 188n9, 189n29, 189–90n31
Sheehan, Thomas, 23
Soskice, Janet, 179n24
Stone, Alison, 82, 172n40, 182n43
suffering, 1, 6–7, 18, 19, 72, 77, 94–96, 117, 133, 142, 143, 144, 182n44, 182n46, 182n47, 184n73, 184–85n81, 186n105, 186n106, 187n109; phenomenology and, 99–107; Christ and, 107–15

Tanner, Kathryn, 48
Taylor, Charles, 41–41
te Velde, Rudi A., 169 n111
theology of culture, 17, 19–20, 48–49, 70–71, 143–45
topology, 15–17, 33, 35–42, 48, 68, 71–74, 84–85, 88, 91–93, 107, 112, 114, 115, 118, 123–27, 131, 136, 138, 139, 140–41, 154n79, 168n65

transcendence, God and, 39, 40–41, 71, 98, 118, 132–33, 136, 139, 162n6, 193n80, 193–94n81, 194n82, 194n89
transfigured goodness, 17–18, 45, 72, 74, 84–85, 91–93, 94, 96, 107, 110, 112, 114–18, 133–34, 137–41
transformation, 35, 84–91, 93, 170n6, 174n59, 175n76
Treanor, Brian, 18–19, 94, 114, 141, 181n39

van Erp, Stephan, 197n7

Walton, John C., 151n25
Webster, John, 153n56
Westermann, Claus, 5, 150n18, 151n24
Westphal, Merold, 8–10
Williams, Rowan, 7, 86, 91, 177n100, 177n102, 194n88
Wiman, Christian, 102, 112, 182n44, 185n83
Wirzba, Norman, 70
Wolfe, Judith, 119, 188n13
world: Heidegger and, 35–38, 123–24

Young, Iris Marion, 81–82, 105–6, 183n71

Zwicky, Jan, 113, 144

Index ■ *219*

Jacob Benjamins is a Postdoctoral Research Fellow at the University of St. Michael's College in the University of Toronto.

Perspectives in Continental Philosophy
John D. Caputo, series editor

Recent titles:

Dimitris Vardoulakis, *The Ruse of Techne: Heidegger's Magical Materialism.*
George Pattison, *A Philosophy of Prayer: Nothingness Language, and Hope.*
Irving Goh, ed., *Jean-Luc Nancy among the Philosophers.*
Neal DeRoo, *The Political Logic of Experience: Expression in Phenomenology.*
John D. Caputo, *Radical Theology: Expositions, Explorations, Exhortations.*
Michael Naas, *Class Acts: Derrida on the Public Stage.*
Adam Kotsko, *What is Theology? Christian Thought and Contemporary Life.*
Galen A. Johnson, Mauro Carbone, and Emmanuel de Saint Aubert, *Merleau-Ponty's Poetics: Figurations of Literature and Philosophy*
Ole Jakob Løland, *Pauline Ugliness: Jacob Taubes and the Turn to Paul.*
Marc Crépon, *Murderous Consent: On the Accommodation of Violent Death.* Translated by Michael Loriaux and Jacob Levi, Foreword by James Martel
Emmanuel Falque, *The Guide to Gethsemane: Anxiety, Suffering, and Death.* Translated by George Hughes.
Emmanuel Alloa, *Resistance of the Sensible World: An Introduction to Merleau-Ponty.* Translated by Jane Marie Todd. Foreword by Renaud Barbaras.
Françoise Dastur, *Questions of Phenomenology: Language, Alterity, Temporality, Finitude.* Translated by Robert Vallier.
Jean-Luc Marion, *Believing in Order to See: On the Rationality of Revelation and the Irrationality of Some Believers.* Translated by Christina M. Gschwandtner.
Adam Y. Wells, ed., *Phenomenologies of Scripture.*
An Yountae, *The Decolonial Abyss: Mysticism and Cosmopolitics from the Ruins.*

Jean Wahl, *Transcendence and the Concrete: Selected Writings*. Edited and with an Introduction by Alan D. Schrift and Ian Alexander Moore.

Colby Dickinson, *Words Fail: Theology, Poetry, and the Challenge of Representation*.

Emmanuel Falque, *The Wedding Feast of the Lamb: Eros, the Body, and the Eucharist*. Translated by George Hughes.

Emmanuel Falque, *Crossing the Rubicon: The Borderlands of Philosophy and Theology*. Translated by Reuben Shank. Introduction by Matthew Farley.

Colby Dickinson and Stéphane Symons (eds.), *Walter Benjamin and Theology*.

Don Ihde, *Husserl's Missing Technologies*.

William S. Allen, *Aesthetics of Negativity: Blanchot, Adorno, and Autonomy*.

Jeremy Biles and Kent L. Brintnall, eds., *Georges Bataille and the Study of Religion*.

Tarek R. Dika and W. Chris Hackett, *Quiet Powers of the Possible: Interviews in Contemporary French Phenomenology*. Foreword by Richard Kearney.

Richard Kearney and Brian Treanor, eds., *Carnal Hermeneutics*.

A complete list of titles is available at http://fordhampress.com.

www.ingramcontent.com/pod-product-compliance
Lightning Source LLC
Chambersburg PA
CBHW020406080526
44584CB00014B/1191